Beginning CouchDB

JOE LENNON

Apress®

Beginning CouchDB

ISBN-13 (pbk): 978-1-4302-7237-3

ISBN-13 (electronic): 978-1-4302-7236-6

Printed and bound in the United States of America 9 8 7 6 5 4 3 2 1

President and Publisher: Paul Manning
Lead Editor: Frank Pohlmann
Technical Reviewer: Paul Davis
Editorial Board: Clay Andres, Steve Anglin, Mark Beckner, Ewan Buckingham, Gary Cornell, Jonathan Gennick, Michelle Lowman, Matthew Moodie, Jeffrey Pepper, Frank Pohlmann, Ben Renow-Clarke, Dominic Shakeshaft, Matt Wade, Tom Welsh
Coordinating Editor: Anne Collett
Copy Editor: Kim Wimpsett
Compositor: Kimberly Burton
Indexer: Potomac Indexing, LLC
Artist: April Milne
Cover Designer: Kurt Krames

Distributed to the book trade worldwide by Springer-Verlag New York, Inc., 233 Spring Street, 6th Floor, New York, NY 10013. Phone 1-800-SPRINGER, fax 201-348-4505, e-mail `orders-ny@springer-sbm.com`, or visit `http://www.springeronline.com`.

For information on translations, please e-mail info@apress.com, or visit `http://www.apress.com`.

Apress and friends of ED books may be purchased in bulk for academic, corporate, or promotional use. eBook versions and licenses are also available for most titles. For more information, reference our Special Bulk Sales–eBook Licensing web page at `http://www.apress.com/info/bulksales`.

The source code for this book is available to readers at `http://www.apress.com`. You will need to answer questions pertaining to this book in order to successfully download the code.

To the memory of my uncle, John, and my grandfather, Seán

Contents at a Glance

Contents

About the Author

Joe Lennon is a web applications and database developer from Cork, Ireland. He has had an interest in computing since he was five years old, when he got his first taste of programming while typing up the code for Telly Tennis from the back of the manual for his Amstrad 6128. This interest continued as he grew up, first discovering the World Wide Web in the early 1990s on his father's black-and-white Windows 3.1 IBM ThinkPad, complete with 14.4Kbps PCMICA modem. He dabbled with web development in the late 1990s and was an expert in HTML, CSS, and JavaScript by the time he finished school.

In 2003, Joe enrolled at University College Cork to study Business Information Systems, where he excelled over four years, achieving a First Class Honours each year. He received a scholarship in 2006 for his performance in that year's examinations and regularly achieved grades of 90%+ for development projects. As part of the program, Joe spent six months in Boston, Massachusetts, working as a systems analyst for Fidelity Investments. He graduated from UCC in 2007.

Later that year, Joe joined Core International as a web applications developer. Since joining Core, he has been involved in the development of several new web-based products, as well as the redevelopment and improvement of some existing ones. He introduced the concept of JavaScript frameworks and Ajax to the company's web division in 2008, developing a PL/SQL and JavaScript framework that is now used in every Core web product.

Aside from his work at Core, Joe has worked on several successful web development projects, including Learn French by Podcast, a language-learning web site that offers its members free high-quality MP3 podcasts and allows them to purchase accompanying professional PDF guides for a small fee. He also maintains a blog on his web site at `http://www.joelennon.ie`, where he has often posted tutorials about topics ranging from Oracle database development to Windows batch scripting. In the past two years, Joe has written more than a dozen articles and tutorials for the IBM developerWorks web site, including articles on Adobe Flex, Facebook applications, ExtJS, Adobe AIR, IBM DB2, and more.

About the Technical Reviewer

 **Paul J. Davis** is a bioinformatician and CouchDB developer from Ipswich, Massachusetts. A native of Agency, Iowa, he attended the University of Iowa graduating in 2005 with a degree in electrical engineering. During his studies at university, he got his first paid programming job as a research assistant under Prof. Michael Mackey. With Prof. Mackey's tutoring, he moved from data analysis to system programming, working on the Large Scale Digital Cell Analysis System (LSDCAS).

After working for four years on LSDCAS, he moved eastward to a position with New England Biolabs. After repeated attempts of trying to force biological data into a relational database, he quickly started searching for a better solution. During this search, he found CouchDB and quickly became convinced that it was just the solution he had been searching for. Nearly two years later, he's now a CouchDB committer.

Beyond CouchDB, Paul contributes to a number of other open source projects. You can find a majority of his contributions via `http://github.com/davisp` or on his web site at `http://www.davispj.com`.

Acknowledgments

Writing this book would not have been possible if it were not for the help and support of many people. First, I'd like to thank Jill, the love of my life, who has been there for me throughout this whole project. She has put up with so much the past few months—and never once complained about it. I am eternally grateful for her love and support.

Second, I'd like to thank my mother, Maria, who has always believed in me and pushed me to get the best out of myself. Thank you to my father, Jim, who has always worked his socks off to make sure that I had everything I could ever need or want. Thank you to my sisters, Laura and Kelly, who can always put a smile on my face, even when I'm being a cranky big brother!

Thank you to my grandparents, my aunts and uncles, and my cousins. I hope you all enjoy this book, because you will be receiving a copy for Christmas this (and every) year. Also a big thank you to the Mac Sweeneys—Jill, Mick, Susie, Patrick, and Sarah—I greatly appreciate all the support you have given me.

Thank you to the many people who have given me invaluable advice and support—Seán Murphy, Darragh Duffy, Jonathan Reardon, Mike Murphy, John Goulding, and everyone at Core International; Dermot O'Sullivan, Troy Mott, Hugh Nagle, and Connor Murphy. I'd also like to make a special thank you to my grandfather, Joe Lennon (Senior), for all his help with my writing career to date.

I owe an enormous debt of gratitude to a number of people who worked on this book project. Without my lead editor, Frank Pohlmann, this book would not have been created. I'd like to especially thank him for all of his guidance and for giving me the opportunity to fulfill one of my ambitions in life. Special thanks to Paul Davis; without his expertise on CouchDB, this book would be far less useful. Thank you to Anne Collett, who managed the difficult task of keeping me on schedule while also keeping me motivated at the same time. Thank you to Kim Wimpsett for the kind words about my writing style, although in truth, her hard work and effort has made my writing look so much better than it really is.

I'd like to thank everyone at Apress who has worked to make this project a success, including Leonardo Cuellar, Matthew Kennedy, Simon Yu, James Markham, and Anna Ishchenko.

Finally, I'd like to thank Damien Katz for creating CouchDB. Without your efforts, this book would never have had a reason for being written.

Introduction

Apache CouchDB is an exciting database management system that is growing in popularity each day. This book introduces you to CouchDB, guiding you through its relatively short history and what makes it different from the other database systems out there. It offers simple, unassuming steps on getting CouchDB up and running on your computer that's running Linux or Mac OS X. It guides you through the process of creating a database and working with data; covers more complex topics such as views and map/reduce; and explores advanced database concepts such as replication, compaction, and deployment. It also shows you how to develop applications that are housed entirely in the database itself, in addition to using Python, Django, and Ruby to interact with CouchDB from a traditional server-side application.

Who This Book Is For

This book is written for anyone with an interest in CouchDB, document-oriented databases, or database development in general. It does not assume any knowledge in relation to CouchDB, although some experience with UNIX commands and basic JavaScript skills are beneficial.

What You Need

To follow the examples in this book, you will need access to a computer running the Linux operating system or Mac OS X. You will need administrative access to this computer in order to install CouchDB. If you are using a Windows PC, see the "CouchDB Resources" section for a link to an unofficial Windows binary installer for CouchDB that you may be able to use. Alternatively, you can get a hosted version of CouchDB from http://couch.io.

CouchDB Resources

This book is written as a guide to help you get started with CouchDB. For further information about CouchDB, consult the following resources:

- http://couchdb.apache.org/
- http://couchdb.apache.org/community/lists.html
- #couchdb on irc.freenode.net
- http://wiki.apache.org/couchdb/
- http://planet.couchdb.org/

- http://hosting.couch.io/
- http://damienkatz.net/
- http://jan.prima.de/plok/
- http://wiki.apache.org/couchdb/Windows_binary_installer
- http://www.ibm.com/developerworks/opensource/library/os-couchdb/index.html
- http://twitter.com/CouchDB

Contacting the Author

If you have any questions, comments, or feedback, you can contact the author by e-mail at joe@joelennon.ie or on Twitter @joelennon.

PART 1

■■■

Getting Started

In this part, you will learn all about the CouchDB database and how it differs from traditional relational database management systems. You will learn how to install CouchDB on Linux and Mac OS X operating systems, and you will see just how easy it is to create a new CouchDB database.

■ ■ ■

CHAPTER 1

Introduction to CouchDB

CouchDB is a relatively new database management system, designed from the ground up to suit modern software applications that tend to be web-based, document-oriented, and distributed in nature. For several decades now, relational database management systems have reigned supreme in application and database development, with the likes of Oracle, SQL Server, and MySQL being used in every type of software application imaginable.

When object-oriented development started to gain traction in the early 1990s, many believed that object-oriented database systems would closely follow suit. Since then, however, there has been a large shift in focus in software development. The breakthrough of dynamic web applications and mobile technology has led to developers looking for lightweight, inexpensive, and well-documented solutions. Many of these developers were prolific at SQL, and open source relational databases such as MySQL simply made the most sense. Today, MySQL is used on millions of web sites across the world.

The relational model that these databases are built on, however, was designed many years ago, when the World Wide Web and Internet were unheard of. Although the strict schema-based structure these databases adhere to is required in some web applications, such as transaction systems, it is not a good fit for many modern web projects, such as blogs, wikis, and discussion forums, which by their nature are a better fit to a document-oriented database.

What Is CouchDB?

CouchDB is a document-oriented database management system, released under the open source Apache License. In contrast to most database systems, it stores data in a schema-free manner. This means that, unlike traditional SQL-based databases, there are no tables and columns, primary and foreign keys, joins, and relationships. Instead, CouchDB stores data in a series of *documents* and offers a JavaScript-based view model for aggregating and reporting on the data.

If you are wondering where the name CouchDB came from, you may be surprised to hear that it is in fact an acronym. According to the CouchDB wiki, Couch stands for "Cluster Of Unreliable Commodity Hardware," indicating that CouchDB is intended to run distributed across a cluster of cheap servers. Anyone who has dealt with replication in databases before will know that it is rarely a simple task, but the exact opposite applies when it comes to CouchDB. Add to this the fact that CouchDB is developed in Erlang OTP, a fault-tolerant programming language that offers excellent concurrency features, and you know that your CouchDB database will scale well without a loss of reliability and availability.

Currently, CouchDB is available for most UNIX-based systems, including Linux and Mac OS X. Binary installers are available for Ubuntu, Fedora, CentOS, FreeBSD, and Mac OS X systems through each system's individual package manager. Windows support is pretty sketchy currently, although an unofficial binary installer is in the works. Alternatively, CouchDB can be built from source on virtually any POSIX system. I will discuss how to install CouchDB on Linux and Mac OS X in the next two chapters. You will also get a look at an unofficial application for Mac OS X called CouchDBX, which allows you to simply download and run a CouchDB server immediately, no installation or configuration necessary.

CouchDB: The Story So Far

In April 2005, Damien Katz posted on his blog about a new database engine he was working on. Details were sparse at this early stage, but what he did share was that it would be a "storage system for a large scale object database" and that it would be called CouchDB. His objectives for the database were for it to become the database of the Internet and that it would be designed from the ground up with web applications in mind.

Katz began working on the database soon after his blog post, choosing C++ as the platform to build it on. Right from the very beginning, CouchDB was designed to be schema-free and indexable, using a combination of append-only storage and atomic updates. It was clear that Katz was heavily influenced by Lotus Notes, the product he worked tirelessly on for many years. The choice of using append-only storage meant that data in a CouchDB database would never be overwritten, but rather it would become "outdated," with the newer data taking precedence.

In November 2005, Katz announced that he was working on the Fabric formula language. Katz was previously involved in the development of the Lotus Notes Formula language, which Fabric inherited many features from. In December 2005, Katz published a blog post outlining his goals and ambitions for CouchDB, stating that it was "Lotus Notes built from the ground up for the Web." It was in this blog post that many of the features that exist in CouchDB today were put forward, such as document orientation, distributed architecture, bidirectional replication, and offline access. Further validating the notion that CouchDB would be the "database for the Web" was Katz's hope that CouchDB would be a great database engine for applications such as e-mail, bug tracking, timesheet management, blogs, and RSS feeds, amongst others.

A big milestone in CouchDB development was the announcement in February 2006 that its underpinning codebase was being moved, in its entirety, from C++ to Erlang. This purpose-built programming language was developed by Ericsson and is heavily used in the telecommunications industry. It is highly centered on the ideas of concurrency control, fault tolerance, and distributed applications, and as a result, Katz believed it was the perfect fit for CouchDB.

Another breakthrough came in April 2006 when it was announced that CouchDB would be solely accessible via an HTTP-based RESTful API. What this means is that rather than connecting to the database server using a client application, you would use any software capable of interacting with an HTTP web server to make requests, which would in turn perform database actions, returning an appropriate response when finished. This means you can manage the database by simply visiting URLs in your web browser, using command-line tools such as `curl` or, more importantly, via any programming language that supports HTTP requests.

The first publically available release of CouchDB, version 0.2, was made available for download in August 2006. At the time, CouchDB would run only on Microsoft Windows. Not much was said about CouchDB over the next 12 months, but in August 2007, Damien Katz announced that he had decided to scrap XML in the favor of JavaScript Object Notation (JSON) and to get rid of the Fabric formula language altogether, instead choosing to use JavaScript as a query engine. This decision is arguably the most important one made to date in the CouchDB project, and it sparked a huge amount of interest in the project.

In November 2007, version 0.7.0 was released, and it came with a host of new features. CouchDB now featured a JavaScript view engine based on Mozilla Spidermonkey and an attractive web-based administration interface (which would later be named Futon). This version of CouchDB was the first version that could actually be used as a proper database, and it quickly drew the attention of IBM, which backed the project, allowing Damien Katz (who previously worked for IBM) to work full-time on developing CouchDB. Soon after IBM got involved, CouchDB's license was changed to use the Apache License rather than the restrictive and cumbersome GNU General Public License (GPL).

In February 2008, it was announced that CouchDB would include support for Map/Reduce. CouchDB views would be defined using a Map function and an optional Reduce function. The Map function would take an input document and emit key/value pairs. The Reduce function then takes each of these pairs and performs further calculation. CouchDB's implementation of Map/Reduce is designed to allow views to be updated incrementally, meaning that it will only reindex any documents that have been modified since the last time the index was updated. This allows large sets of partitioned data to be queried extremely quickly, as the view has been generated over time.

In June 2008, version 0.8.0 was launched, and the following month, a usable version of CouchDBX, a one-click packaged version of CouchDB for Mac OS X, was made available. This meant that potential CouchDB developers could get their feet wet by sampling what CouchDB has to offer, without getting their hands dirty with a full install. In November 2008 CouchDB became a top-level Apache project, alongside the likes of the Apache HTTP Server, Tomcat, Ant, and Jakarta. If anything, this certified CouchDB as a credible project to developers around the world and has definitely worked to the project's advantage.

In April 2009, version 0.9.0 was released, followed by the release of version 0.9.1 in late July 2009. The first beta version of CouchDB, 0.10.0, was released in October 2009. At the time of writing, there is no fixed release date for version 1.0, although many predict it will be sometime in the next 12 months.

Document-Oriented Databases

A key feature of CouchDB is that it is a document-oriented database management system. Basically, this means that the data stored in a CouchDB database comprises a series of documents, each of which can contain a series of fields and values. Each document is independent of one another, and there is no strict schema that they must adhere to. Traditional databases that adhered to the relational model stored data in a series of tables; they were made up of rows and columns of data. In a relational database, you must predefine the schema that all data in each table will adhere to, and all the data contained in the table must strictly conform to that schema.

If you are used to SQL-based databases like Oracle, SQL Server, and MySQL, you are probably quite familiar with the concepts of relationships, primary keys, foreign keys, referential integrity, and so forth. If you are not, don't panic, because these concepts don't exist in CouchDB. In fact, it may take some time for a SQL developer to grasp the idea of a database without relationships and a row/column layout. Instead of a primary key field, each document in a CouchDB database has a unique ID. This unique ID can be assigned by the user or application, or it can use a universally unique identifier (UUID)—a random number generated by CouchDB that greatly reduces the chance of duplicate IDs being used. All data relevant to the document in question is stored directly in that document itself.

The fact that CouchDB is a schema-free database management system is very important. When developing a relational database, you must carefully think about how your database should be modeled before you create it. Altering a SQL database can be a devastating experience for any database administrator, because a series of dependency and integrity issues come into play. This is not the case with a document-oriented database like CouchDB. Each document is self-contained, so you do not need to store redundant null values, and you can define new fields for each document independently of one another.

It may be easier to think of CouchDB as a collection of paper documents. On a paper document, it doesn't make any sense to list a field as null. For example, if a person does not have a middle name, would you write their name as "John NULL Smith"? Of course not. You would simply leave out the middle name altogether. The same principle applies to a document-oriented database.

Naturally, a schema-free architecture has some disadvantages, such as a lack of defined structure and unnecessary replication of data across documents. Of course, in cases where these criteria are of the utmost importance, CouchDB is probably not the database for you. In fact, the developers openly state that they do not intend for CouchDB to be a direct replacement for a relational SQL-based database. Instead, they see it as an alternative in scenarios where a document-oriented architecture is a viable solution. In applications such as wikis, document management systems, discussion forums, blogs, support management systems, and so forth, documents are the way forward. For years now, web developers have retrofitted their application model to fit around a relational database. Thanks to CouchDB, this may no longer be necessary.

CouchDB Documents

Data in a CouchDB database is stored in a series of uniquely named documents, objects made up of various named fields. The values stored in the document can be strings, numbers, dates, booleans, lists, maps, or other data types. Each document in the database has a unique ID, and the documents are stored in the database on a flat address space. There is no limit to the number of fields a document may have or on the size of values stored in the document. In addition to data fields, each document includes metadata that is maintained by the CouchDB server itself, such as a revision number and more.

The use of document revisions is important, because CouchDB itself does not impose a locking mechanism on data. If two users are editing the same data at the same time, the first to commit their update will succeed, while the other will receive a conflict error. When a conflict is detected, the user will be presented with the latest revision of the document and offered the opportunity to make their changes again. Also important to note is that CouchDB will never overwrite existing documents, but rather it will append a new document to the database, with the latest revision gaining prominence and the other being stored for archival purposes. This works in a similar way to the revision control of a document management system, except that it is taken care of by the database itself.

■ **Note** Although CouchDB stores previous revisions of documents, it is not safe to assume that these revisions will be available permanently. To keep the size of the database to a minimum, CouchDB provides a feature allowing a database administrator to compact the database. This will delete any previous revisions of documents, and hence the revision history will be lost. If you are developing an application that requires revision history, it is highly recommended that you build an additional versioning layer rather than use CouchDB's internal layer.

The CouchDB layout and committing system adheres to the ACID properties (atomicity, consistency, isolation, and durability), which guarantee the reliable execution of database transactions. *Atomicity* basically means that database transactions should be all or nothing—either the entire transaction completes successfully or none of it does. *Consistency* refers to the database being in the same state before and after every database transaction. *Isolation* means that each transaction must be isolated from others in that its new state should not be available until the transaction is complete. Finally, *durability* means that when a transaction is complete and the user has been notified of the fact, the transaction cannot be reversed, even by a complete system failure or shutdown.

The JavaScript View Engine

Because CouchDB is schema-less by design, the data stored in the database is highly unstructured. Although this means the data is flexible and the fields can be easily changed without disrupting database integrity, it also means that the flat data can be difficult to report on. Although it might be suitable and fast for general-purpose querying, it starts to become more cumbersome when you try to perform aggregation and reporting.

Fortunately, CouchDB provides a Spidermonkey-based JavaScript view engine that allows you to create ad hoc views that can perform aggregation and joins, allowing you to report on the documents in the database. These views are not physically stored in the database, but rather they are generated when required, and as a result, they do not impact the actual data being reported on. There is no limit to the number of views you can use.

In CouchDB, views are defined inside design documents, and just like data documents, they can be replicated across instances of the database. Inside these design documents are JavaScript functions that run queries using CouchDB's implementation of Map/Reduce. In addition to stored views, ad hoc queries and reports can be run using a temporary view, although for performance reasons, this is not recommended.

Each time a client makes a read request, CouchDB will make sure that the requested views are up-to-date. If the requested view does not contain the most recent database changes, these edits are incrementally inserted into the view. This alleviates the performance issues associated with generating a view dynamically each and every time it is run, especially on databases that store millions of records of data.

RESTful HTTP API

Traditional relational databases are typically accessible using a client software application or module, and database transactions are committed using a language known as Structured Query Language (SQL). CouchDB does things somewhat differently, depending on a RESTful HTTP API to provide users access to the data. Before we continue, let's deal with those acronyms.

Representational State Transfer (REST) in this sense refers to the fact that data access is available via a series of simple web services that are implemented in Hypertext Transfer Protocol (HTTP) and adhere to the principles of REST. JavaScript Object Notation (JSON) is a light, text-based data format for representing data. An application programming interface (API) is the basic interface offered to developers so they can build applications that interact with the database. Typically, programming languages would each have a client library for interacting with a particular database. Although client libraries exist for CouchDB (for the sole purpose of making it easier to interact with the database), any platform that supports HTTP requests can interact with CouchDB without requiring any additional client libraries to be installed.

To use the CouchDB API, you issue an HTTP request to the CouchDB server. What the server does with your request depends on the URI you are issuing the request to, the request method you are using (GET, POST, PUT, DELETE), and the data you send along with your request. When the server has finished processing your request, it will return the data (or details of any error that may have been encountered) or a suitable JSON response. You can then parse the JSON in your application and display the results of the transaction accordingly.

Parsing JSON is quite simple, and using a JavaScript framework such as Prototype or jQuery makes sending HTTP requests and parsing JSON responses very simple using Ajax methods. As JSON increases in popularity, many languages are including support in their standard library. For languages that don't have built-in support, there is a wide selection of third-party extensions to almost all popular languages.

Futon

If all this API nonsense isn't making much sense to you, feel free to park it for now, because I will be covering it in more detail later, with detailed examples of how to use the API in your very own CouchDB applications.

Thankfully, the developers of CouchDB decided that you shouldn't need a degree in computer science in order to interact with the database. To allow users to interact with the database immediately, they created Futon, the web-based CouchDB administration tool (Figure 1-1). This visually stunning web application comes bundled with every CouchDB install, and it actually runs on the same server as CouchDB. As a result, when you start the CouchDB database, Futon is automatically available to you.

Futon is exceptionally feature rich for such a young piece of software. It allows you to create, modify, and delete databases and documents as you please, and it has advanced pagination and sorting functionality on every screen. It also allows you to easily compact your database, as well as run a series of diagnostics to ensure your database is working as it should be.

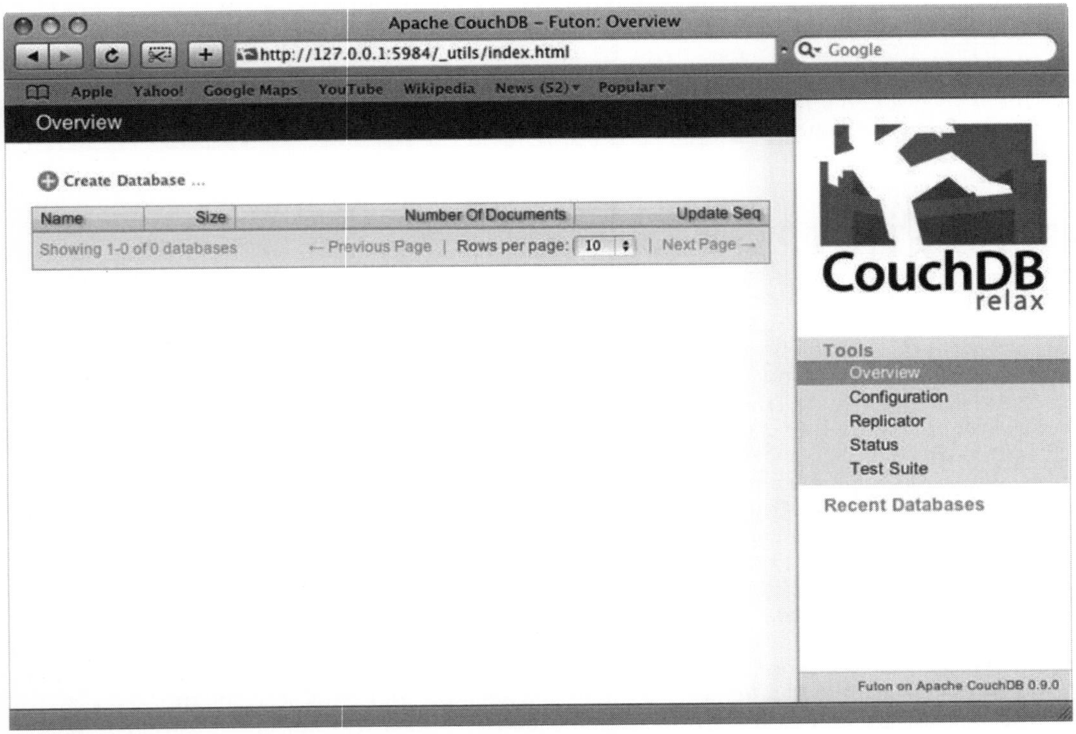

Figure 1-1. Futon, the CouchDB administration interface

So...Now What?

Now that you've learned what CouchDB is and how it works, you're going to dive right in and get a CouchDB development environment up and running. Over the next two chapters, I will walk you through the process of installing CouchDB on Linux and Mac OS X operating systems. Then, in Chapter 4, you shall delve deep into CouchDB development by creating your first database. If you already have some experience with CouchDB, feel free to plough ahead to Part 2 of this book, where I'll discuss practices for managing CouchDB databases.

■ ■ ■

CHAPTER 2

Installing CouchDB on Linux

In this chapter, you will learn how to install CouchDB on the Linux operating system. When it comes to setting up Couch on Linux, several options are available, depending on the particular Linux distribution you use. Precompiled binary versions of CouchDB are available via various package managers; for example, you can use aptitude on newer versions of Ubuntu Linux and yum on Fedora Linux. Even if your system's package manager does not include CouchDB itself in its repository, it's quite likely that it does feature some of Couch's dependencies (Erlang, ICU, Spidermonkey, libcurl, and so on). If your operating system does not support one of these package managers (or for some reason you can't get it to work), all is not lost, because it is not that difficult to compile CouchDB (and its prerequisites) from source code.

■ **Note** International Components for Unicode (ICU) is an open source set of libraries for Unicode support and software internationalization. CouchDB uses it for Unicode collation. Mozilla Spidermonkey is a JavaScript engine that CouchDB uses for creating views using JavaScript code. libcurl is a library that provides support for transferring data over URLs. You use it so that Spidermonkey can make HTTP requests.

I will cover all these options in great detail over the course of this chapter. First, I will walk you through installing CouchDB on Ubuntu Linux 8.10. I will then show how to use the yum package manager to install CouchDB on Fedora Linux. Finally, you will learn the more difficult task of building CouchDB and all dependencies from source code.

Installing CouchDB on Ubuntu Linux 8.10

In this section, I will walk you through the installation of CouchDB on Ubuntu Linux 8.10. You should also be able to follow this guide to install CouchDB on later versions of Ubuntu. If you are using an earlier version of Ubuntu, however, skip ahead to the "Building CouchDB (and Prerequisites) from Source Code" section for instructions on building CouchDB and its dependencies from source. I will show you how to install CouchDB's dependencies using the apt-get command, before downloading the latest release version of CouchDB (0.10.0 at the time of writing) and building it from source. If you want to build the trunk version of CouchDB, you can simply follow the instructions here up until the point of building CouchDB and then follow the CouchDB build instructions from the later section of this chapter.

You will be installing CouchDB and its dependencies using command-line tools, so open a Terminal window. If you are using GNOME, you will find this option under Applications ▶ Accessories ▶ Terminal, as shown in Figure 2-1.

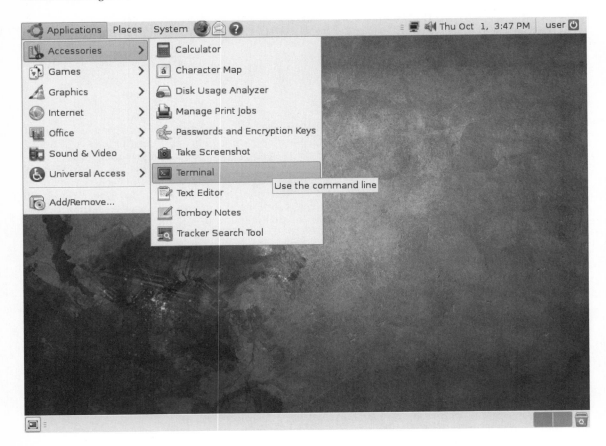

Figure 2-1. *Opening Terminal in Ubuntu Linux*

Before you can install CouchDB, you need to install a series of dependency packages. If you are using version 8.10 or later of Ubuntu Linux, you can use the `apt-get` package manager utility to install all these dependencies. In the Terminal window, issue the following commands to automatically download and install CouchDB's dependencies. If any of these packages have further dependencies, `apt-get` will automatically download and install them, too.

```
$ sudo apt-get install automake autoconf libtool help2man
$ sudo apt-get install build-essential erlang libicu-dev libmozjs-dev libcurl4-openssl-dev
```

With CouchDB's dependency packages installed, you are now ready to download and build CouchDB. In this section, you will download the latest release version of CouchDB (0.10.0 at the time of writing) from an Apache mirror. In this example, I'm downloading from an Irish Apache mirror site—if you want to find one closer to your location, visit the CouchDB web site at http://couchdb.apache.org. The following commands will download and unpack the tarball for CouchDB 0.10.0.

```
$ wget http://apache.mirrors.esat.net/couchdb/0.10.0/apache-couchdb-0.10.0.tar.gz
$ tar xzvf apache-couchdb-0.10.0.tar.gz
```

This will create a new directory beneath your working directory, named apache-couchdb-0.10.0. Let's enter this directory and configure and build CouchDB from the source code:

```
$ cd apache-couchdb-0.10.0
$ ./configure
$ make
$ sudo make install
```

You now have CouchDB installed on your system, but you need to do some final configuration before you can launch the CouchDB server. First, let's create a user account, couchdb, which will own the CouchDB system directories:

```
$ sudo adduser couchdb
```

You will be asked a series of questions in order to set up the user account. When asked for a password, repeatedly hit the Enter key (providing no password) until it stops asking for one. You can accept the default options for every field. With the user account created, let's create the CouchDB system directories and assign ownership of them to the couchdb user.

```
$ sudo mkdir -p /usr/local/var/lib/couchdb
$ sudo mkdir -p /usr/local/var/log/couchdb
$ sudo mkdir -p /usr/local/var/run
$ sudo chown -R couchdb /usr/local/var/lib/couchdb
$ sudo chown -R couchdb /usr/local/var/log/couchdb
$ sudo chown -R couchdb /usr/local/var/run
```

Finally, you need to copy the couchdb service to the correct folder and configure the service to run at startup:

```
$ sudo cp /usr/local/etc/init.d/couchdb /etc/init.d
$ sudo update-rc.d couchdb defaults
```

With that completed, you are now ready to launch the CouchDB server. Use the following command to start CouchDB as a background service, which will be automatically started when you boot your machine:

```
$ sudo /etc/init.d/couchdb start
```

You should see a message that the system is "starting database server couchdb," which will be processed in the background. Let's check that the server has started successfully:

```
$ curl http://127.0.0.1:5984
```

If CouchDB is running, you should see a message like the one shown in Figure 2-2.

■ **Note** It is quite possible that `curl` is not installed by default on Ubuntu Linux. If you get a message informing you that `curl` is not available, simply use the command `sudo apt-get install curl` to download and install it automatically.

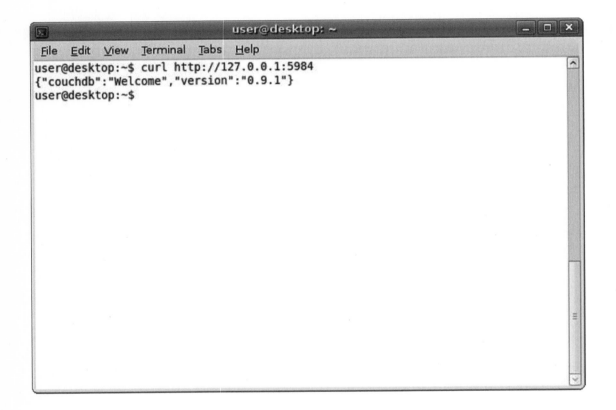

Figure 2-2. CouchDB welcome response message

With CouchDB up and running, now is a good time to open the Futon web administration interface and run the Test Suite, ensuring that every component of the CouchDB server is running properly. Open your favorite web browser, and navigate to the URL `http://127.0.0.1:5984/_utils`. On the right side of the page, click the Test Suite link. On the page that follows, click the Run All button near the top left of the page to begin the tests. Your browser may become slow and unstable while the tests run, so be patient. If all is well, you should receive a "Success" response for each test in the list (Figure 2-3).

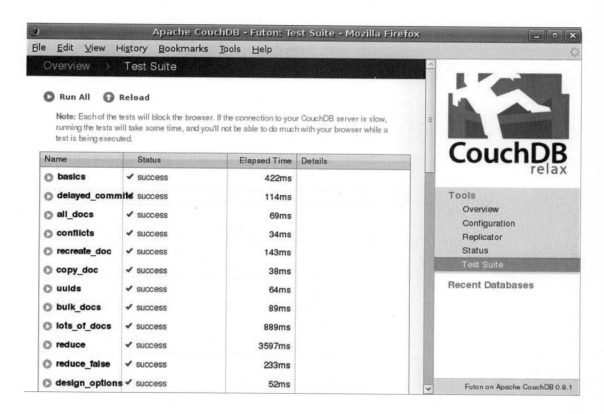

Figure 2-3. *Futon Test Suite results*

■ **Note** If you are experiencing problems with the replication test failing, make sure you entered the IP address 127.0.0.1 rather than localhost in the URL. If you have IPv6 enabled on your system, localhost will resolve to an IPv6 address first, and because CouchDB listens only on IPv4, the connection cannot be established. If you're set on using localhost, disabling IPv6 will also fix this issue.

That's it—you now have a working CouchDB server on your Ubuntu system! Feel free to play around with CouchDB using the Futon interface, and when you're ready, continue to Chapter 4 to learn how to create your first CouchDB database.

Installing CouchDB on Fedora Linux Using yum

Installing CouchDB on Fedora Linux is very simple thanks to the inclusion of the YellowDog Updater, Modified (yum). This command-line based software management utility will automatically update itself before fetching the requested software and any dependency packages required. I am installing CouchDB on Fedora 11, but the process should be the same for earlier versions of Fedora.

The first thing you will need to do is open a Terminal window. You can find the Terminal application in Applications ▶ System Tools ▶ Terminal, as shown in Figure 2-4.

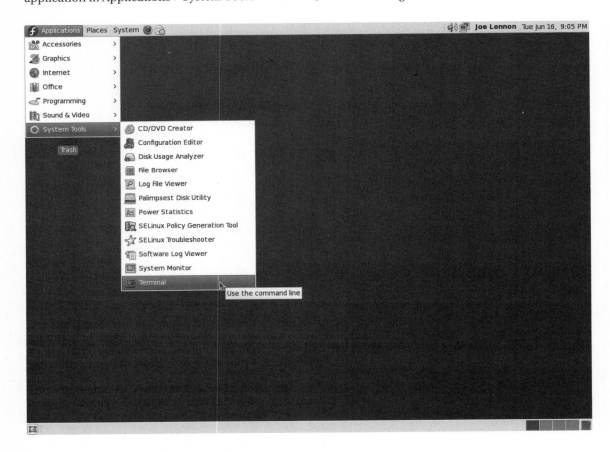

Figure 2-4. Opening Terminal in Fedora Linux

You will now tell the yum application to install the couchdb package. It is highly likely that you are logged in to Fedora as a standard user and hence will not have sufficient privileges to install packages with yum. There's no need to log out, however; we can use the su command to run a shell command as the root user. Issue the following command in your Terminal window to begin the installation process:

```
$ su -c 'yum install couchdb'
```

You will be asked for a password. Enter your system administrator (root) password and hit Enter. yum will search for any dependencies, before presenting a summary of what package and prerequisites are to be installed. It will ask you to confirm before the installation starts, as shown in Figure 2-5.

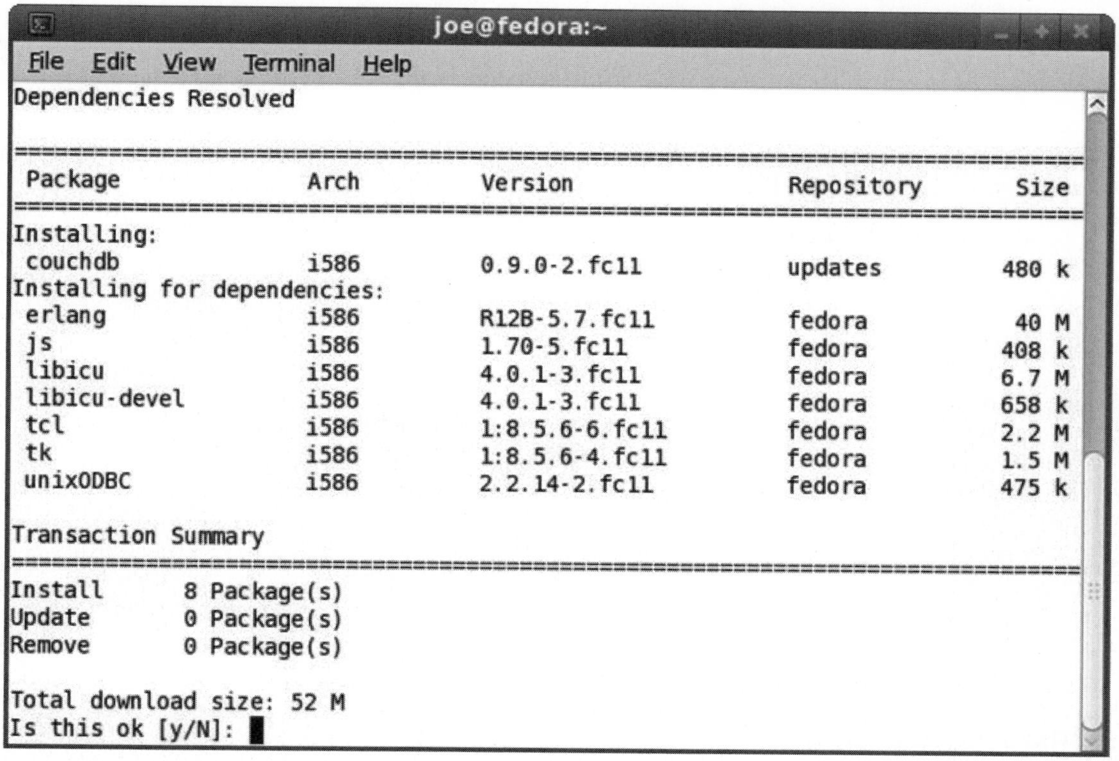

Figure 2-5. Installing CouchDB using the yum package manager

Press the Y key on your keyboard, and hit Enter to begin the installation process. On my system, the total download size amounted to 52 megabytes (MB). If you already have the latest version of Erlang installed, this download size will be significantly less (CouchDB itself is less than half a megabyte!). When it has finished downloading all the required packages, it will automatically install them for you. When it is done, it will give you a summary of what package was installed and what dependencies were installed along with it. This should look something similar to Figure 2-6.

17

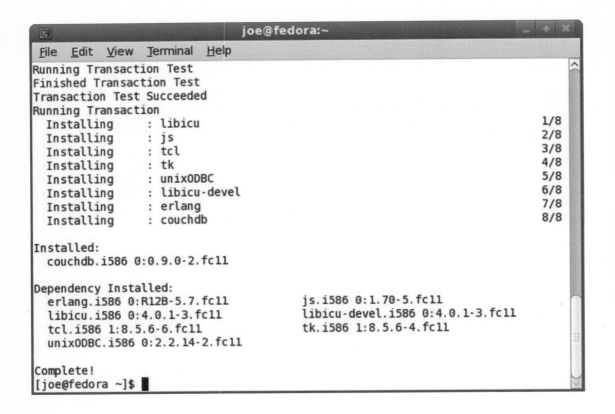

Figure 2-6. CouchDB installation complete

When the installation has finished, you will need to start the CouchDB server. This is very simple; just issue the following command:

```
$ su -c 'couchdb'
```

You should see a message similar to the one shown in Figure 2-7.

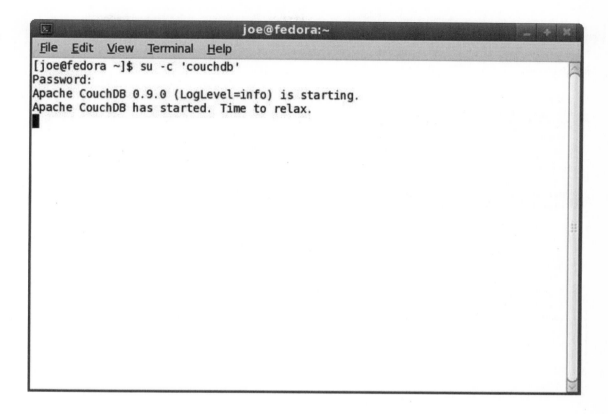

Figure 2-7. Apache CouchDB has started.

You may notice that you no longer have a prompt in this terminal window. Not to worry, just open another Terminal tab by hitting Shift+Ctrl+T. You will now verify that the server is running properly using `curl`. It is highly likely that you already have `curl` installed on your system, but if you do not, installing it is as simple as issuing the following command:

```
$ su -c 'yum install curl'
```

If `curl` is not installed, `yum` will automatically install it for you. If you have an out-of-date version of `curl` installed, `yum` will update it for you. If you already have the latest version of `curl`, `yum` will tell you that it has nothing to do and will quit. When `curl` has installed, you can verify that the CouchDB server is running with the following command:

```
$ curl http://127.0.0.1:5984
```

The server should return the following response:

```
{"couchdb":"Welcome","version":"0.9.0"}
```

Congratulations, you have now set up CouchDB on your Fedora Linux system! Before you proceed to Chapter 4, it might be a good time to check that Futon, CouchDB's web-based administration utility, is up and running correctly. Fire up your favorite web browser, and point it to the following URL:

`http://127.0.0.1:5984/_utils`

If Futon is working, you should see an attractive user interface like the one shown in Figure 2-8.

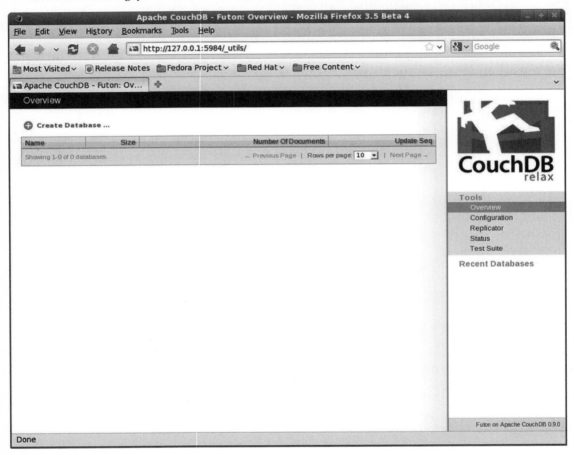

Figure 2-8. CouchDB's Futon Admin utility in action

I will now show how to run Futon's Test Suite to perform several diagnostic checks on the CouchDB server. Click the Test Suit link in the menu on the right side of the Futon screen. On the Test Suite page, click the Run All link near the top left of the page to begin the tests. The process should not take long, and with any luck, all the tests will return a success message, as per Figure 2-9.

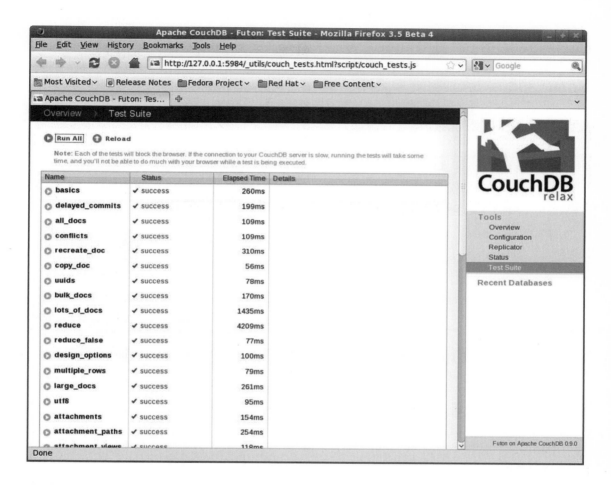

Figure 2-9. *Futon Test Suite results*

You are now ready to drive ahead and start developing CouchDB databases and applications. Feel free to skip ahead to Chapter 4, where you'll see how to create a CouchDB database.

Building CouchDB (and Prerequisites) from Source Code

If your system does not have a package manager with a CouchDB package available or you want to be sure that you are installing the latest version of Couch, your best bet is to compile CouchDB from source code. In this section, I will not only walk you through the process of building CouchDB from the source code for the latest trunk version, but you will also learn how to manually build the prerequisite applications you will need in order to use CouchDB—Erlang, libcurl, ICU, Spidermonkey, and Subversion.

■ **Caution** It is worth mentioning at this point that building software from source code is not for the fainthearted. Things often go wrong, and you are pretty much on your own when it comes to fixing any issues that arise. The following procedure is recommended for advanced users only. At the very least you should be comfortable working at the Linux command line. You have been warned!

This procedure has been tested on Slackware Linux 12.2, but they should work on any Linux distribution. It is assumed that you have OpenSSL installed, as well as the following development tools:

- GNU Automake (version 1.6.3 or newer)
- GNU Autoconf (version 2.59 or newer)
- GNU Libtool
- GNU help2man
- GNU Make
- GNU Compiler Collection (gcc)

■ **Note** Older versions of the client version of Ubuntu Linux did not install these tools by default. Fortunately, installing these tools is very simple on Ubuntu. Just run the following command:

```
$ apt-get install build-essential automake autoconf libtool help2man
```

If you have any trouble installing a particular package, the best place to look for help is the relevant application's documentation or manual.

Let's get started. For the most part, you will be entering commands in the Terminal window, and you will need to run these commands with administrative privileges. To do this, you will need to prefix your commands with su -c and wrap the command you are calling in single quotes. You may be asked to authenticate the first time you use this.

For the most part, I will be working from my home directory. Most of the software will be installed to various locations throughout the Linux filesystem, so where exactly you download and compile the applications is not important. If you're not sure where you are, use the command pwd to print your working directory.

Building Erlang

The first application you are going to download and build is Erlang. In the following command listing, Erlang R13B01 is downloaded. This was the latest stable release available at the time of writing. Feel free to change the download URL to a newer version of Erlang if you want. Download the Erlang source distribution using wget as follows:

```
$ wget http://erlang.org/download/otp_src_R13B01.tar.gz
```

When the download has completed (it may take a while, because it's quite a large file—around 50–60MB), issue the following commands to create a new directory from which you will build Erlang:

```
$ su -c 'mkdir /usr/local/erlang'
$ cd /usr/local/erlang
```

Now you decompress and extract the source code archive:

```
$ su -c 'tar xvzf /root/otp_src_R13B01.tar.gz'
```

This will create a new directory called otp_src_R13B01 under /usr/local/erlang. Change into this directory using this:

```
$ cd otp_src_R13B01
```

Now you are ready to go ahead and build your Erlang installation. The following commands will configure and compile Erlang. Please note that each of these commands will take a considerable amount of time to run, because you are compiling the source code for the entire Erlang programming language.

```
$ su -c './configure'
$ su -c 'make && make install'
```

When Erlang has finished compiling, you can test that it is working by running the Erlang prompt. Simply enter the command erl to open the compiler, and you should see a prompt similar to that in Figure 2-10.

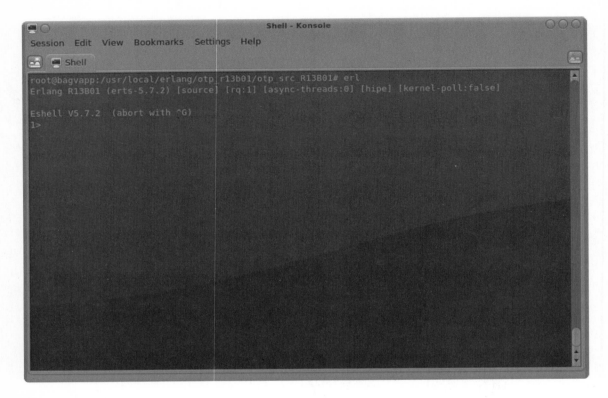

Figure 2-10. Testing your Erlang installation

When you are satisfied that Erlang is working, you can return to your Linux shell by entering the following command in the Erlang shell (don't leave out the period at the end; it's required!):

```
q().
```

Next you will build libcurl. Before you do so, return to your home directory (or wherever you're using as your base for downloading packages) by issuing the following:

```
$ cd ~
```

Building libcurl

The libcurl library is very simple to build. Download libcurl (and curl) using the following command:

```
$ wget http://curl.haxx.se/download/curl-7.19.6.tar.gz
```

Now extract the contents of the archive using the following command:

```
$ tar xvfz curl-7.19.6.tar.gz
```

This will create a new directory called `curl-7.19.6`. Enter this directory using the following:

```
$ cd curl-7.19.6
```

Now issue the following commands to configure and build `curl` and libcurl:

```
$ su -c './configure'
$ su -c 'make'
$ su -c 'make install'
```

That's all there is to installing libcurl. In the next section, you will build ICU.

Building ICU

Installing ICU is relatively straightforward, and the steps are similar to those you followed to build Erlang. The first step is to download the ICU source distribution. The latest version of ICU available at the time of writing was 4.2. Check the ICU web site for newer versions if you so wish.

```
$ wget http://download.icu-project.org/files/icu4c/4.2.0.1/icu4c-4_2_0_1-src.tgz
```

When the download has finished, decompress and extract the archive file using the following command:

```
$ tar xvfz icu4c-4_2_0_1-src.tgz
```

This will extract the contents of the archive into the `icu` directory. I will now show how to change to the source subdirectory inside this new directory and change the permissions of a few files to make sure they are ready for the build process:

```
$ cd icu/source
$ chmod u+x runConfigureICU configure install-sh
```

Next, you need to run the configuration script and start the compilation process itself:

```
$ su -c './runConfigureICU Linux'
$ su -c 'make && make install'
```

That's it for ICU. The next dependency for CouchDB you need to install is Spidermonkey. Once again, navigate back to your home directory before proceeding to the next section.

Building Spidermonkey

To build Spidermonkey, you will need to have several prerequisite packages installed on your system. Most of these packages (Perl, gcc, GNU make, and so on) are preinstalled on most Linux distributions. If you are using an older version of Ubuntu Linux, it is possible that you may not have all of these dependencies installed. You can install all of Spidermonkey's dependencies using the following commands:

```
$ sudo apt-get build-dep firefox
```

```
$ sudo apt-get install mercurical libasound2-dev libcurl4-openssl-dev libnotify-dev libxt-
dev libiw-dev
```

Ensure you are in your home directory, and you can proceed to download and build Spidermonkey. First, let's download the source distribution from Mozilla. I'm going to install Spidermonkey 1.7.0, because it works well with recent versions of CouchDB. If you want to use 1.8.0, be sure to build CouchDB from trunk.

■ **Note** Version 0.9.0 of CouchDB specifically requires version 1.7 of Spidermonkey to be installed. If you are building this version of CouchDB, ensure you use Spidermonkey 1.7.

```
$ wget http://ftp.mozilla.org/pub/mozilla.org/js/js-1.7.0.tar.gz
```

When the distribution package has finished downloading, use the following command to decompress and extract it:

```
$ tar xvzf js-1.7.0.tar.gz
```

Now navigate into the **src** subdirectory of the **js** directory:

```
$ cd js/src
```

From here you can compile Spidermonkey using the following commands:

```
$ JS_DIST=/usr/local/spidermonkey make -f Makefile.ref export
$ export LD_LIBRARY_PATH=/usr/local/spidermonkey/lib
$ ln -s /usr/local/spidermonkey/lib/libjs.so /usr/local/lib/libjs.so
$ ln -s /usr/local/spidermonkey/include /usr/local/include/js
```

Spidermonkey is now installed! The final prerequisite you need to build before building CouchDB itself is the Subversion, the version control system you need to use to get the latest "trunk" version of CouchDB.

Building Subversion

The CouchDB source code is maintained in a Subversion repository on Apache's servers. To download the latest build of CouchDB from trunk, you need to have a Subversion client installed on your machine. In this section, I will show how to build Subversion from source code.

■ **Note** Subversion is only required to retrieve the latest version of CouchDB from trunk. If you are building a release version of CouchDB, you can skip this step and download the source code from the CouchDB project web site instead.

Subversion has a number of dependencies that are required, which vary based on whether you are installing Subversion client or server. Fortunately, an archive containing the dependencies for the client is available, which can be extracted so that the prerequisites are automatically built along with Subversion. If you follow these instructions, you will not need to take any further steps to install Subversion's dependencies.

First, download the Subversion source code and the dependency archive using the following commands (make sure you're in your home directory):

```
$ wget http://subversion.tigris.org/downloads/subversion-1.6.5.tar.gz
$ wget http://subversion.tigris.org/downloads/subversion-deps-1.6.5.tar.gz
```

The dependency archive will extract the dependencies into the same directory as the Subversion source code archive was extracted to. Now enter the Subversion source directory and build Subversion:

```
$ cd subversion-1.6.5
$ su -c './configure'
$ su -c 'make && make install'
```

Subversion is now installed on your system. In the next section, you will use Subversion to get the latest version of CouchDB from trunk, before building CouchDB itself.

Building CouchDB

First and foremost, congratulations for making it this far! Building applications from source distributions is not light work. The good news is that you're almost there. You will now download the CouchDB source distribution from trunk using Subversion. Navigate back to your home directory, and use the following command to check out the latest version of CouchDB from the project's Subversion repository.

```
$ svn co http://svn.apache.org/repos/asf/couchdb/trunk couchdb
```

This will create a new folder named couchdb. Navigate into this folder using the following command:

```
$ cd couchdb
```

The first thing you need to do is bootstrap the source code. This is performed using the following command:

```
$ su -c './bootstrap'
```

When the bootstrapping has completed, you will see the message "You have bootstrapped Apache CouchDB, time to relax." Now you will run the configuration script.

```
$ su -c './configure'
```

When the configuration process has completed, enter the following command to install CouchDB:

```
$ su -c 'make && make install'
```

You're nearly there! Before you start the CouchDB server, you just need to create a user for couchdb, create a few directories, and set some permissions. Firstly, create a couchdb user by issuing the following command:

```
$ su -c 'adduser couchdb'
```

The system will ask you to enter a series of details for the new user. Simply accept the default options, and make sure you supply no password when prompted. You should see a message "Account setup complete" when the account has been created. Now you will create some directories and change the ownership of those directories to the couchdb user.

```
$ su -c 'mkdir -p /usr/local/var/lib/couchdb'
$ su -c 'chown -R couchdb /usr/local/var/lib/couchdb'
$ su -c 'mkdir -p /usr/local/var/log/couchdb'
$ su -c 'chown -R couchdb /usr/local/var/log/couchdb'
$ su -c 'mkdir -p /usr/local/var/run'
$ su -c 'chown -R couchdb /usr/local/var/run'
$ su -c 'cp /usr/local/etc/rc.d/couchdb /etc/init.d/'
```

With all that done, you are now ready to start the CouchDB server. The following command will start the CouchDB server in the background:

```
$ su -c '/etc/init.d/couchdb start'
```

You should see a message "Starting database server couchdb" to confirm that the server is indeed starting. Let's perform a quick check to see that it is indeed working:

```
$ curl http://127.0.0.1:5984
```

If the CouchDB server is running, you should see a message like this:

```
{"couchdb":"Welcome","version":"0.10.0a809125"}
```

If, for some reason, the server is not running and you get an error message when you try the previous line, it may be an issue with the initialization script. Try simply entering the following command:

```
$ couchdb
```

If the build was successful, you should see a message saying "Apache CouchDB has started – Time to relax." Open up a second Terminal window, and try the curl command shown previously again—this time it should work.

Before you move on, now would be a good time to test that Futon, CouchDB's administration utility, is working correctly. Futon provides a suite of diagnostic tests that will ensure that your CouchDB installation is healthy. Open your favorite web browser, and go to http://127.0.0.1:5984/_utils. You should see a screen like Figure 2-11.

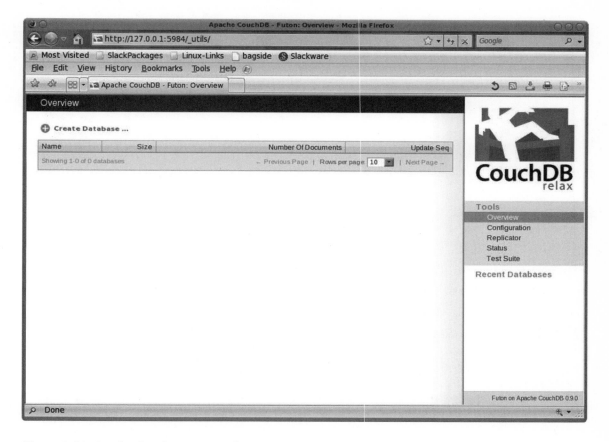

Figure 2-11. *Apache CouchDB Futon administration utility*

Now that you have Futon open, click the Test Suite link in the navigation menu on the right side of the screen. From here, click the Run All link near the top left of the page to start the Futon diagnostic tests. Ideally, all the tests will run and return a "success" status message, as in Figure 2-12.

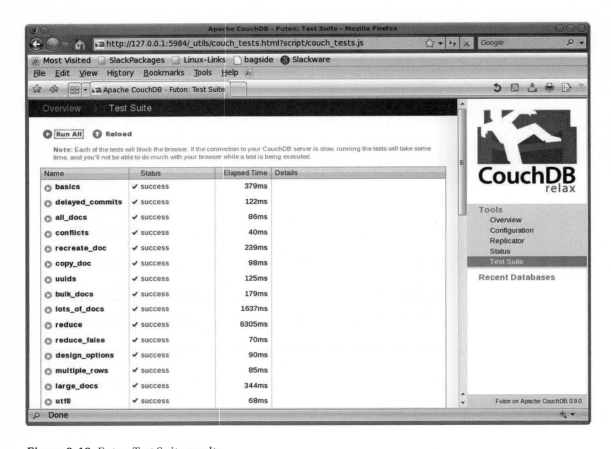

Figure 2-12. Futon Test Suite results

Congratulations, you have just successfully built CouchDB and its prerequisite packages from source code. You are now armed with all the tools you need to go forward and start learning how to create CouchDB databases. In the next chapter, you will learn how to install CouchDB on Mac OS X. In Chapter 4, you will learn how to create your first CouchDB database.

CHAPTER 3

■ ■ ■

Installing CouchDB on Mac OS X

In this chapter, you will learn how to install the CouchDB database on Mac OS X. There are several ways of installing CouchDB on the Mac. An unofficial "one-click" package, CouchDBX, is available and provides an easy-to-use way of trying CouchDB, if you don't like to get your hands dirty. I will talk about this in more detail later in this chapter. At the other end of the spectrum is the option to build CouchDB directly from source code. This is quite complicated and is recommended only to power users who want the highest level of flexibility with their CouchDB installation. Thankfully, there's a happy medium that offers relative simplicity in terms of installation while allowing you a high level of control in the configuration of your CouchDB setup. This method is what I refer to as the "MacPorts" method.

Before you can install CouchDB using MacPorts, you need to take care of a few dependency issues. First, you need to install Apple's Xcode developer tools. You can install the tools from your Mac OS X installation CDs/DVD, or alternatively you can download them from the Apple Developer Connection web site. Then you need to install MacPorts, an excellent open source package manager for Mac OS X. Once you have these dependency issues sorted out, installing CouchDB is a piece of cake.

Installing the Xcode Developer Tools

The Xcode developer tools are a suite of utilities for creating software applications that run on Mac OS X. Although not installed by default, Xcode can be found on your Mac OS X installation DVD/CDs and installed in a few simple steps. If you have lost the DVD/CDs that came with your Mac, you can download Xcode from Apple's Developer Connection (ADC) web site free of charge. In this section, I will walk you through the process of downloading Xcode from ADC and installing it on Mac OS X Leopard (10.5).

■ **Note** In the following steps I will be showing how to install Xcode version 3.0, because I am running Mac OS X Leopard (10.5). If you are installing Xcode on an earlier version of Mac OS X, you will need to download a different release of Xcode, because version 3.0 is not supported on older Mac OS X releases. Mac OS X Tiger (10.4) users should look for Xcode version 2.5, while those using Mac OS X Panther (10.3) will need Xcode version 1.5.

The first thing you need to do is download the latest version of the Xcode developer tools from ADC. Open your favorite web browser, and visit this location:

`http://developer.apple.com/technology/xcode.html`

You should see a page similar to that in Figure 3-1.

Figure 3-1. *The ADC web page for downloading Xcode*

On this page you will see two options; Xcode for iPhone and Mac Development and Xcode for Mac-only Development. Click the Download Now button next to the second option.

Note that if your Mac has an Intel (not a PowerPC) processor, you can install the Xcode for iPhone and Mac Development option. In addition to registering for ADC membership, you will need to register as an iPhone developer. Please note that there may be small differences in the following steps if you choose to go down this path.

The next screen (Figure 3-2) asks you to log in as an ADC member with your Apple ID and password. If you are not an ADC member but you have an Apple ID, enter those credentials; you will be brought to a page to complete your ADC membership registration. If you do not have an Apple ID, you will need to use the "sign up" link at the bottom of the page to get one before you can log in and download the Xcode tools.

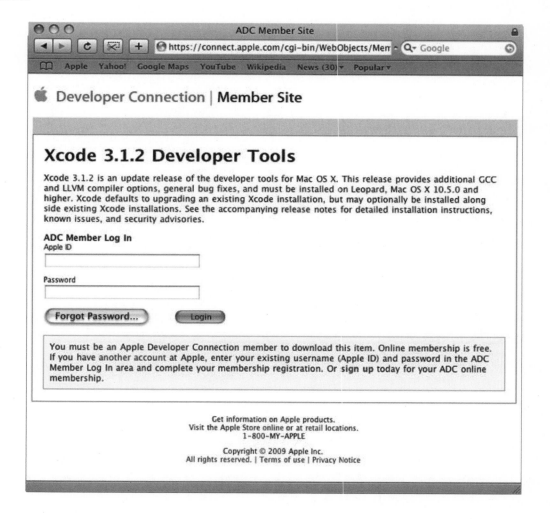

Figure 3-2. Log in to Apple Developer Connection to download the Xcode developer tools.

Once you have logged in to ADC, you will see a page similar to that shown in Figure 3-3. At the time of writing, the latest available version of Xcode was 3.1.2. Click the Xcode 3.1.2 Developer Tools DVD (Disk Image) link to commence the download.

■ **Note** The Xcode developer tools package is quite large (the disk image for version 3.1.2 weighed in at 996 megabytes), so it is highly recommended that you download the package over a high-speed Internet connection. Even on a decent broadband connection, the download may take over an hour. If this is not an option for you, I recommend that you install Xcode from your Mac OS X installation media instead.

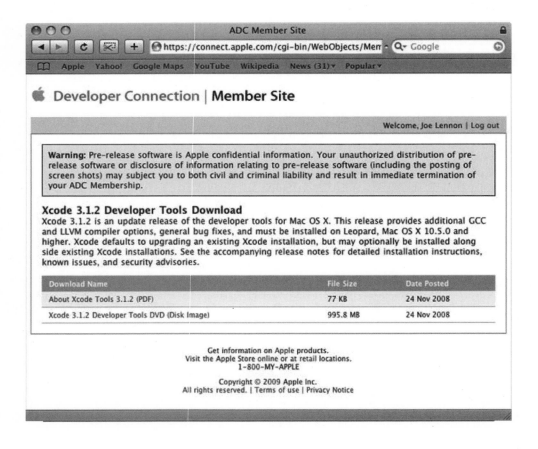

Figure 3-3. Xcode developer tools download page

Although the download page says that this is a DVD disk image, it does not mean that you need to burn it to DVD before you can use it. When the download has completed, the disk image should automatically mount and pop up a Finder window. From here, you can launch the Xcode installation application by double-clicking the XcodeTools.mpkg icon, as shown in Figure 3-4.

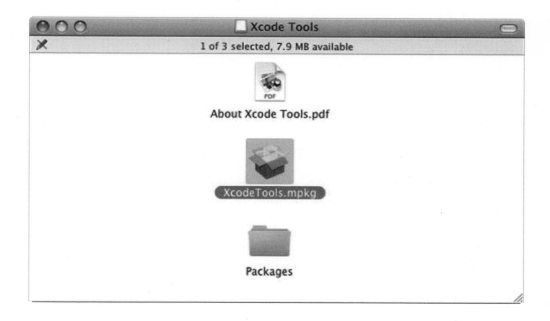

Figure 3-4. Xcode developer tools disk image

The Xcode Tools Installer will now load, and you can click the Continue button to begin the install. On the screen that follows, click the Continue button once again, which will pop up a confirmation dialog box, asking you to agree to the terms of the software license agreement. Click Read License to read these terms, and once you are satisfied, click the Agree button to move on. On the Custom Install on "Macintosh HD" screen, you can accept the default selections and click the Continue button to advance to the next screen. If you want to change the location where Xcode will be installed, you can click the Change Install Location button here; otherwise, simply click Install to begin the installation procedure.

You will now be asked for your Mac OS X system password. Enter it (if you have one), and click OK to continue. The installation procedure will now begin, and depending on your hardware, the process should take approximately ten minutes.

When the installation process has completed, you should see something similar to the screen shown in Figure 3-5.

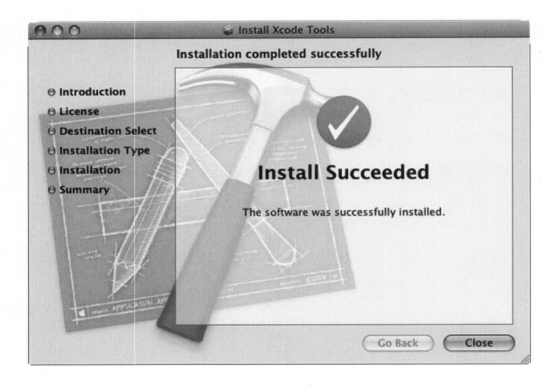

Figure 3-5. Xcode developer tools installation succeeded message

Installing MacPorts

I am going to show how to install CouchDB using an excellent, open source package manager for Mac OS X called MacPorts. Unfortunately, MacPorts is not included as part of Mac OS X, and therefore you need to install it before you can use it to install CouchDB. You will install MacPorts by downloading the latest binary package from the MacPorts project web site. Before beginning, please ensure that you have installed Xcode (see the previous section for detailed instructions on how to do this), because some of its components are required in order to install MacPorts.

Let's dive in and get MacPorts up and running on your system. Open your favorite webs browser, and visit the Installing MacPorts page on the MacPorts project web site:

```
http://www.macports.org/install.php
```

This page should look something like the one shown in Figure 3-6.

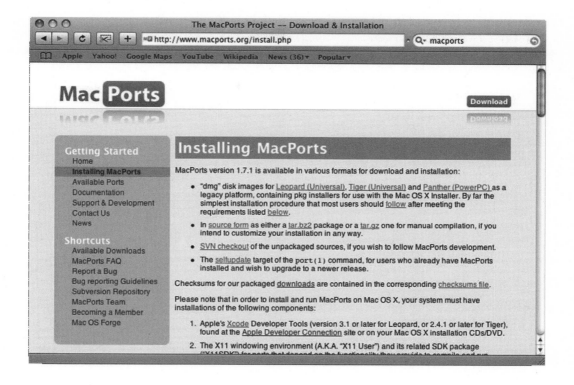

Figure 3-6. The MacPorts Project web site—Installing MacPorts page

The first bullet point on this page has links to three binary DMG image files, one each for the Snow Leopard (10.6), Leopard (10.5), Tiger (10.4), and Panther (10.3) versions of Mac OS X. Simply click the relevant link for the version of the operating system installed on your Mac, and the download will start. Unlike Xcode, MacPorts is a very lightweight piece of software (the current version at the time of writing, 1.7.1, weighed in at 415 kilobytes when I downloaded it). As soon as it has downloaded, the disk image will mount, and the installation application should open immediately.

When the installer starts, you will be informed that the package contains a program that determines whether the software can be installed, and it will ask whether you are sure that you want to continue. Simply click the Continue button to close this message, and you will be brought to the MacPorts installer, which should look similar to Figure 3-7.

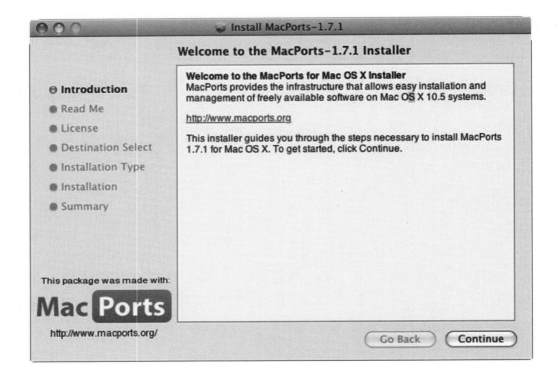

Figure 3-7. *Welcome to the MacPorts installer*

When this window appears, click the Continue button to move to the next part of the installation, which gives you information about MacPorts, its requirements, where it will be installed, and how to use it. Click Continue to skip forward to the next section. On the Software License Agreement screen, click Continue to bring up the confirmation dialog box asking you to agree to the terms of the software license agreement. If you like, read the license, and when you're ready, click the Agree button to continue with the installation. I don't recommend changing the installation target location, but if you feel the need to do so, you can click the Change Install Location button on the next screen to change it. Otherwise, just hit Install, and the installation procedure will commence.

As with Xcode, you will now be asked for your Mac OS X system password. Enter it, if you have one, and click OK to start the install. The entire process should only take a couple of minutes to complete. When it is finished, you should see a message like the one in Figure 3-8.

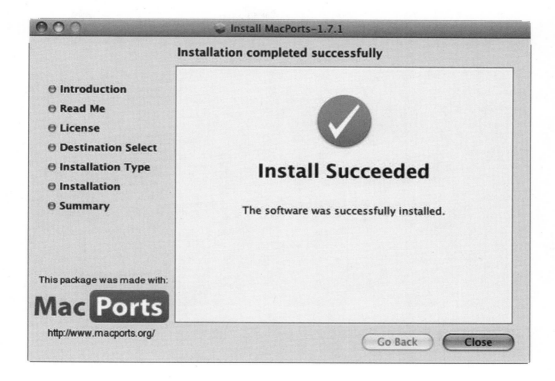

Figure 3-8. *MacPorts install succeeded.*

Before we move ahead and install CouchDB itself, let's perform a quick test to ensure that MacPorts is working as expected. To do this, open the Mac OS X Terminal application. The easiest way to do this is to open Spotlight (Cmd+Spacebar) and enter **Terminal** into the Spotlight text box. You should see *Terminal* as the Top Hit items and under the Applications section, as shown in Figure 3-9.

Figure 3-9. Terminal in Mac OS X Spotlight

Alternatively, you can find Terminal in the folder Applications ▶ Utilities. When you launch the Terminal application, you should see a prompt like the one shown in Figure 3-10.

Figure 3-10. Mac OS X prompt in Terminal window

To verify that MacPorts is working correctly, type in the following command in the Terminal window:

```
$ port search couchdb
```

If MacPorts has been installed and configured as required, you should see output similar to that in Figure 3-11.

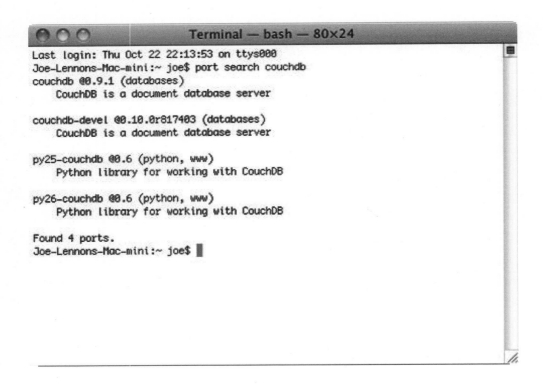

```
Last login: Thu Oct 22 22:13:53 on ttys000
Joe-Lennons-Mac-mini:~ joe$ port search couchdb
couchdb @0.9.1 (databases)
    CouchDB is a document database server

couchdb-devel @0.10.0r817403 (databases)
    CouchDB is a document database server

py25-couchdb @0.6 (python, www)
    Python library for working with CouchDB

py26-couchdb @0.6 (python, www)
    Python library for working with CouchDB

Found 4 ports.
Joe-Lennons-Mac-mini:~ joe$ █
```

Figure 3-11. Verifying MacPorts is installed in Terminal

Now that you have MacPorts installed, you are only a short section away from having CouchDB up and running on your Mac OS X system. Enter the quit command to exit the MacPorts interactive prompt and return to the shell. Let's move on and install CouchDB!

Installing CouchDB

In this section, you will use MacPorts to install CouchDB on your Mac. CouchDB has many dependencies, but fortunately you do not need to worry about sourcing all of these because MacPorts will automatically download and install them for you prior to installing CouchDB. As a result, installing CouchDB itself is not difficult at all.

At the end of the previous section, you checked that MacPorts was installed by opening the Mac OS X Terminal application and starting the MacPorts interactive prompt. If you closed that window, simply follow the same steps to open a new Terminal window. This time, enter the following command:

```
$ sudo port install couchdb
```

You may be presented with a warning about improper use of the sudo command and will then be asked to enter your password. Enter your password, and after a short time MacPorts will begin fetching and automatically installing all of CouchDB's dependency packages. Please note that this may take some time (about an hour or maybe even longer on some systems), so it might be a good time to take a break!

■ **Caution** In Mac OS X Leopard (10.5), the sudo command will not work if the user you are logged in as does not have a password set. If you simply hit the Return key when prompted for your password, sudo will just exit, and nothing will happen. In the Accounts preferences pane in your Mac OS X System Preferences, set up a password for your user account before you attempt to use MacPorts to install CouchDB. You can remove it after the installation has been completed if you want.

You'll know that the installation of CouchDB and its dependencies is completed when you are returned to the prompt and your Terminal window looks like the one in Figure 3-12.

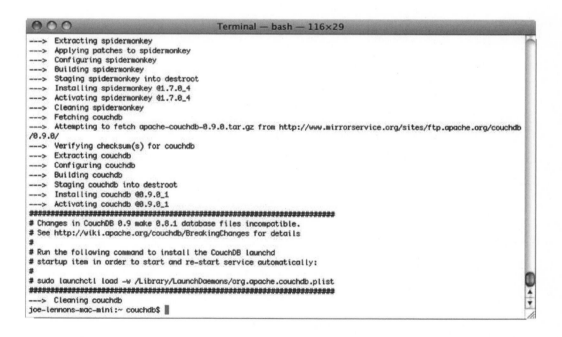

Figure 3-12. MacPorts installation of CouchDB completed

Before you take CouchDB out for a test-drive, let's make sure that all the dependencies are up-to-date. Back in the Mac OS X Terminal application, enter the following command (you'll need to provide your password again):

```
$ sudo port upgrade couchdb
```

In most cases, there should be nothing that needs updating, but if you already had MacPorts installed before reading this book, this command will ensure that any CouchDB dependencies that were already previously installed are up-to-date.

The final command you are going to run will configure CouchDB to run as a Mac OS X service and tell it to run CouchDB every time Mac OS X boots up. This step is optional, but if you don't complete, it you will need to start CouchDB manually every time you want to use it.

```
$ sudo launchctl load -w /Library/LaunchDaemons/org.apache.couchdb.plist
```

This command will have started CouchDB, but if you have chosen not to install as a Mac OS X service, you will need to manually start the server. Remember, you do not need to do this if you ran the previous command.

```
$ sudo launchctl start org.apache.couchdb
```

If, for some reason, you need to stop the CouchDB server at any stage, you can use the following command to do so:

```
$ sudo launchctl stop org.apache.couchdb
```

Now, let's run a couple of quick checks to make sure your CouchDB setup is running nice and smoothly! First, you will make sure that the CouchDB server is working correctly. The easiest way to do this is to use curl to make a CouchDB request. At the Mac OS X Terminal, issue the following command:

```
$ curl http://127.0.0.1:5984
```

If the CouchDB server is running, you should see a message similar to the following:

```
{"couchdb":"Welcome","version":"0.9.0"}
```

You can perform the same test by simply visiting http://127.0.0.1:5984 in your favorite web browser. Doing so, you should see a result similar to the one shown in Figure 3-13.

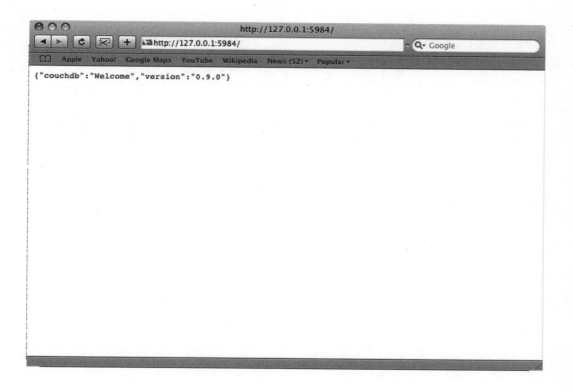

Figure 3-13. *Checking the CouchDB server is running*

The final test you will run is a quick check that Futon, the CouchDB web-based administration interface, is up and running. To check this, visit `http://127.0.0.1:5984/_utils/index.html` in your favorite web browser. You should see a rather pretty page, like the one in Figure 3-14.

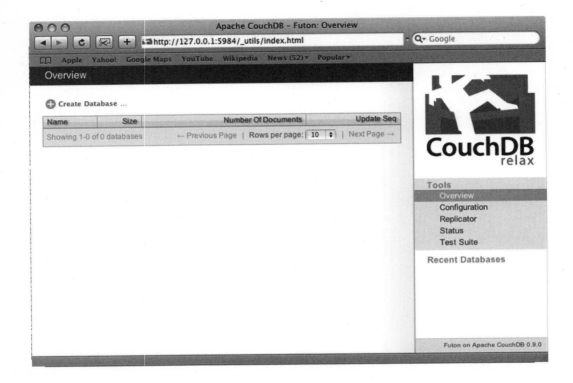

Figure 3-14. Futon, the CouchDB administration interface

From the Tools menu on the right side of the Futon interface, click the Test Suite link. This will bring you to a page where you can run a series of diagnostic tests to make sure that all aspects of your CouchDB server are running as they should. Click the Run All link at the top of this page to begin the tests. All going well, you should have zero failures, and the result should look something like the page in Figure 3-15.

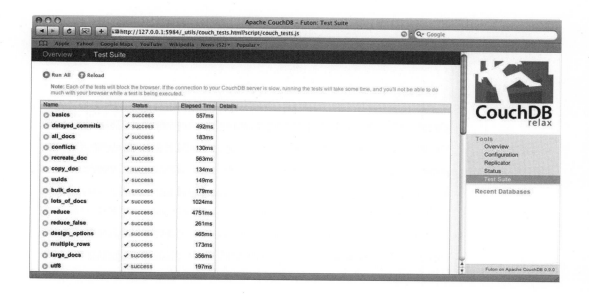

Figure 3-15. *Futon's CouchDB Test Suite results*

Congratulations! You now have a fully operational installation of CouchDB running on your Mac OS X system. If you chose to run the command to install CouchDB as a service, it will start up automatically each time you boot up your Mac. Feel free to skip ahead to the next chapter, where you will learn how to create a database and the basics of database development with CouchDB.

CouchDBX: A One-Click CouchDB Package for Mac OS X

If the idea of installing Xcode, installing MacPorts, and getting down and dirty with the Mac OS X Terminal are not your cup of tea, there is an alternative! An unofficial one-click CouchDB package known as CouchDBX will get you up and running with a CouchDB server without installing anything. It doesn't offer the flexibility or configurability of a full install, but it's great for trying out CouchDB quickly. It can even be used on a machine that has a full version of CouchDB installed!

To get CouchDBX, visit `http://janl.github.com/couchdbx/`, and click the Download link. At the time of writing, the latest version was 0.10.0-R13B02, which includes Apache CouchDB 0.10.0, Erlang R13B02, Spidermonkey 1.7, and ICU 3.8. This particular version is approximately 12 megabytes in size, so it shouldn't take too long to download, even on slower Internet connections.

When the download has completed, you should have a CouchDB icon in the folder where your browser downloads are stored. Simply double-click this icon to run CouchDBX, and you should see a screen similar to that shown in Figure 3-16.

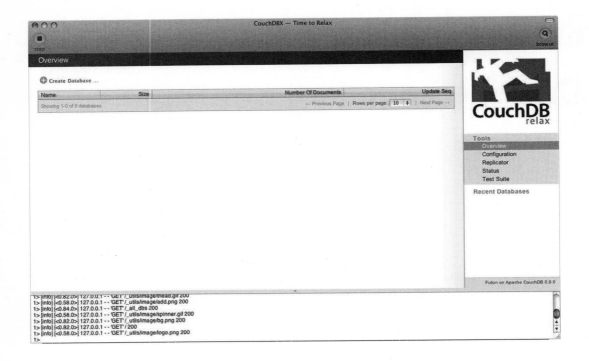

Figure 3-16. CouchDBX—the "one-click" CouchDB package

That was much simpler, now wasn't it? There's no doubting the fact that CouchDBX is the fastest and easiest way of getting a CouchDB environment up and running on your Mac. You can use CouchDBX to work through most of the content of this book, although if you are serious about CouchDB development, I highly recommend that you consider installing CouchDB on your system, either using MacPorts or building from the source code. It offers far superior performance and higher levels of reliability and flexibility when it comes to your CouchDB setup.

CHAPTER 4

■ ■ ■

Creating Your First CouchDB Database

In this chapter, you will learn how to interact with the CouchDB database server—primarily by means of learning how to perform basic tasks using the HTTP API, including the following:

- Creating a new database

- Creating, updating, and deleting database documents

- Adding file attachments to documents

- Retrieving documents from the database

- Creating a database view

If you have experience with traditional database management systems that use Structured Query Language (SQL) to interact with the database, the concepts introduced in this chapter may be quite alien at first. Unlike SQL-based databases, CouchDB does not come with its own client application; rather, you communicate with the server using any application or language that supports HTTP requests.

Another thing that might seem strange is that I won't discuss the design of your database before you go ahead and create it. You don't need to define the table structure for your database, because there are no tables. You don't need to draw up an entity relationship diagram (ERD) because there are no relationships. CouchDB is a *schema-free* database management system, meaning you don't have to worry about these things before you create your database; you can change any of these as required without negatively impacting your existing data.

Tools of the Trade

As mentioned, CouchDB does not come with a client application for connecting to the database server (well, actually it does, in the form of a web-based interface called Futon, but I'll discuss that in more detail later). Instead, you can interact with the CouchDB server using any piece of software or any programming language that supports making HTTP requests to a web server. CouchDB's API defines a series of methods that allow you to create databases, create documents, modify existing documents, and do all the other features you'd expect from a database management system. CouchDB then sends a response to the application in the form of JavaScript Object Notation (JSON), which can easily be parsed by most modern programming languages. JSON also has the advantage in that it is quite easily read by humans.

■ **Note** Up until this point, all UNIX commands have been prefixed with the prompt symbol ($). This is the final chapter in which I will include the prompt before these commands.

In this chapter, you will issue commands to your CouchDB server using the `curl` utility. If you followed an installation procedure from Chapter 2 or Chapter 3, you already came across `curl` when you verified that CouchDB was installed correctly. If you want to check that `curl` is installed on your system, open a Terminal window or command prompt, and enter the following command:

```
$ curl http://127.0.0.1:5984
```

If `curl` is installed (and assuming you have CouchDB running on your own computer), you should receive a response like the following:

```
{"couchdb":"Welcome","version":"0.9.0"}
```

Later in this book you will use other tools to interact with the CouchDB database, including CouchDB's very own Futon web-based administration interface, the JavaScript client-side web development language, and the PHP, Ruby, and Python programming languages.

HTTP Requests

To communicate with the CouchDB server over HTTP, it's important to have a basic understanding of how HTTP actually works. HTTP is a protocol that is primarily used to serve documents over the World Wide Web. You probably recognize it from the start of web addresses (for example, `http://www.apress.com`). HTTP is a client-server architecture where the client makes a request, and the server processes that request before returning a response to the client.

HTTP defines eight methods that are used to describe the desired action to be performed on the resource being requested. In CouchDB, you really need to be concerned with only four of these methods—GET, POST, PUT, and DELETE. CouchDB also uses an extension method provided by the HTTP protocol—COPY. What each method is used for is actually quite self-explanatory: GET is used to retrieve data from the database, PUT is used to insert new data and modify existing data (POST can also be used, but it is not recommended in most cases), DELETE is used to delete data from the database, and COPY is used to copy documents in the database. You will learn a lot more about how these request methods are used as you progress through this chapter.

JSON Response

When the CouchDB server processes an HTTP request, it returns a response in JSON. JSON is a light format for transporting data that is easy for humans to read but at the same time is simple for machines to parse. The data is written in the form of a JavaScript object, which is where the name comes from. JSON parsers are available for virtually every programming language, making it simple to use in your applications.

JSON supports various basic data types, including numbers, strings, booleans, nulls, arrays, and objects. A JSON object is opened and closed with curly braces, with a collection of comma-separated key/value pairs enclosed within these braces. A typical JSON object may look like the following:

```json
{
    "firstName": "Joe",
    "lastName": "Lennon",
    "email": [
        "joe@joelennon.ie",
        "joe@joelennon.com"
    ],
    "web": "http://www.joelennon.ie"
}
```

Using curl

curl is a lightweight command-line tool for transferring data to or from a server using various protocols, such as HTTP, HTTPS, and FTP. In this chapter, you will be using it to interact with CouchDB's HTTP interface. The most basic use of curl is to simply pass it a URL as an argument, and by default it will issue an HTTP GET request to the URL supplied. You have already seen an example of this earlier in this chapter, where you passed http://127.0.0.1:5984 as an argument to the curl utility.

curl has a host of options, most of which you don't need now. Three options are very important, however. First, the -X flag allows you to tell CouchDB which HTTP request method you want to use. This is important because the HTTP request method will define what exactly the CouchDB server will do (for example, GET retrieves, PUT creates/modifies, and DELETE destroys).

Another important curl flag is the -H option. This allows you to define HTTP headers in your requests to the CouchDB server. When you create documents in CouchDB, you define your documents in JSON and send this JSON data to the server. Unfortunately, older versions of the CouchDB server have no way of knowing what type of content this is unless you explicitly tell it. Luckily, you can use the -H flag and pass the string Content-Type: application/json, which does just that.

The final option you need to know about is the -d option. This allows you to include data (the message part of the HTTP request) when communicating with the CouchDB server. This is essential when you want to create meaningful documents or make any changes to existing documents. You will be using the -d flag to send your JSON document definitions and JavaScript view definitions to CouchDB.

If this doesn't make any sense to you at this point, don't worry—it should become a lot clearer in the next section when you actually start working with the database.

Creating Your First Database

Let's dive right in and create your first CouchDB database—a simple contacts database where you will store information much like that in an address book or phone book.

■ **Note** In all the following examples, I am assuming that you have the CouchDB server installed and running on your local machine. If you are interacting with a remote CouchDB server, replace the IP address 127.0.0.1 with the IP address of the machine where CouchDB is installed.

Creating the database is simple—just issue the following command in your Terminal window or command prompt:

```
$ curl -X PUT http://127.0.0.1:5984/contacts
```

Here you are making an HTTP PUT request to the **/contacts** resource of the CouchDB server. CouchDB translates this as "Create a new database named contacts." When the database has been created, CouchDB responds with the following JSON object:

```
{"ok":true}
```

The previous message basically means that the operation was successful and CouchDB encountered no errors in the process of creating the contacts database. That's great, but what would happen if CouchDB did encounter an error? Let's investigate by trying to create another database with the same name. Hit the up arrow in your Terminal window or, if required, retype the previous command:

```
$ curl -X PUT http://127.0.0.1:5984/contacts
```

This time around, you should receive a much different response than the last time:

```
{"error":"file_exists","reason":"The database could not be created, the file already
exists."}
```

As you can see, the CouchDB server attempted to create another database called contacts but could not do so because it already exists. It then sent a JSON response with two fields—the error field with the error code value **file_exists** and the reason field with a user-friendly error message informing you that the database could not be created because the file already exists.

Now that you have created a database, let's ask CouchDB to specify what databases are currently available on the server. Issue the following command:

```
$ curl -X GET http://127.0.0.1:5984/_all_dbs
```

You should receive the following response:

```
["contacts"]
```

This is a JavaScript array of all the databases currently stored on the CouchDB server. Let's see how it looks when there are multiple databases; create a second database called books:

```
$ curl -X PUT http://127.0.0.1:5984/books
```

Once again, you should receive the following response:

```
{"ok":true}
```

Now let's ask CouchDB once more to list all the databases available:

```
$ curl -X GET http://127.0.0.1:5984/_all_dbs
```

This time, it should return the following array:

```
["books","contacts"]
```

You'll be working on the contacts database for the remainder of this chapter, so you have no need for the books database. Let's get rid of it by issuing the following command:

```
$ curl -X DELETE http://127.0.0.1:5984/books
```

You should see a familiar response:

```
{"ok":true}
```

Now let's see whether you can generate another CouchDB error message. Press the up key to bring back the last-issued command or, if required, reenter the following:

```
$ curl -X DELETE http://127.0.0.1:5984/books
```

This time, the response you receive should be an error message saying that the database doesn't exist:

```
{"error":"not_found","reason":"Missing"}
```

Before moving on to working with documents in your newly created database, let's issue a command that will provide some information about the contacts database:

```
$ curl -X GET http://127.0.0.1:5984/contacts
```

This should return a response similar to the following:

```
{"db_name":"contacts","doc_count":0,"doc_del_count":0,"update_seq":0,"purge_seq":0,"compact_
running":false,"disk_size":4096,"instance_start_time":"1246103330612270"}
```

This response has some useful information fields, notably `doc_count`, which tells you how many documents are contained in the contacts database, and `disk_size`, which informs you how much disk space the database is taking up. These values should change substantially over the course of the coming sections as you work with documents.

Creating Documents in Your Contacts Database

If you were working with a traditional relational database management system, at this point you would be defining the schema for your database and mapping out the various tables, columns, and relationships that are required for a contacts database. You would be trying to work out all the different fields that may be required—for example, some contacts may have a fax number, an MSN Messenger account, or a Skype account that you want to include. So, in your table design, you would need to have columns for each of these fields. You may want to allow each contact to have several phone numbers and put these into a separate table that holds the type of number and the number itself, as well as a foreign key to map these numbers back to the contact record.

With CouchDB, however, you don't have to do any of this. CouchDB databases are schema-free, meaning that their structure is not strictly defined, and as a result you can change them on the fly as your needs require. If one contact has a fax number, you include it in that contact's document. If another contact doesn't have a fax number, you simply don't include it. If a contact has several phone numbers, you can set the `phone_number` field to be an array of phone number objects—there is no need to define separate tables.

In the contacts database, each contact that you create is considered to be an individual document. It may help to think of how a contact would be represented on a physical document—such as a business card. Every business card is a separate document, and the same applies to the contacts in the CouchDB database. Let's go ahead and create a contact:

```
$ curl -X PUT http://127.0.0.1:5984/contacts/johndoe -d '{}'
```

This should return a response similar to the following:

```
{"ok":true,"id":"johndoe","rev":"1-795358690"}
```

You've just created a document with the document ID of johndoe. The CouchDB server has automatically generated a revision number and included this in its response.

■ **Tip** When passing data to a CouchDB API using the `-d` flag, it is recommended that you encapsulate your JSON code using single quotes rather than double quotes. JSON objects use double quotes around key names and string values. Therefore, if you wrapped your `-d` argument in double quotes, you would need to escape every double quote you used in the code.

Now that your document is in the database, let's issue a command to retrieve it from CouchDB:

```
$ curl -X GET http://127.0.0.1:5984/contacts/johndoe
```

You should receive a response like the following:

```
{"_id":"johndoe","rev":"1-795358690"}
```

At this point you're probably thinking that this contact isn't very useful. All it has is a unique ID and a revision number; it has no contact-related data whatsoever. So, let's just delete this contact altogether. Deleting a document in CouchDB is quite similar to deleting a database, except you must specify the latest revision number of the document you want to delete. Issue the following command to delete your johndoe document from the database (be sure to replace the revision number after **?rev=** with the actual revision number of your document):

```
$ curl -X DELETE http://127.0.0.1:5984/contacts/johndoe?rev=1-795358690
```

All going well, you should receive a response similar to the following:

```
{"ok":true,"id":"johndoe","rev":"2-2789254104"}
```

■ **Note** If you pass the wrong revision number as a parameter when attempting to delete a document, you will get an error such as "Document update conflict." If you get this error, make sure your revision number is correct and try again.

Let's make sure the johndoe record is deleted by trying to retrieve the document once again:

```
$ curl -X GET http://127.0.0.1:5984/contacts/johndoe
```

If the document has been deleted, you should receive the following response:

```
{"error":"not_found","reason":"deleted"}
```

Now you will create a new contact, but this time around you will actually include some data for the document. A document in CouchDB is simply a JSON object, and you simply include this JSON in your curl request using the **-d** flag to send it along with your HTTP request. I am now going to create document of my own contact details with fields for my first name, last name, and e-mail address. In nicely formatted JSON, this document looks like the following:

```
{
        "firstName":"Joe",
        "lastName":"Lennon",
        "email":"joe@joelennon.ie"
}
```

Let's create this document now by issuing the following command:

```
$ curl -X PUT http://127.0.0.1:5984/contacts/joelennon -d
'{"firstName":"Joe","lastName":"Lennon","email":"joe@joelennon.ie"}'
```

When the contact has been created, you should receive a response like the following:

```
{"ok":true,"id":"joelennon","rev":"1-45597617"}
```

■ **Caution** You need to be careful of a couple of things when entering JSON data through `curl`. The first is that although the JSON code may run over several lines, it's important that you do not cause line breaks by pressing Enter or Return yourself. Just let the commands wrap onto the next line themselves. Second, JSON data must be escaped when passed as data in `curl`. As you can see in the previous example, I am escaping every double quote character by inserting a backslash in front of it. If you do not do this, you can expect an `invalid_json` error to be returned by the CouchDB server.

Now let's get back this document from the database, with the following command:

```
$ curl -X GET http://127.0.0.1:5984/contacts/joelennon
```

You should see a more interesting result, like this one:

```
{"_id":"joelennon","_rev":"1-45597617","firstName":"Joe","lastName":"Lennon","email":"joe@joelennon.ie"}
```

As you can see, your contact document now includes the data you specified as well as the document ID and revision number. Let's create another contact, but this time around let's copy the existing contact details instead of starting from scratch. Issue the following command:

```
$ curl -X COPY http://127.0.0.1:5984/contacts/joelennon -H "Destination: johnsmith"
```

The response this time just gives the revision ID for the new document:

```
{"rev":"1-4152282996"}
```

Let's check that the document looks right using a GET request:

```
$ curl -X GET http://127.0.0.1:5984/contacts/johnsmith
```

You should get back something like this:

```
{"_id":"johnsmith","_rev":"1-4152282996","firstName":"Joe","lastName":"Lennon","email":"joe@joelennon.ie"}
```

As you can see, all the details from the joelennon contact were copied to a new document with the document ID johnsmith. Now let's update this document with John Smith's actual contact details. In this example, you are also going to include a phone number and a second e-mail address. John Smith's contact document in nicely formatted JSON looks like the following:

```
{
    "firstName":"John",
    "lastName":"Smith",
    "email": [
        "johnsmith@example.com",
        "jsmith@example.com"
    ],
    "phone":"(555) 555-5555"
}
```

To update an existing document, you must include the revision field in your JSON document, with the revision identifier that the changes are based on. This is for conflict detection purposes and will prevent multiple users from making changes to the same document at the same time. So, to update the johnsmith contact, you can use the following:

```
$ curl -X PUT http://127.0.0.1:5984/contacts/johnsmith -d '{"_rev":"1-
4152282996","firstName":"John","lastName":"Smith","email":["johnsmith@example.com","jsmith@e
xample.com"],"phone":"(555) 555-5555"}'
```

The response should be similar to this:

```
{"ok":true,"id":"johnsmith","rev":"2-843046980"}
```

Let's check it out with a GET request at any rate:

```
$ curl -X GET http://127.0.0.1:5984/contacts/johnsmith
```

This time you should get a response like the one shown here:

```
{"_id":"johnsmith","_rev":"2-
843046980","firstName":"John","lastName":"Smith","email":["johnsmith@example.com","jsmith@ex
ample.com"],"phone":"(555) 555-5555"}
```

Getting Started with CouchDB Views

If you have ever used a traditional relational database management system, you're probably wondering at this stage how you are going to actually perform meaningful queries on the data in your database. This is handled by CouchDB's powerful view engine. I will discuss this and provide in-depth examples of CouchDB views in Chapters 8 and 9, but for now let's get your feet wet by taking a look at some of the built-in views that you can use to query your data right away.

■ **Note** In this example, you will write your view using the JavaScript view engine that ships with CouchDB. Views can be written in any language that has an engine written for it—at the time of this writing, engines existed for languages including Python, PHP, Ruby, and Erlang. It is worth noting that support for native Erlang views is planned for CouchDB 0.10.0.

The first view I'll cover is the _all_docs view. This specialized built-in view returns a listing of all documents in a CouchDB database. To use the view, you simply issue a GET request to the URI /databasename/_all_docs. Let's try this on the contacts database:

```
$ curl -X GET http://127.0.0.1:5984/contacts/_all_docs
```

This will return a response with a count of the documents in the database, as well as document IDs and revision numbers for each document, as shown here:

```
{"total_rows":2,"offset":0,"rows":[
```

```
{"id":"joelennon","key":"joelennon","value":{"rev":"1-45597617"}},
{"id":"johnsmith","key":"johnsmith","value":{"rev":"2-843046980"}}
]}
```

The `total_rows` field tells you the number of documents stored in the database. The results are ordered by document ID. You can reverse the order by issuing the query string `descending=true`:

```
$ curl -X GET http://127.0.0.1:5984/contacts/_all_docs?descending=true
```

As you can see, the results are identical except the contents of the rows array appear in the reverse order:

```
{"total_rows":2,"offset":0,"rows":[
{"id":"johnsmith","key":"johnsmith","value":{"rev":"2-843046980"}},
{"id":"joelennon","key":"joelennon","value":{"rev":"1-45597617"}}
]}
```

You can limit the number of documents to return using the `limit` query parameter. In the following example, I am limiting the results of the `_all_docs` view to just one, with the order still set to `descending`. Be sure to escape the `&` character by prefixing it with a backslash.

```
$ curl -X GET http://127.0.0.1:5984/contacts/_all_docs?descending=true\&limit=1
```

This should return output similar to the following:

```
{"total_rows":2,"offset":0,"rows":[
{"id":"johnsmith","key":"johnsmith","value":{"rev":"2-843046980"}}
]}
```

From version 0.9.0 of CouchDB onward, you can also request that the actual document data itself be returned along with the metadata when using the `_all_docs` view. This will not work in versions prior to 0.9.0.

```
$ curl -X GET http://127.0.0.1:5984/contacts/_all_docs?include_docs=true
```

This returns similar results to the previous queries, except that it also returns the actual data stored in each document. The response should be similar in format to the following text:

```
{"total_rows":2,"offset":0,"rows":[
{"id":"joelennon","key":"joelennon","value":{"rev":"1-
45597617"},"doc":{"_id":"joelennon","_rev":"1-
45597617","firstName":"Joe","lastName":"Lennon","email":"joe@joelennon.ie"}},
{"id":"johnsmith","key":"johnsmith","value":{"rev":"2-
843046980"},"doc":{"_id":"johnsmith","_rev":"2-
843046980","firstName":"John","lastName":"Smith","email":["johnsmith@example.com","jsmith@ex
ample.com"],"phone":"(555) 555-5555"}}
]}
```

The second and final built-in view I'll cover is the `_all_docs_by_seq` view. This view returns all documents in the database, including deleted ones, ordered by the last time they were modified. To use this view, simply issue the following:

```
$ curl -X GET http://127.0.0.1:5984/contacts/_all_docs_by_seq
```

This should return both of the documents that currently exist in the database, along with the johndoe contact you created and subsequently deleted earlier in this chapter:

```
{"total_rows":2,"offset":0,"rows":[
{"id":"johndoe","key":2,"value":{"rev":"2-2789254104","deleted":true}},
{"id":"joelennon","key":5,"value":{"rev":"1-45597617"}},
{"id":"johnsmith","key":7,"value":{"rev":"2-843046980"}}
]}
```

All the view parameters you passed when using the _all_docs view will also work with the _all_docs_by_seq view.

Summary

That concludes Part 1 of the book. In Chapter 1, you discovered what CouchDB is and how it differs from traditional relational database management systems. You learned about CouchDB's history and all about the building blocks of the database server.

In Chapter 2, you learned how to install the CouchDB server on the Linux operating system. You first learned how to install CouchDB from source code on Ubuntu Linux, installing dependencies using the apt-get package utility. You then used the yum package manager to install CouchDB 0.9.0 on Fedora Linux 11. Finally, you undertook the brave task of downloading and building CouchDB and its dependencies—Erlang, ICU, and Spidermonkey—from source code.

In Chapter 3, you learned how to install CouchDB on a Mac OS X machine. You downloaded and installed Apple's developer tools package, Xcode. You also sourced and configured the MacPorts package manager, before using MacPorts to retrieve the CouchDB binary package and install it. I also briefly discussed the CouchDBX one-click package available for Mac OS X.

Finally, in this chapter, you undertook the task of creating your first CouchDB database using the command-line tool curl. You learned how to create and delete databases and how to retrieve a list of all available databases. Next you looked at database documents and how they are created, deleted, copied, and modified. I rounded up this chapter and this part of the book by covering some of CouchDB's built-in specialized views for retrieving all documents and some of the parameters that can be used to manipulate the resultset returned by these views.

In the next part of the book, you will take an in-depth look at managing CouchDB databases, namely, using the Futon web-based administration interface, a more detailed investigation of CouchDB's API, an overview of the concept of map/reduce and how to use it in CouchDB, and the creation of views using the JavaScript view engine.

PART 2

■■■

Managing CouchDB Databases

Now that you have a working installation of CouchDB up and running and you've learned the basics of how a CouchDB database works, let's investigate some of the CouchDB features that you can use to manage your database. In this part, you will start with a detailed look at Futon, the web-based administration tool that comes bundled with every CouchDB installation. You will then learn about JavaScript Object Notation and how it is used to store documents in CouchDB databases. Next, you will see how to create views of your data in special design documents and how the concept of map/reduce applies to CouchDB. You then conclude this part of the book with a chapter about creating advanced views.

CHAPTER 5

■ ■ □ □

Using Futon: The CouchDB Administration Interface

As you saw in Chapter 4, CouchDB offers a powerful RESTful API that can be interacted with via any software that supports making HTTP requests. You used the `curl` command-line utility to create a database and documents, modify documents, and delete documents. Although the syntax and process of using `curl` for this purpose is quite straightforward, it's not ideal for day-to-day database management. Imagine retrieving all the documents in a database that contains thousands, or even millions, of documents. The results would be completely unreadable.

Fortunately, CouchDB also comes with a graphical interface to the database: Futon. Futon is a web-based administration tool that is built in HTML, CSS, and JavaScript. It is an interface that is as simple to use as it is easy on the eye. You may remember Futon from Chapters 2 and 3, when you tested the installation of CouchDB.

By default, you can access Futon by the `/_utils` URI of the CouchDB server. So, if you have CouchDB installed on your local machine, you can access Futon via the URL `http://127.0.0.1:5984/_utils`. Enter this URL into your favorite web browser to launch Futon.

On Futon's start page (Figure 5-1), you will notice that the interface is divided into two key sections: the navigation bar located on the right and the main area on the left. The navigation bar has links to some useful CouchDB tools, as well as links to some recent databases you have worked on. This list may be empty at this point, but you will notice it populating as you start to use Futon. You will take a look at the tools Futon provides later in this chapter. The main area of the CouchDB interface is where you will spend most of your time interacting with CouchDB databases—creating databases and documents, uploading attachments, modifying documents, compacting databases, and deleting databases.

In the main section of the Futon interface, you should see an "Overview" heading at the top. This is a breadcrumbs navigation trail, and when you start navigating into databases and documents, this area will give you an easy way of getting back to previous pages. Beneath the heading bar, you should see a plus icon (+) and a Create Database link. As you might expect, this link simply allows you to create a new CouchDB database. You'll come back to that feature in a moment. Below this link, you should see a table with four columns: Name, Size, Number Of Documents, and Update Seq. If you followed Chapter 4 of this book, you should see a single row for the contacts database. You'll notice that the name of the database is highlighted in bold and is red. This is because this is a link to navigate to a page where you can manage that particular database.

In the footer of the databases table, there is a pagination bar, which will tell you the total number of databases on the server, as well as allow you to define how many databases should be displayed per page (ten is the default setting). If you have at least ten databases, you can navigate from page to page using the Previous Page and Next Page links on the right side of the pagination bar.

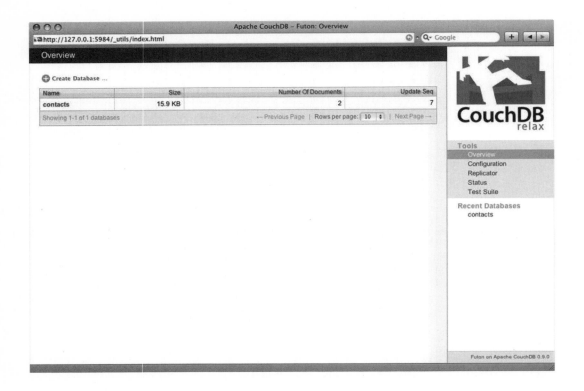

Figure 5-1. *The Futon start page, or Overview page*

■ **Note** If you see more than one database, it's quite likely that you did not delete the databases that were automatically generated by the Futon Test Suite in Chapters 2 and 3. Don't worry about these databases; you can delete them through Futon in due course if you so wish. Alternatively, you can just leave them there; they're not doing any harm.

That's all there is to the Futon start page. As you create more CouchDB databases, the table on this page will start to populate with more rows. Let's move forward and create a new database.

Creating a Database

Click the Create Database link near the top of the page, just beneath the Overview header. This will pop up a modal dialog box, like the one shown in Figure 5-2.

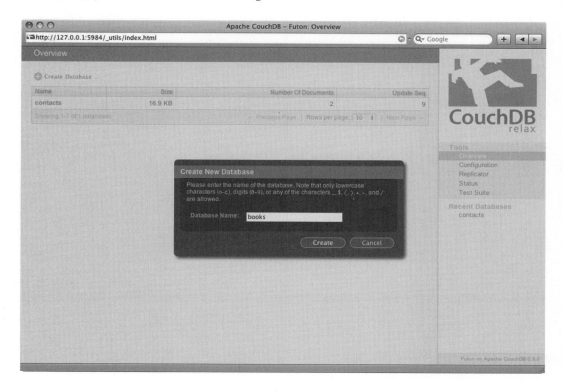

Figure 5-2. *Create New Database dialog box*

The dialog box asks you to enter a name for the database. It informs you that the database name must contain only lowercase characters (a–z), digits (0–9), or any of the characters _, $, (,), +, -, and /. As a general rule of thumb, I prefer to name databases using only lowercase characters and the underscore (_) character. This avoids any potential issues with URL encoding and escaping characters when using the API. In this dialog box, enter **books** in the Database Name field, and click the Create button.

CouchDB will create a new database with the name books and will take you directly to its Futon page, `http://127.0.0.1:5984/_utils/database.html?books`. Figure 5-3 shows the default view of this page.

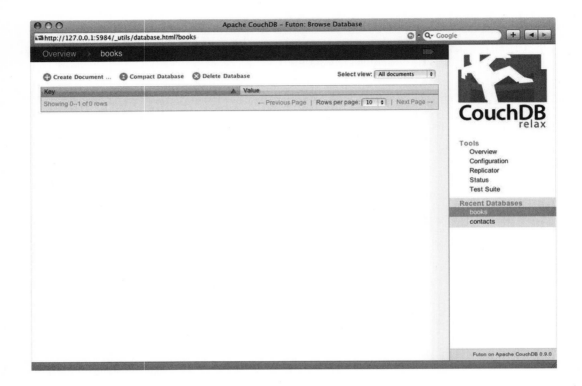

Figure 5-3. *The New books database page*

You may notice that the books database has been added to the Recent Databases list. Also, notice that in the heading bar in the main section of Futon, alongside Overview you have an arrow and the name of the database. Also notice that the text Overview is now clickable. This will bring you back to the Futon start page. On the right side of the heading bar, you will notice a small gray shape that looks like a signpost. This is a link to the raw view of the database, showing the JSON code that it is made up of. Click that link now to view what the raw code looks like.

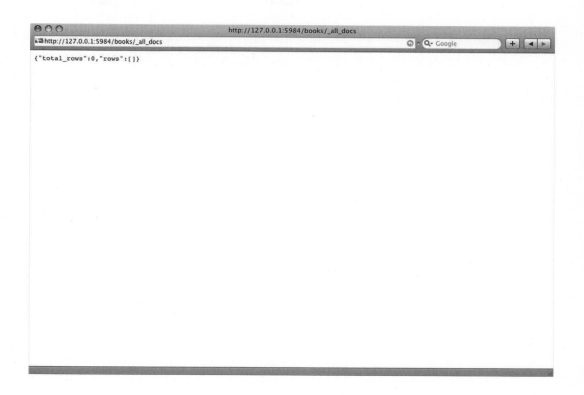

Figure 5-4. *Raw JSON view of the database*

As you can see in Figure 5-4, this page displays the results of the specialized view **_all_docs** for the books database. You may recall this specialized view from Chapter 4, when you used `curl` to get this same data from the contacts database. You will notice that the URL is `http://127.0.0.1:5984/books/_all_docs`. Try changing the books segment of the URL to contacts and see what happens. If you followed Chapter 4, you should see a result like the one shown in Figure 5-5.

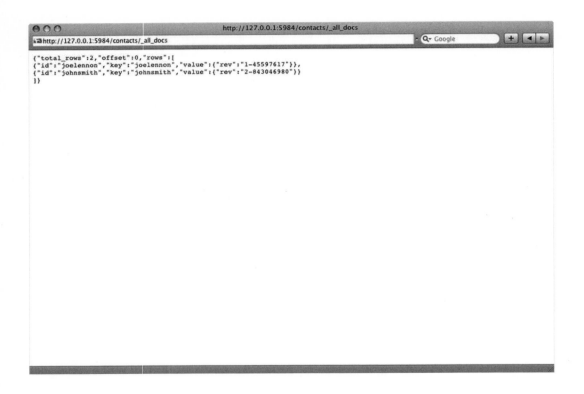

Figure 5-5. The raw view of the contacts database from Chapter 4

Now, go back to the Browse Database page for the books database using your web browser's Back button. You should be back at the page that looks like Figure 5-3. Below the heading bar, you should see three links: Create Document, Compact Database, and Delete Database. These links are pretty self-explanatory, and you will learn about them in more detail in a moment.

A bit further to the right of these links you'll notice a "Select view" drop-down box. Currently, "All documents" is selected. If you expand the list, you should also see the Design Documents and Temporary View options. Neither of these will be particularly useful right now, but you will learn a lot more about views in Chapters 7, 8, and 9.

Below these links and the "Select view" drop-down box, there is another table, similar to the one you saw on the Futon start page. This time, however, there are only two columns: Key and Value. You'll notice that the Key column has a darker shade of gray background, and there is an arrow on the right side of the column heading. This is used to change the sort order of the data in the table, and you will see it in action shortly when you start working with documents. This table's footer is identical to the one you saw previously, with pagination information and links. It works exactly the same as the one in the table of databases.

Click the Overview link in the heading bar to return to the Futon start page. You'll notice that there are now two rows in this table—one for the books database and one for the contacts database (Figure 5-6). Rows in this table are ordered alphabetically, so books will appear above contacts.

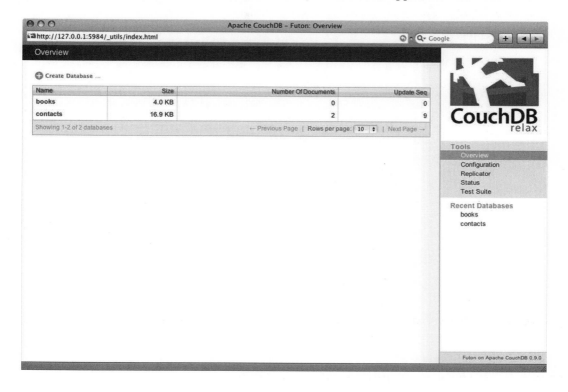

Figure 5-6. *The Futon Overview page—now with the books database*

Let's create a third database. Click the Create Database link once more. Enter whatever you like for the database name. I used the name games, but it really doesn't matter. When CouchDB has created the database, you will be brought to the database's page on Futon. It should be pretty much identical to the page you saw moments ago for the books database. This time, however, you're just going to go ahead and delete the database. Click the Delete Database link beneath the heading bar. Futon will ask you to confirm that you want to delete it, because it is irreversible (Figure 5-7).

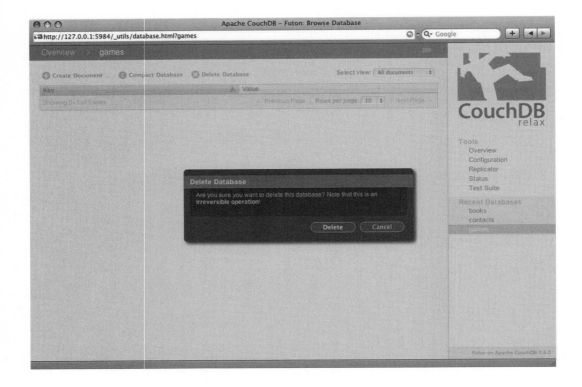

Figure 5-7. Delete Database dialog box

Click the Delete button to confirm the deletion. You will now be back at the Futon start page, and you'll notice that there is no sign of the database you just deleted. Next you will look at creating documents in your database.

Creating a Document

Click books to open the Futon page for that database once again. This time, click the Create Document link. A modal dialog box will appear asking you to enter a unique ID of the document or to leave the field empty to get an autogenerated ID (Figure 5-8).

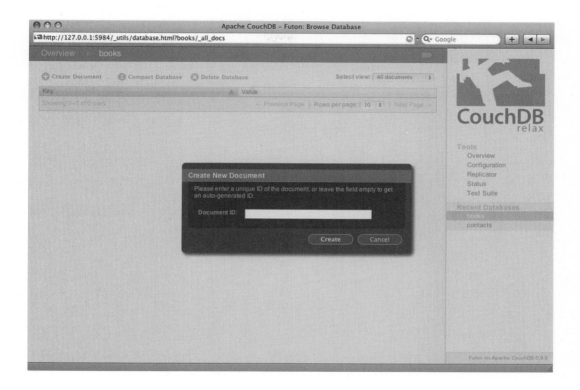

Figure 5-8. *Create New Document dialog box*

For the first document, leave the Document ID field blank, and click the Create button. CouchDB will automatically assign the document a universally unique identifier (UUID) and revision number. When the document has been created, you will automatically be brought to a page that allows you to work with that document. This page will look similar to Figure 5-9. Please note that the values of the `_id` and `_rev` fields will be different from the ones shown in the figure.

Figure 5-9. *New document page*

In the heading section, you will notice that the document ID has been added to the breadcrumbs trail. Like in the database view page, you also get a link to view the raw data. Below the heading, there are four links: Save Document, Add Field, Upload Attachment, and Delete Document. Again, these links are self-explanatory. Below these links once again is a table, with Field and Value columns. Currently there should be two rows, one for the _id field and one for the _rev field. You will notice at the top right of the table there are two tabs: Field (currently selected) and Source. Click the Source tab to view the JSON source code of the document. The footer in this table is not like the ones you have seen previously, but rather it has Previous Version and Next Version links (which are likely grayed out at this point) for viewing other versions of the document. As I pointed out in Chapter 1, every time you update a document in CouchDB, the existing document is not in fact modified, but rather a new revision is created to reflect the changes. These links allow you to flick through previous versions of the document as you require.

■ **Caution** Previous versions of CouchDB documents are deleted when the database is compacted, so don't assume that old revisions will always be available.

Let's remove this document altogether by clicking the Delete Document link. Again, you'll be asked to confirm that you want to delete the document. Click the Delete button, and you will be brought back to the books database page. Now create another document, but this time give it a meaningful ID, rather than asking CouchDB to generate one. Click the Create Document link, and this time when asked for a document ID, enter **978-1-4302-7237-3**. That is the International Standard Book Number (ISBN) for this book. Once again, you will see a page similar to the page for the previous document you created, except that this time the _id field value will be 978-1-4302-7237-3.

Right now, this data isn't exactly very useful; it merely tells you the ISBN of some book. Let's make it more useful by entering some more fields. Click the Add Field link. A new row will be added to the table, with a text box shown in the Field column, with the value "unnamed" selected. After the text box, you will see two tiny images, a green check and a red cross. Clicking the green check mark saves any changes you make; clicking the red cross cancels and reverts it to the previous value. You can see this field in Figure 5-10.

Figure 5-10. Adding a field to a document

Enter **title** as the field name, and press Enter to close the text box. You will notice that the text will now be a noneditable label, and it has a gray *x* icon to the left of it. This allows you to delete the field. Try clicking the icon; the field will be removed immediately. Once you have done this, add the field again. Changing the field name is very simple—simply double-click the name, and it will show up as an editable text box once again. You can change the name of any field except for the **_id** and **_rev** fields. In the Value column, you will see that the title field is set to null. This is modified in the same way as the field name column is, by double-clicking the current value to display an editable text box. Enter **Beginning CouchDB** in this text box, and press Enter to leave the edit mode. If you have entered it correctly, the text should turn green.

■ **Caution** It is important to include the surrounding double quotes when entering string values into the database—these tell CouchDB that you are entering a string. If you forget the quotes, you will get an error message: "Please enter a valid JSON value (for example: "string")." Simply wrap your value in double quotes, and it should save.

Let's add some more fields to the document now. The following are the field names and values I have entered for this document:

Field	Value
author	"Joe Lennon"
print_price	34.99
ebook_price	24.49
publisher	"Apress"
tags	["database", "couchdb", "beginner"]

In Figure 5-11, you will see how these fields look on the document page in Futon.

Figure 5-11. *The complete "Beginning CouchDB" document*

You will notice that the two price fields do not have double quotes wrapped around them. The reason for this is that these values are numeric, not strings. You will also notice that the tags field has an array of three string values: **"database"**, **"couchdb"**, and **"beginner"**. Futon nicely displays these values each on a separate line, prefixed by each tag's index in the array.

An important thing to note at this point is that all these new fields have not yet been saved to the database. To do so, you need to click the Save Document link above the table, which will commit these changes to the server. When you do so, the page will refresh, and you will notice that the revision number has changed, and in the footer it will say that it is "Showing revision 2 of 2." You will also be able to click the Previous Version link to look at the old revision.

Next, let's take a look at how all of this looks in JSON representation. Click the Source tab, located at the top right of the document table. The source should look something like this:

```
{
    "_id": "978-1-4302-7237-3",
    "_rev": "2-1751458128",
    "title": "Beginning CouchDB",
    "author": "Joe Lennon",
```

```
    "print_price": 34.99,
    "ebook_price": 24.49,
    "publisher": "Apress",
    "tags": [
        "database",
        "couchdb",
        "beginner"
    ]
}
```

You can see a similar view of the data, albeit not as nicely formatted and without the syntax highlighting, by clicking the gray shape on the right side of the heading bar. This will show the raw JSON data, as it is retrieved from the database.

Uploading Attachments

CouchDB features built-in support for attaching files to documents in the database. These are referenced in a special `_attachments` attribute of the document, in a JSON structure consisting of the name of attachment, the content type (MIME type), and the attachment data itself, encoded in base64. There are no limits on the number of attachments a document can have.

Futon makes it very easy to attach files to documents. On the document's page in Futon, click the Upload Attachment link. A modal dialog box will appear asking you to select the file you want to attach to the document. It informs you that a new revision of the document will be created immediately after the upload has completed, so there is no need to save the document to commit the changes. Figure 5-12 shows the dialog box.

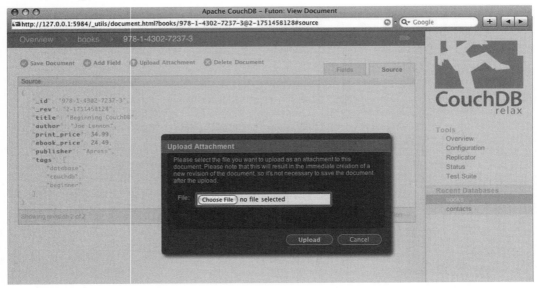

Figure 5-12. Upload Attachment dialog box

In this example, I am going to attach an image file, specifically the cover image for this book. If you want to download this image, you can find it at the following URL: `http://www.apress.com/resource/bookcover/9781430272373?size=medium`. The image is in GIF format and is less than 4KB in size. In the Upload Attachment dialog box, click the Choose File/Browse button, and select the file you want to attach. Then click the Upload button to save the attachment to the database. When the upload has finished, you will be brought back to the document page, and you will notice that there is now an `_attachments` field, and a new revision of the document has been created, as shown in Figure 5-13.

Figure 5-13. *A document with an attachment*

You'll also notice that the name of the file that is attached to the document is in fact a link. Clicking this link will display the image itself, because it is stored in the database. You can delete attachments using the small delete icon to the left of the attachment filename. You will not be asked to confirm the deletion, but it is worth noting that the attachment will not be deleted from the document until you click the Save Document link.

Feel free to add some more documents to the database. For each book you add, you can have different fields if you so want. There is no strict schema to adhere to, so if you have a book that does not have an e-book version and hence has no e-book price, you do not need to include that field in the document. Figure 5-14 shows how my books database looks, after I added some more book documents.

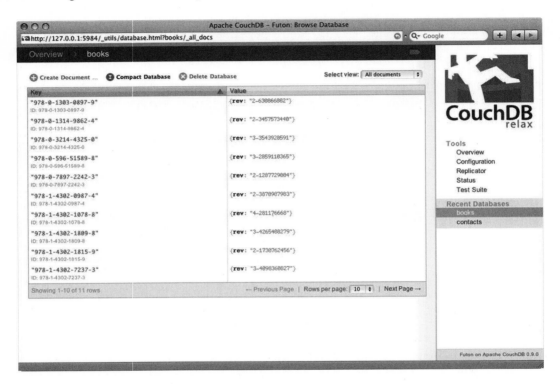

Figure 5-14. *A more complete example*

Compacting the Database

At this point, you should have several books in the database. I have 11 in my database, but whatever the number is, it doesn't really matter. Return to the Futon start page by clicking the Overview link in the breadcrumbs trail in the heading section of Futon. The information about your books database should be significantly different from what it was earlier. Mine tells me that it is 419.6KB in size, with 11 documents and an Update Seq value of 33. This is quite a large size for a database with only 11 documents. This is caused in part by the fact that I have included image attachments for several of those documents. This size is further padded, however, by the fact that the database retains deleted documents and older revisions of documents, including the attachments. This can lead to wasted disk space, because much of the data is merely duplicated with each revision.

If you are satisfied that you do not need previous revisions and that you won't need to restore previously deleted documents, you can help reduce the database size by compacting the database.

Futon includes a link to compact the database—simply click the database name on the Futon start page (in this case, the books database). On this page, next to the Create Document link, you will see the link for Compact Database. Click this to begin compacting. Before the process starts, you will be warned that deleted documents and previous revisions will be removed and that the operation is irreversible and can take a while for large databases (Figure 5-15). Click the Compact button.

■ **Note** When a CouchDB database is compacted, the database file is rewritten, permanently removing out-of-date revisions and previously deleted documents from the file. Once you run compaction, there is no way of recovering this data.

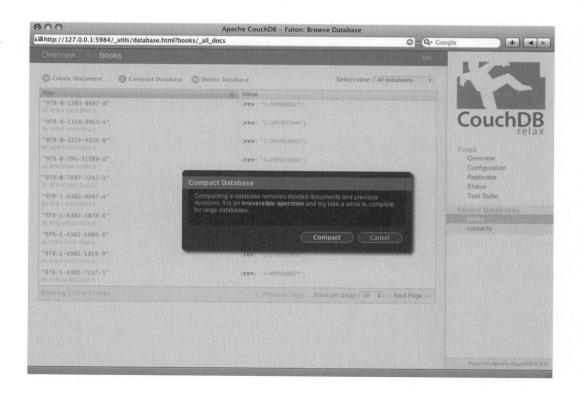

Figure 5-15. Compact Database dialog box

Because the database is still quite small, compaction will complete very quickly. When it is done, you may be wondering what is different, because you will simply be returned to the database page in

Futon with no indication of anything being changed. The first thing that will be different will be that previous revisions will no longer exist. Click any document ID that has been previously revised to open that document's page. Now try to click the Previous Version link in the footer of the table. You should get a message similar to that shown in Figure 5-16.

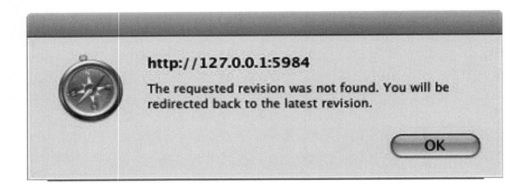

Figure 5-16. Revision not found error message

The next major difference is the database size. Click the Overview link at the top of the page to return to the Futon start page. The size of the books database should be much smaller. My 419.6KB database was reduced to just 105.7KB by compacting it. As I'm sure you can imagine, these savings become even more important as the database grows in size.

Futon Tools

In Futon's navigation bar, you will see a series of tools: Overview, Configuration, Replicator, Status, and Test Suite. You have already seen two of these links in great detail. The Overview link simply brings you to the Futon start page, from where you can work with the databases stored on your CouchDB server. The Test Suite option runs a series of tests to ensure that your CouchDB server is running and working properly. You ran the Test Suite in Chapters 2 and 3, after you installed CouchDB. So, now let's look at the three options that you have not yet visited at this point.

Click Configuration to open the CouchDB Configuration page (Figure 5-17). This page lists all the different CouchDB configuration options, which can be found in the configuration files on the server. It is can be easier to read and update the different options here than it is to change the settings in the configuration files. Please note, however, that you will still need to restart the CouchDB server in order for some of these changes to take effect.

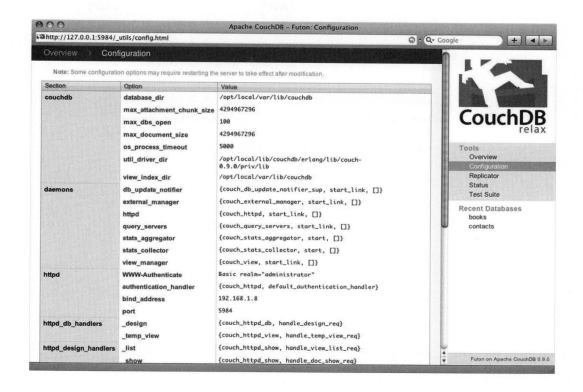

Figure 5-17. *Futon Configuration page*

Generally speaking, you will not want to mess with these settings, because doing so could break your CouchDB installation. One change you may want to make is the `bind_address` option in the `httpd` section. By default this is set to 127.0.0.1. If you try to connect to your CouchDB database from another computer on your network, you'll notice that it will fail. For example, my CouchDB server is on a Mac OS X machine with the IP address 192.168.1.8. I have a Windows laptop that should be able to access this CouchDB server's Futon interface by visiting `http://192.168.1.8:5984/_utils` in my web browser. However, when I do so, Firefox (my web browser of choice on Windows) gives a page load error. This is because a `bind_address` value of 127.0.0.1 allows only the computer running the server to access CouchDB.

By changing the bind address from 127.0.0.1 to 0.0.0.0, you can allow remote connections to your CouchDB database, from any machine (local or remote) that can access the server. By doing so, I was successfully able to open Futon on my Windows machine, as shown in Figure 5-18. You do not need to restart the server for this particular change to take effect.

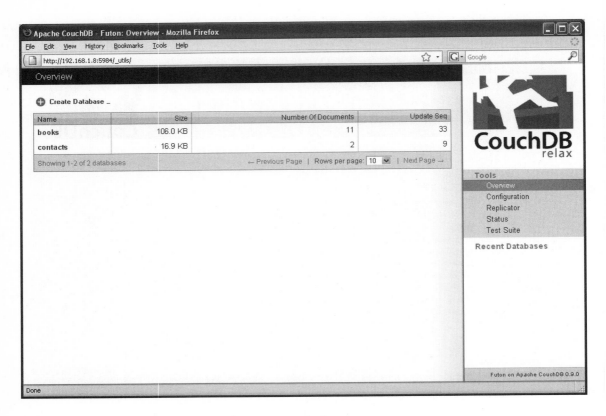

Figure 5-18. *Accessing Futon remotely from a networked computer*

■ **Caution** If you change your bind address to something other than 0.0.0.0, you will no longer be able to access Futon (or CouchDB itself) using the local loopback IP address 127.0.0.1. Instead, you will need to use the IP address you set in the `bind_address` configuration option (for me it is 192.168.1.8).

Now let's take a brief look at the Status page. This will not be of much use to you at this point, because you will have no processes or tasks running that you can view on this page. This is useful when you have large databases and are using the Futon Replicator to replicate these databases between instances or if you are compacting a large database. Right now, however, all you should see is something similar to Figure 5-19.

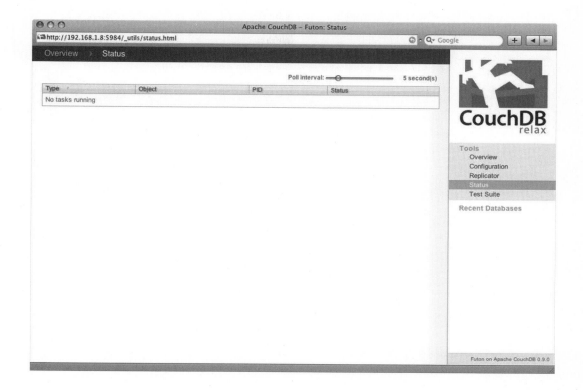

Figure 5-19. Futon Status page

Finally, let's take a look at the Replicator tool. One of the key features of CouchDB is that it is easy to replicate across instances and servers, making it an excellent option for a highly scalable database. Futon includes an easy-to-use replicator that allows you to replicate changes from one database to another. The databases can reside on the same machine or on a remote machine; it does not matter. You will revisit the topic of replication later in this book, but for now, let's check out Futon's Replicator tool by replicating the books database to a second local database.

First, click the Overview link (either at the top of the page or in the Tools menu in the right navigation bar) to return to the Futon start page. From here, click Create Database, and give the database the name more_books. If you like, you can create some new book documents in this database, but it's not necessary. To open Futon's replication tool, click the Replicator link in the Futon navigation bar. On this screen, you will see a box with some options for replicating a database. Under the "Replicate changes from:" option, make sure the "Local database" radio button is selected, and from the drop-down list, ensure that you pick the books database. Under the "to:" label, make sure that Local database is selected also, but from this drop-down, select the more_books database. You can see these options in Figure 5-20.

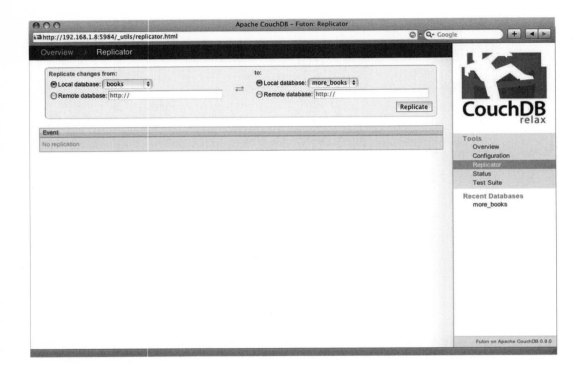

Figure 5-20. *Futon Replicator page*

When you're ready to replicate the database, click the Replicate button. CouchDB will immediately begin the replication process, and it shouldn't even take a second because the database is so small. When it has completed, the Replicator screen will look similar to that in Figure 5-21.

Figure 5-21. Futon Replicator result

■ **Note** If you created some books in the more_books database before you performed the replication, those books will still be available, alongside the newly replicated books documents (assuming no conflicts between the two databases, of course).

Now return to the Overview page, and you'll notice that the more_books database will have the same number of documents as the books database. The size may be larger, but that is because it has kept placeholders for each revision of the database. If you want, you can compact the more_books database to get it to match the size of the books database.

Of course, in a real scenario, replicating a database on the same server doesn't have much use, and you'd be far more likely to replicate the database across a network to a remote CouchDB server. This example simply shows how easy it is to replicate a CouchDB database.

Summary

In this chapter, you learned all about Futon, CouchDB's web-based administration tool. You learned how to create and delete databases, create documents, add fields, upload attachments, delete documents, compact databases, replicate databases, and more. As you have seen, Futon itself is quite powerful and is a very simple client for managing your CouchDB database.

In the next chapter, you will learn about JSON (JavaScript Object Notation), the format in which CouchDB documents are stored.

■ ■ ■

CHAPTER 6

Introduction to JSON

Documents in a CouchDB database are, put simply, data structures defined using JavaScript Object Notation (JSON). In this chapter, you will learn all about JSON. Starting with the basics, you will learn what exactly JSON is and how it works. You will see the different data types that a JSON object can work with, and then you'll get your hands dirty by creating JSON structures and testing them using JavaScript and a web browser. You will then investigate how CouchDB uses JSON, providing you with the knowledge you need to leverage the simplicity and power of this format in your CouchDB applications.

What Is JSON?

JSON is an open, text-based, human-readable data interchange format derived from the JavaScript programming language. It is extremely lightweight, and despite its close connection to JavaScript, it is language-independent, with parsers available for virtually every programming language in existence.

JSON is most commonly used in web application development, particularly those applications that employ Ajax requests to asynchronously fetch data from the server. This does not mean it is restricted to web applications, however; it can be used as a data format in any situation where information needs to be stored as text.

If you are already familiar with JSON, you may want to skim through this chapter, at least up until the "CouchDB and JSON" section, which introduces how JSON is employed in CouchDB.

Why JSON?

The main advantage of using JSON as a data format is its pure simplicity. It is very simple to write and read JSON, from both human and computer perspectives. At its core, JSON is merely a collection of name/value pairs defined inside an object, and its basic structure makes it perfect for transporting data in an independent and lightweight manner.

Another advantage of JSON is its syntax, which uses conventions that programmers familiar with languages such as C, C++, Java, PHP, Python, and JavaScript should be able to follow. JSON parsers are available for most modern programming languages; a comprehensive list is available at http://www.json.org. The popular server-side web development language PHP includes native JSON support from version 5.2, and Python and JavaScript also have built-in JSON support.

For web applications, JSON makes a lot of sense. Some modern web browsers include support for native JSON encoding and decoding. Many web services and feed providers are making their APIs available with the option to return a response in JSON format. Yahoo! Pipes allows you to take one or more existing feeds, regardless of the format they are available in, and mash them up to produce output in a number of formats, including JSON.

■ **Note** At the time of writing, native JSON support is available in Firefox 3.5 and Microsoft Internet Explorer 8. For browsers that do not support JSON natively, the `eval()` function can be used to translate a string containing JSON code into JavaScript objects.

These are the other benefits of JSON:

- It is an open standard.

- It has internationalization support because it uses Unicode.

- It is easy to map to object-oriented frameworks.

- It is simple to map data from an existing database or XML to a JSON structure.

JSON 101: Syntax and Data Types

In JSON, data structures are defined as either an object or an array. You will now look at each of these concepts in more detail.

An object is an unordered collection of name/value pairs. These pairs each contain a piece of data that describes the object to which it belongs. The name is the description of what the data represents, and the value is the data itself. For example, a `Car` object may have the name/value pairs listed in Table 6-1.

Table 6-1. Car Object

Name	Value
Make	"Ford"
Model	"Mustang"
Year	2009
Body	"Coupe"
Color	"Red"

In JSON, objects are defined between an opening brace ({) and a closing brace (}). Each name/value pair is defined in the format `name:value` (*name colon value*), and pairs are separated using a comma (`,`). Listing 6-1 shows this syntax.

Listing 6-1. JSON Object Syntax

```
{
    name1: value1,
    name2: value2,
    name3: value3,
    ...,
    nameN: valueN
}
```

An *array* is an ordered list of values, indexed by the position of the value in the list. An example of an array would be a list of the days of the week, as illustrated in Table 6-2.

Table 6-2. "Days of the Week" Array

Index	0	1	2	3	4	5	6
Value	"Sunday"	"Monday"	"Tuesday"	"Wednesday"	"Thursday"	"Friday"	"Saturday"

You define arrays in JSON using an opening bracket ([) and a closing bracket (]), separating each value with a comma (,). Listing 6-2 shows the syntax of an array.

Listing 6-2. JSON Array Syntax

```
[value1, value2, value3, …, valueN]
```

It is important to note that both of these structures can be nested. In other words, an object can contain a value, which is itself an object or an array. Likewise, an array can contain a value, which is itself an array or an object.

Each value in a JSON object or array must be represented using a valid data type. There are six basic types available for use in JSON:

- **String**: This is used for character data such as names, addresses, and e-mail addresses. These are defined in Unicode and are wrapped in double quotes ("). If your string needs to include a double quote, you can escape it with the backslash character (\). An example of a string value is `"Joe Lennon"`.

- **Number**: This is used for numeric data, including integers and floating-point numbers. An example of a number value is `-901.8563`.

- **Boolean**: This is a logical data type having one of two values: `true` or `false`.

- **Null**: This is used where a field has no value or an unknown value. Denoted simply as `null`.

- **Object**: A value can itself be an object, another collection of name/value pairs. In the previous `Car` example, you may have a field `engine`, which could be an object itself with fields such as `gas_type` and `cubic_capacity`.

- **Array**: A value can also be an array, representing another list of ordered values. Again, take the example of a `Car` object. This could have a field called `previous_owners`, which would be an array of previous owners. Each value in this array could be a `Person` object.

Let's look at examples of both of these structures. First translate the `Car` object from Table 6-2 into a JSON object, as shown in Listing 6-3.

Listing 6-3. Car Object in JSON

```
{
    make: "Ford",
    model: "Mustang",
    year: 2009,
    body: "Coupe",
    color: "Red"
}
```

Now let's take a look at the "days of the week" array from Table 6-2 and how it would be represented in JSON (see Listing 6-4).

Listing 6-4. "Days of the Week" in JSON

```
["Sunday", "Monday", "Tuesday", "Wednesday", "Thursday", "Friday", "Saturday"]
```

Each value in the array is automatically assigned a numeric index based on its position in the array. This index starts with 0 and increments by 1 for each consecutive value. Later in this chapter, you will see the significance of this index value and the order in which array values are defined. Finally, let's make some adjustments to the `Car` object, adding some of the fields I suggested when discussing the data types earlier in this section, namely, `engine` and `previous_owners` (see Listing 6-5).

Listing 6-5. Modified Car Object in JSON

```
{
    make: "Ford",
    model: "Mustang",
    year: 2009,
    body: "Coupe",
    color: "Red",
    engine: {
        gas_type: "Petrol",
        cubic_capacity: 4600
    },
    previous_owners: [
        {
            name: "John Smith",
            mileage: 1000
        },
        {
```

```
            name: "Jane Hunt",
            mileage: 2500
        }
    ]
}
```

As you can see in Listing 6-5, you have added a field called `engine`, which is itself a JSON object, made up of two fields—`gas_type` and `cubic_capacity`. You have also added a field `previous_owners`, which is an array of objects, each of which contains two fields—`name` and `mileage`.

In the next section, you will investigate further examples and see how you can actually work with this data using JavaScript.

Working with JSON

The best way to get to grips with JSON structures is to actually define and use them. In this section, you will use some basic JavaScript to define objects and arrays and to access the data they contain. To follow these examples, simply enter the code from the listings into a text file using your favorite text editor, save it to a location on your hard disk, and then open that file using your web browser.

Defining JSON Structures

Let's get a basic outline HTML document together so you can start working on some examples. Open your favorite text editor, and create a new plain-text file. Save the file as `index.html`, and store it somewhere on your hard disk that will be easy to find. For example, on my Mac OS X environment, I have created a folder in my home folder (`/Users/joe`) called `json` and saved `index.html` in it. Next, add the contents of Listing 6-6 to the file and save it again.

Listing 6-6. `index.html`—Basic Structure

```
<html>
    <head>
        <title>My Cars</title>
    </head>
    <body>
        <h1>My Cars</h1>
        <script type="text/javascript">

        </script>
    </body>
</html>
```

Now open this file in your favorite web browser; you should see something like Figure 6-1.

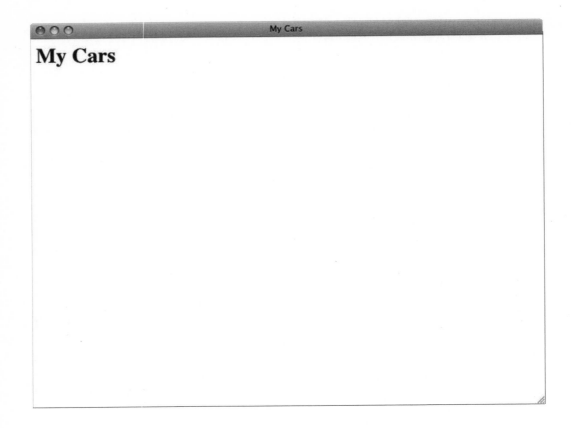

Figure 6-1. Viewing index.html in a web browser

The first thing you are going to do is create your JSON object. You do this between the opening and closing `<script>` tag. The object definition is exactly as was illustrated in Listing 6-5, except that you are also assigning the object to a JavaScript variable name, which is in this instance `car` (Listing 6-7).

Listing 6-7. index.html—Adding the JSON Object

```
<html>
    <head>
        <title>My Cars</title>
    </head>
    <body>
        <h1>My Cars</h1>
        <script type="text/javascript">
```

```
            var car = {
                make: "Ford",
                model: "Mustang",
                year: 2009,
                body: "Coupe",
                color: "Red",
                engine: {
                    gas_type: "Petrol",
                    cubic_capacity: 4600
                },
                previous_owners: [
                    {
                        name: "John Smith",
                        mileage: 1000
                    }, {
                        name: "Jane Hunt",
                        mileage: 2500
                    }
                ]
            }
        </script>
    </body>
</html>
```

If you save the file and reload your web browser, you'll notice that nothing has changed. The reason is that you have simply defined your JavaScript object; you have not yet done anything with it. Let's make sure everything is working as it should be by adding some code to output the car's details to the screen (Listing 6-8).

Listing 6-8. index.html—Outputting the Car's Details

```
<html>
    <head>
        <title>My Cars</title>
    </head>
    <body>
        <h1>My Cars</h1>
        <script type="text/javascript">
            var car = {
                make: "Ford",
                model: "Mustang",
                year: 2009,
                body: "Coupe",
                color: "Red",
                engine: {
                    gas_type: "Petrol",
                    cubic_capacity: 4600
                },
                previous_owners: [
                    {
```

```
                    name: "John Smith",
                    mileage: 1000
              }, {
                    name: "Jane Hunt",
                    mileage: 2500
              }
           ]
       }

       document.write('<h2>'+car.make+' '+car.model+'</h2>');
       document.write('<strong>Year:</strong> '+car.year+'<br />');
       document.write('<strong>Body Type:</strong> '+car.body+'<br />');
       document.write('<strong>Engine:</strong> ');
       document.write(car.engine.cubic_capacity+'cc '+car.engine.gas_type);
       document.write('<h3>Previous Owners:</h3>');
       document.write('<ul>');
       for(person in car.previous_owners) {
           document.write('<li>');
           document.write(car.previous_owners[person].name+' (');
           document.write(car.previous_owners[person].mileage+' miles)');
           document.write('</li>');
       }
       document.write('</ul>');
    </script>
  </body>
</html>
```

This time around, when you save the file and open it in your browser, you should see a more interesting result—like the one shown in Figure 6-2.

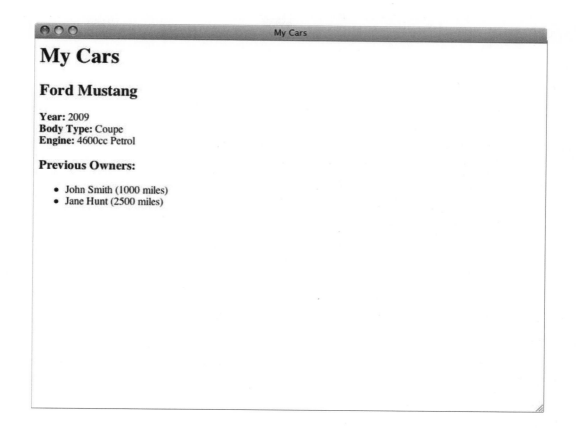

Figure 6-2. Viewing `index.html` *output in the browser*

In Listing 6-8, you'll notice that you are using the function `document.write` repeatedly. This merely tells JavaScript to output the value between the parentheses to the document. In this example, you are creating a level-two HTML heading with the `car` object's `make` and `model` values. Notice how you access the values in the `car` object using the syntax `object_name.field_name`. You then use a similar technique to get the `year` and `body` values. As you saw previously, the field `engine` is itself an object, with two fields—`gas_type` and `cubic_capacity`. To access these fields, you use the syntax `object_name.sub_object_name.field_name`.

The field `previous_owners` is a little trickier, because it is an array. You are using the unordered list HTML tag (`<ul>`) to create a new list. You need to use the array index to tell JavaScript which item in the array you want to display. So, you could simply use `car.previous_owners[0].name` and `car.previous_owners[1].name`, and it would work the same way as in this coding example. But how do you know how many values are in the array? It's easy in this example because the number is small, but if it were large, it would be very difficult to keep track of, not to mention the amount of repetitive code to output all the values. Also, if the contents of the array were to change in the object definition, you would also need to change the output code.

Looping Through JSON Arrays

A much easier solution is to use a **for** loop to iterate through the items in the array and output them. In this example, we are saying that "For every person in the field **car.previous_owners**, execute the code between the braces." As you can see, this code outputs a list item with the person's name and the amount of mileage they have driven.

You are not restricted to just outputting the values in the object; you can also manipulate them and perform calculations on them where relevant. Let's modify the car example slightly. First let's create a current owner object. This will be the same type of object as each object in the **previous_owners** array, with two fields—**name** and **mileage** (Listing 6-9). When you are outputting your data to the screen, you will then calculate the total mileage for the car and output that too.

Listing 6-9. index.html—Working with the Object Data

```html
<html>
    <head>
        <title>My Cars</title>
    </head>
    <body>
        <h1>My Cars</h1>
        <script type="text/javascript">
            var car = {
                make: "Ford",
                model: "Mustang",
                year: 2009,
                body: "Coupe",
                color: "Red",
                engine: {
                    gas_type: "Petrol",
                    cubic_capacity: 4600
                },
                current_owner: {
                    name: "Joe Lennon",
                    mileage: 500
                },
                previous_owners: [
                    {
                        name: "John Smith",
                        mileage: 1000
                    }, {
                        name: "Jane Hunt",
                        mileage: 2500
                    }
                ]
            }
```

```
        var mileage_total = 0;

        document.write('<h2>'+car.make+' '+car.model+'</h2>');
        document.write('<strong>Year:</strong> '+car.year+'<br />');
        document.write('<strong>Body Type:</strong> '+car.body+'<br />');
        document.write('<strong>Engine:</strong> ');
        document.write(car.engine.cubic_capacity+'cc '+car.engine.gas_type);
        document.write('<h3>Owners, Past and Present:</h3>');
        document.write('<ul>');
        mileage_total += car.current_owner.mileage;
        document.write('<li>');
        document.write(car.current_owner.name+' (');
        document.write(car.current_owner.mileage+' miles)');
        document.write('</li>');
        for(person in car.previous_owners) {
            mileage_total += car.previous_owners[person].mileage;
            document.write('<li>');
            document.write(car.previous_owners[person].name+' (');
            document.write(car.previous_owners[person].mileage+' miles)');
            document.write('</li>');
        }
        document.write('</ul>');
        document.write('<strong>Total Mileage:</strong> '+mileage_total);
    </script>
  </body>
</html>
```

The first major change to this file is that you have added a new field to your Car object, current_owner. This is an object with two fields, name and mileage, which are the same type as each object in the previous_owners array. The next change is that you have added a line after your object definition, which creates a mileage_total variable and sets its value to 0. You will use this variable to hold the total mileage the car has done between all owners, past and present. The next important modification is that before you loop through the previous_owners array, you add the mileage the current_owner has done to the mileage_total, and you output the current owner's details to the list. It is important that this is done outside the previous_owners loop, because the current_owner is not part of that array but rather an independent object field. Moving down to the for loop, you'll notice that you add the mileage of the previous_owners to the mileage_total variable. This will occur, of course, for every iteration of the loop, so each previous owner's mileage will be added to the total. Finally, after the loop has finished, you output the mileage_total to the screen.

If all goes according to plan, when you save your index.html file and reload it in your browser, you should see a result similar to that shown in Figure 6-3.

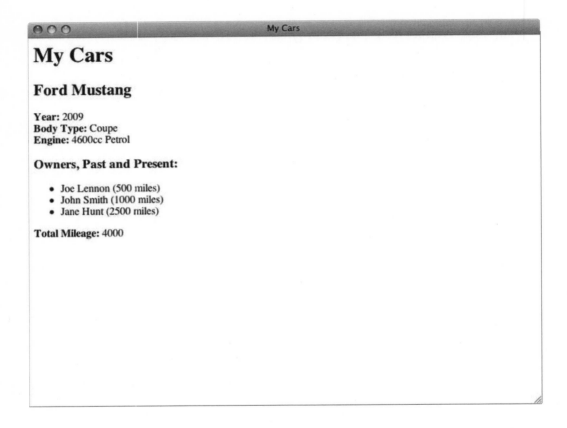

Figure 6-3. Viewing index.html with current owner and mileage total

---

■ **Note** If you are familiar with HTML, you may be thinking that this is all well and good, but couldn't you do the same thing with some really basic HTML using many fewer lines of code? Yes, of course you could, but remember this is a very simple example. In the real world, you might have cars stored in a database and use a programming language like PHP, Python, Ruby, and so on, to retrieve these records. You could then leverage these languages to output the data into JSON, which can be returned to JavaScript as the response to an asynchronous HTTP request. JavaScript can easily read the JSON response and update the web page without needing to refresh the page. Figure 6-4 illustrates where JSON data fits in the flow of a typical asynchronous web application.

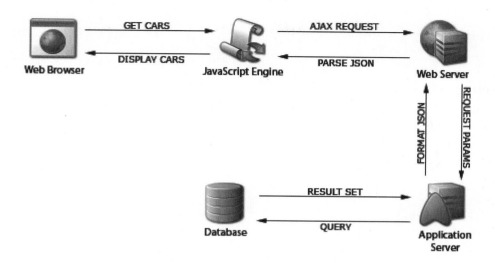

Figure 6-4. Where JSON fits in the traditional web application data flow

Before moving on to the next section, let's make one final modification to the JSON example. Let's assume that the web site you are working with is one for a car dealership. Also assume that this dealership will have more than one car for sale, so let's add a couple of other vehicles into the mix.

If you have followed the example and you are not familiar with programming, your instinct may be to create a second object, `car2`, and to copy and paste the code for outputting the data to output the second car's details. Again, this will work, but it becomes extremely tedious to manage with each subsequent car you create. Instead, let's create an array of car objects and then create a loop that will iterate through this array to output the details of each car (Listing 6-10).

Listing 6-10. `index.html`—The Final Example

```html
<html>
    <head>
        <title>My Cars</title>
    </head>
    <body>
        <h1>My Cars</h1>
        <script type="text/javascript">
        var cars = [
            {
                make: "Ford",
                model: "Mustang",
                year: 2009,
                body: "Coupe",
                color: "Red",
                engine: {
                    gas_type: "Petrol",
```

```
            cubic_capacity: 4600
        },
        current_owner: {
            name: "Joe Lennon",
            mileage: 500
        },
        previous_owners: [
            {
                name: "John Smith",
                mileage: 1000
            },{
                name: "Jane Hunt",
                mileage: 2500
            }
        ]
    }, {
        make: "Chevrolet",
        model: "Camaro",
        year: 2001,
        body: "Convertible",
        color: "Blue",
        engine: {
            gas_type: "Petrol",
            cubic_capacity: 3800
        },
        current_owner: {
            name: "John Daly",
            mileage: 10500
        },
        previous_owners: [
            {
                name: "Tony Bellic",
                mileage: 47000
            },{
                name: "Lisa McIntyre",
                mileage: 12050
            },{
                name: "John Thornton",
                mileage: 18500
            }
        ]
    }, {
        make: "Dodge",
        model: "Challenger",
        year: 2008,
        body: "Coupe",
        color: "Orange",
        engine: {
            gas_type: "Petrol",
            cubic_capacity: 6100
        },
```

```
                current_owner: {
                    name: "Susan Long",
                    mileage: 800
                },
                previous_owners: [
                    {
                        name: "David White",
                        mileage: 750
                    }
                ]
            }
        ]

    for(car in cars) {
        var mileage_total = 0;
        document.write('<hr />');
        document.write('<h2>'+cars[car].make+' '+cars[car].model+'</h2>');
        document.write('<strong>Year:</strong> '+cars[car].year+'<br />');
        document.write('<strong>Engine:</strong> ');
        document.write(cars[car].engine.cubic_capacity+'cc ');
        document.write(cars[car].engine.gas_type);
        document.write('<h3>Owners, Past and Present:</h3>');
        document.write('<ul>');
        mileage_total += cars[car].current_owner.mileage;
        document.write('<li>');
        document.write(cars[car].current_owner.name+' (');
        document.write(cars[car].current_owner.mileage+' miles) - current');
        document.write('</li>');
        for(person in cars[car].previous_owners) {
            mileage_total += cars[car].previous_owners[person].mileage;
        document.write('<li>');
        document.write(cars[car].previous_owners[person].name);
        document.write(' ('+cars[car].previous_owners[person].mileage);
        document.write(' miles)');
        document.write('</li>');
        }
        document.write('</ul>');
        document.write('<strong>Total Mileage:</strong> '+mileage_total);
    }
    </script>
  </body>
</html>
```

In this example, you are creating an array named cars, which contains three items, each of which is a car object. You then loop through this array, and for each iteration you create a total mileage variable, set it to zero, and create a horizontal rule, followed by output of the car details. You'll notice that in this example the notation has changed from object_name.field_name to array_name[array_index].field_name. Save your index.html file, and reload your browser window. The final result should look like Figure 6-5.

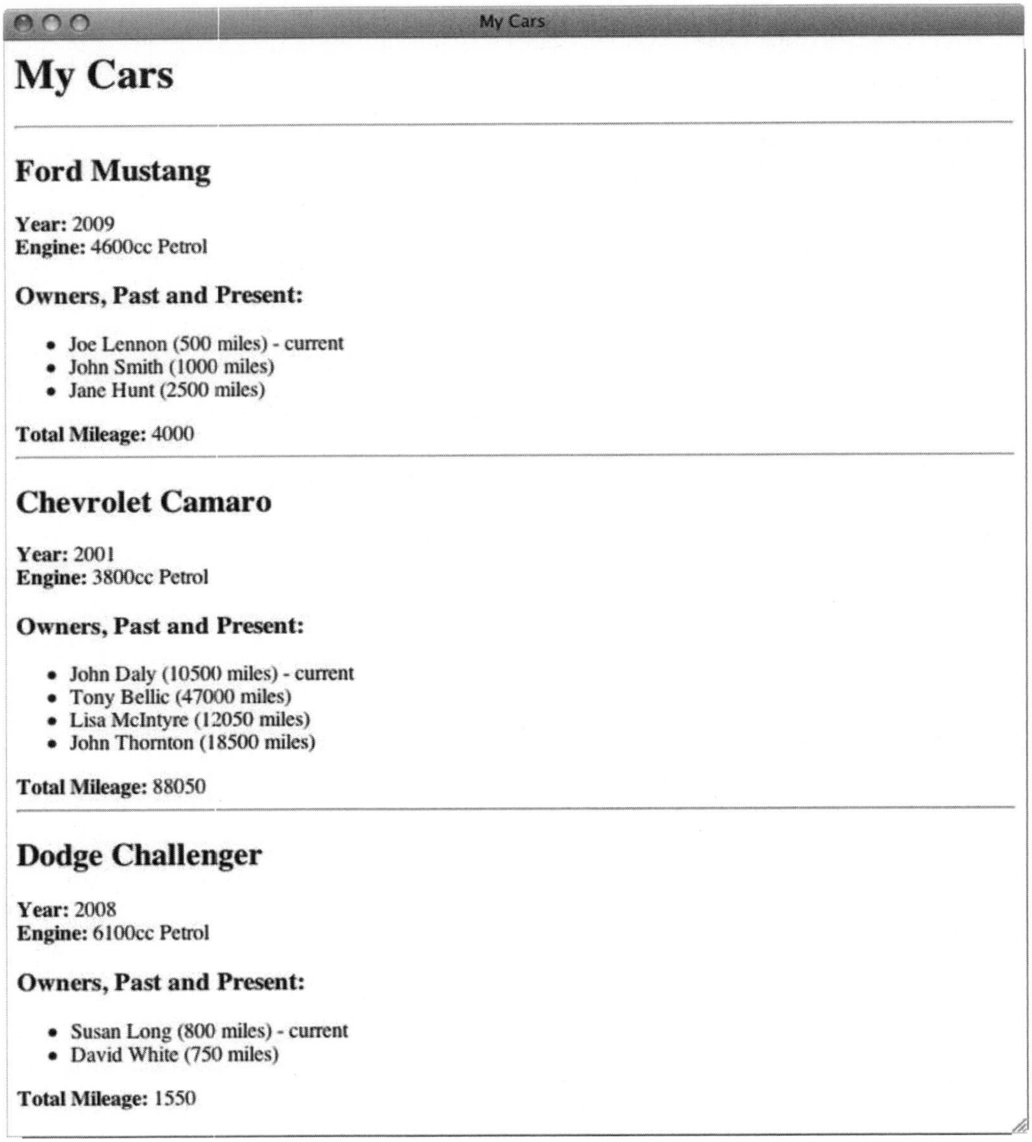

My Cars

Ford Mustang

Year: 2009
Engine: 4600cc Petrol

Owners, Past and Present:

- Joe Lennon (500 miles) - current
- John Smith (1000 miles)
- Jane Hunt (2500 miles)

Total Mileage: 4000

Chevrolet Camaro

Year: 2001
Engine: 3800cc Petrol

Owners, Past and Present:

- John Daly (10500 miles) - current
- Tony Bellic (47000 miles)
- Lisa McIntyre (12050 miles)
- John Thornton (18500 miles)

Total Mileage: 88050

Dodge Challenger

Year: 2008
Engine: 6100cc Petrol

Owners, Past and Present:

- Susan Long (800 miles) - current
- David White (750 miles)

Total Mileage: 1550

Figure 6-5. The final index.html

In this section, you have seen a practical example of how to define JSON objects and arrays and how to access the data in these containers using JavaScript. I hope the practical nature of this section has provided you with some insight into how useful JSON is for storing simple data structures and how easy it is to read and produce.

CouchDB and JSON

Up until this point, the primary focus of this chapter has been to serve as a primer for JSON. In this section, you will explore the different ways CouchDB uses JSON. The most important aspect of CouchDB's use of JSON lies in the structure of the documents in the CouchDB database. In essence, CouchDB documents are plain and simple JSON objects. Every document can have as many fields as required, and these can be of any valid JSON type, such as strings, numbers, booleans, nulls, objects, or arrays.

In addition to the data fields, each document has at least two meta fields: _id and _rev. These house the unique identifier for the document and the document revision number. CouchDB allows base64-encoded binary attachments to be included in a document, each of which is stored in the _attachments field, which contains each attachment as a separate object, identified by its file name and containing the data itself, the MIME type, and the file size of the content. Listing 6-11 shows an example of a CouchDB document.

Listing 6-11. An Example of a CouchDB Document

```
{
    _id: "0ff345433e3464ae346453",
    _rev: "4-18435343",
    name: "John Smith",
    salary: 38000,
    department: "Accounts"
}
```

CouchDB's special design documents, which house the views in a CouchDB database, are also defined as JSON objects. Like regular documents, they have at least an _id field and a _rev field, and they usually have a language field to denote what view server the view should be executed by. The view functions are stored in a views field, which stores an array of the views contained in the design document. Each item in this array represents an individual view, and each of these views contains a map and, optionally, a reduce function. Listing 6-12 shows an example of a design document.

Listing 6-12. An Example of a Design Document

```
{
    _id: "_design/ordering",
    _rev: "2-233320815",
    language: "javascript",
    views: {
        order_by_salary: {
            map: "function(doc) { emit(doc.salary, doc); }"
        },
        order_by_department: {
            map: "function(doc) { emit(doc.dept, doc); }"
```

```
        }
    }
}
```

CouchDB uses JSON not only to define documents and design documents but also to return the results of a view. This is the case for all views, be they special views included with CouchDB, views stored in design documents, or temporary views that are executed ad hoc. The simplest example of this is the `_all_dbs` resource, which simply returns a JSON array with the names of all the databases stored on the CouchDB server. Point your web browser to `http://127.0.0.1:5984/_all_dbs` (assuming CouchDB is installed on your local machine) to see this in action. In my case, it returned the following:
`["contacts","oracle","employees","documents"]`

Let's take a look at a more complex example. This time, let's look at the special `_all_docs` resource for one of the databases that was returned in the previous example. In this case, I'm using the employees database, so I point my browser to `http://127.0.0.1:5984/employees/_all_docs`. Listing 6-13 shows the result I get. Please note that I have reformatted the output to make it easier to read.

Listing 6-13. *Result of the _all_docs Resource*

```
{
        "total_rows": 3,
        "offset": 0,
        "rows": [
            {
                "id": "0ff58e85219e87cbd049985916ae6011",
                "key": "0ff58e85219e87cbd049985916ae6011",
                "value": {
                        "rev": "4-1095527712"
                }
        }, {
                "id": "2c6ac90a0837c5fdec59840b59ad0d25",
                "key": "2c6ac90a0837c5fdec59840b59ad0d25",
                "value": {
                        "rev": "2-929410300"
                }
        }, {
                "id": "3eccc869c36c87149b1dca2a67fec8ce",
                "key": "3eccc869c36c87149b1dca2a67fec8ce",
                "value" :{
                        "rev": "2-149107265"
                }
            }
        ]
}
```

As you can see, this resource returns a JSON object with three fields: `total_rows`, `offset`, and `rows`. The `rows` value is a JSON array with each of the documents in the database represented as a JSON object, with three values: `id`, `key`, and `value`. You will learn more about CouchDB views and how to create your own temporary and permanent views in the coming chapters.

Summary

In this chapter, you learned about JavaScript Object Notation. You discovered how it came to be and what the advantages are of using JSON as a data interchange format. You then learned the basics of JSON structures, namely, data types and the syntax of JSON objects and arrays. You also looked at some practical examples of JSON in action using JavaScript, before discovering how it is used to power many aspects of CouchDB.

What you learned about JSON in this chapter should arm you with the knowledge you need to proceed through the next three chapters, which all relate to CouchDB views. In Chapter 10, you will meet JSON again as you build full CouchDB applications in JavaScript using CouchApp.

CHAPTER 7

■ ■ ■

Introduction to CouchDB Views

Up to this point, your main focus has been on performing CRUD-style operations on your CouchDB data—creating, updating, and deleting documents and attachments and using the Futon web-based interface to manage your database. In this chapter, you will investigate how to get some meaningful data out of your CouchDB database, using the built-in JavaScript view engine.

If you have experience with traditional relational database management systems such as Oracle, Microsoft SQL Server, or MySQL, you will be used to using Structured Query Language (SQL) queries to retrieve data from your database. SQL offers a straightforward and simple means of retrieving, aggregating, and sorting data from a structured database with a strictly defined schema. CouchDB databases, however, do not have a schema, and therefore using structured queries does not make much sense.

The best way to illustrate this is by means of an example. Let's take a basic contacts table and see how that might be represented in a traditional relational database (Figure 7-1).

Table 7-1. *Traditional RDBMS contacts table*

id	name	phone	email	fax
1	John Smith	555-372589	jsmith@example.com	555-372590
2	Jane Thomas	555-210897	jthomas@example.com	null
3	Emma Watson	555-726531	emma@example.com	555-726532
4	Charles Bing	555-821345	charlesb@exmaple.com	null
5	Eric Quinn	555-012796	null	555-098245

As you can see in Table 7-1, the contacts table in a relational database has a strict structure, with each record or row in the table having a value for each column. If a particular contact doesn't have a value for a particular column—for example, Jane Thomas and Charles Bing have no fax number, and Eric Quinn has no e-mail address—then a `null` value is inserted in that column. Now, say you wanted to retrieve the name, e-mail address, and fax number of all your contacts. To do this, you could use a SQL statement like the following:

```
SELECT name, email, fax FROM contacts
```

This would successfully return all contacts from table, returning `null` values where no value is present in a particular column. It can do this because although there is no value in that column, there is still physical data stored in that column in the form of a `null` value.

Now, let's look at the same data but in a CouchDB database (Figure 7-1).

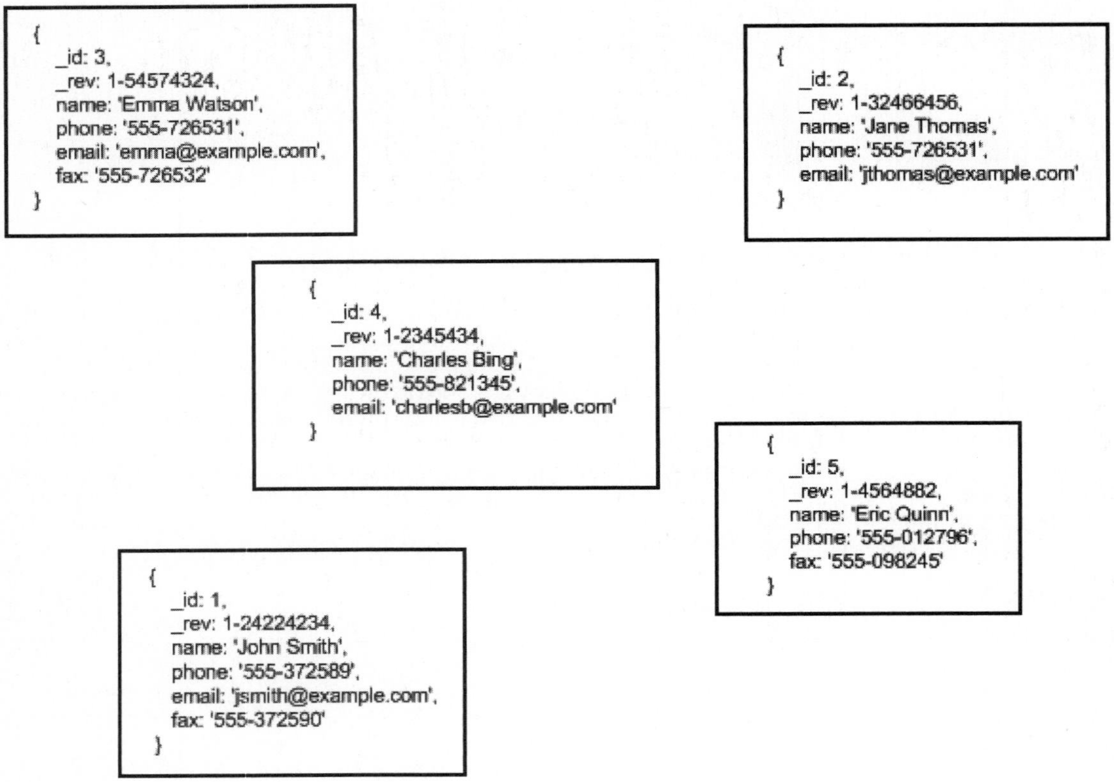

```
{
    _id: 3,
    _rev: 1-54574324,
    name: 'Emma Watson',
    phone: '555-726531',
    email: 'emma@example.com',
    fax: '555-726532'
}
```

```
{
    _id: 2,
    _rev: 1-32466456,
    name: 'Jane Thomas',
    phone: '555-726531',
    email: 'jthomas@example.com'
}
```

```
{
    _id: 4,
    _rev: 1-2345434,
    name: 'Charles Bing',
    phone: '555-821345',
    email: 'charlesb@example.com'
}
```

```
{
    _id: 5,
    _rev: 1-4564882,
    name: 'Eric Quinn',
    phone: '555-012796',
    fax: '555-098245'
}
```

```
{
    _id: 1,
    _rev: 1-24224234,
    name: 'John Smith',
    phone: '555-372589',
    email: 'jsmith@example.com',
    fax: '555-372590'
}
```

Figure 7-1. CouchDB contact documents

As you can see in Figure 7-1, CouchDB does not store data in a tabular, structured way but rather as individual, self-contained documents. Because there is no strict schema to adhere to, documents do not include `null` values for fields they do not have data for. Jane Thomas and Charles Bing have no fax numbers in their documents, and Eric Quinn has no e-mail address in his. Because of this, it would be much more difficult to use a SQL `SELECT` statement to retrieve this data, because not all documents have a value for `email` and `fax`.

This is where CouchDB's support for row-oriented view engines comes into play. Using views, you can aggregate and report on the documents in your CouchDB database. CouchDB views are completely separate from the documents they report on, and there is no restriction on the number of views you can have of any one document. These views are stored in CouchDB in the form of special design documents and are replicated along with regular data documents. As you will see later in this book, this means you can actually replicate entire web applications across CouchDB instances.

When a CouchDB view is queried for the first time, CouchDB runs through every document in the database and runs the view function against it. It then takes the result of the view, which is stored in the form of rows of key/value pairs, and stores it in an individual B-tree file. Although this can take quite some time, it occurs only the first time the view is queried. With each subsequent change of a document, the view function is executed against that document only—everything else is already stored in the B-tree and remains unchanged.

Permanent views are views that are stored inside design documents in the database. They are calculated as described in the previous paragraph. These views are stored and used until such time as their definition changes. You can also create ad hoc temporary views, which are deleted when they are no longer being used. These views are not stored in a design document, and they require the result to be calculated almost every time they are queried. As a result, they are highly inefficient and should be avoided on production systems if possible.

Creating Views

The easiest way to get started creating views is to run some temporary views using the Futon interface. For a detailed overview of Futon, see Chapter 5 of this book. I have created a database called contacts and populated it with the five records, as shown in in Figure 7-1. This database looks like Figure 7-2 in Futon.

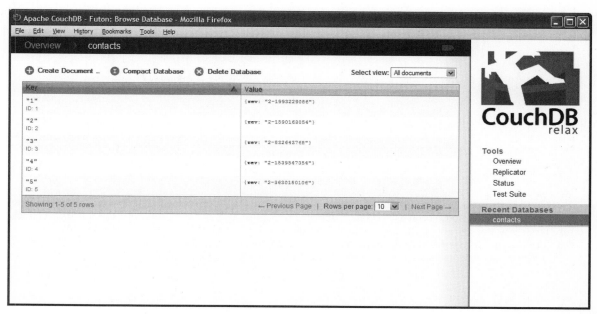

Figure 7-2. The contacts database in Futon

Futon makes it very simple to create temporary views of this data. To the top right of the key/value table, you will see a "Select view" drop-down box. Currently, "All documents" should be selected. Choose "Temporary view" from this list to navigate to the temporary view builder page (Figure 7-3).

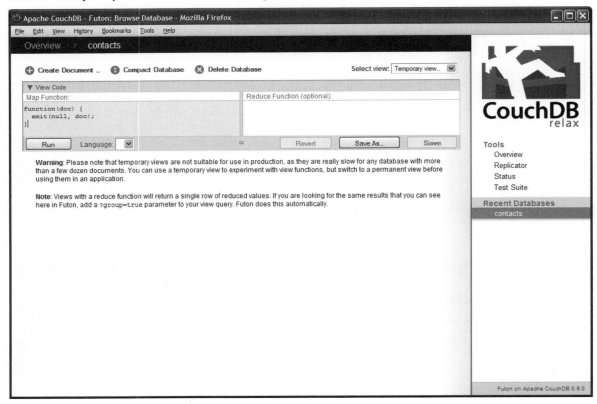

Figure 7-3. Temporary view builder

On this page, you will notice that the key/value table has been replaced by a two-column View Code box. In the left column you have the map function, and in the right column you have the optional reduce function. Don't worry about the reduce function for now, because I will discuss this in much further detail in Chapter 8 when you look at the concept of map/reduce in detail.

In the Map Function column, you will see the code shown in Listing 7-1.

Listing 7-1. *The Default Map Function*

```
function(doc) {
        emit(null, doc);
}
```

This is an example of the map function of a CouchDB view. It takes the document object **doc** as an argument and outputs results using the **emit(key, value)** function. Each call to **emit** corresponds to a row in the view, assuming that the document is successfully processed for all views in the design document. Every time a view is requested, all documents that have been added, updated, or deleted will be processed and inserted in the view, before returning a response.

Beneath the Map Function column you will find a Run button. Click this button to execute the temporary view (Figure 7-4).

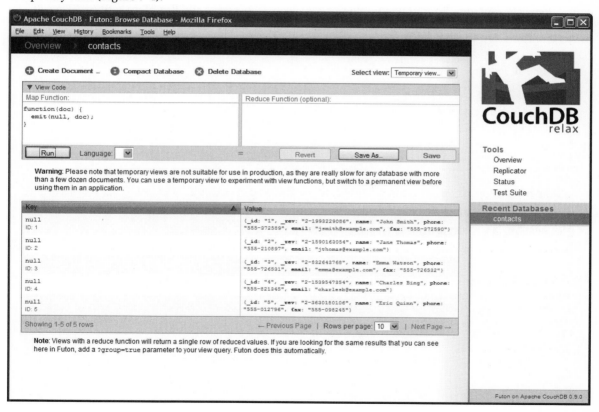

Figure 7-4. *Temporary view results*

As you can see, the results include key/value pairs that match up to the key and value you passed to the emit function in your view. You passed `null` as the key and `doc` (the document object) as the value. In the results, for each document the key is `null`, and the document itself is the value. Let's modify the temporary view function, this time passing the document ID as the key argument to the emit function. This allows you to filter and sort your view by the document ID (Listing 7-2).

Listing 7-2. Using Document ID as a Key

```
function(doc) {
        emit(doc._id, doc);
}
```

Click the Run button to execute the view. This time, the results in the Value column should be the same as before, but in the Key column you'll see that it is showing the document ID for each document.

Because your view is written in JavaScript, you can use its power and flexibility to filter the results. For example, you may want to return the names and phone numbers of only those contacts who have a fax number. Let's create this view now (Listing 7-3).

Listing 7-3. Returning Records for Contacts with Fax Numbers

```
function(doc) {
        if(doc.fax && doc.name && doc.phone)
                emit(doc._id, {Name: doc.name, Phone: doc.phone});
}
```

■ **Note** CouchDB views use a style of dynamic typing known as *duck typing* to determine the semantics of an object based on its current properties. You can see an example of this in Listing 7-3, where you check that a document has fax, name, and phone properties before calling the emit function.

This view returns three only contacts—John Smith, Emma Watson, and Eric Quinn. In addition, it returns the value for each contact as a key/value pair object with the fields Name and Phone. The results are shown in Figure 7-5.

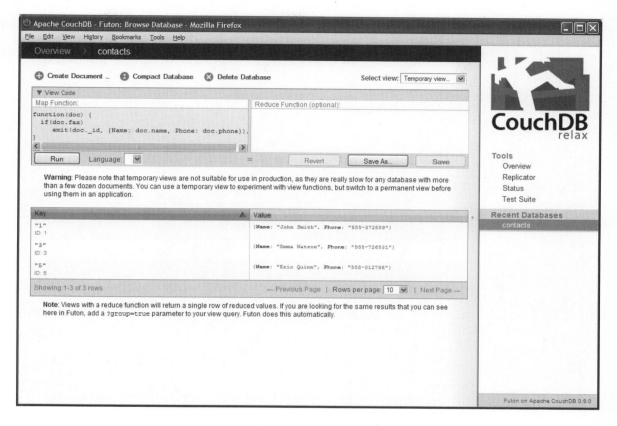

Figure 7-5. Names and phone numbers of contacts with fax numbers

Permanent Views

The easiest way to create a permanent view in Futon is to first create a temporary view as described in the previous section. When you are happy with the results your view returns, you can use the Save As button, found in the Reduce Function column, to save your view as a design document in the database.

To see this in action, let's save the view you created to return the names and phone numbers of only those contacts with fax numbers in the previous section. In the temporary view builder page, make sure the Map Function column contains the code from Listing 7-3, and check that it works as expected by clicking the Run button. If the results look correct, save the view as a design document by clicking the Save As button.

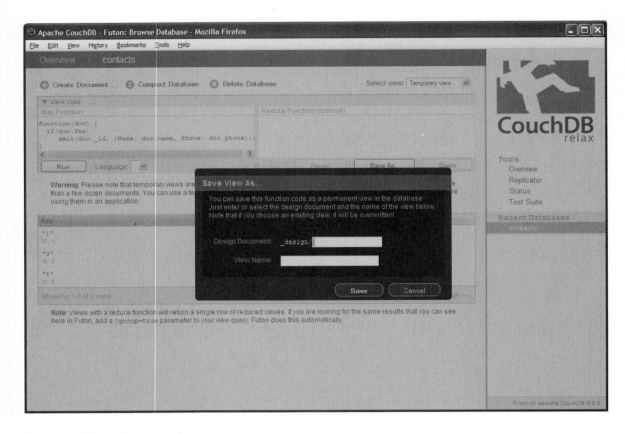

Figure 7-6. *Save View As dialog box*

In the Save View As dialog box that appears, as shown in Figure 7-6, save the view to the design document contacts (**_design/contacts**), and give it a name such as **get_fax_contacts**. When you're ready, click the Save button to persist the view to a design document.

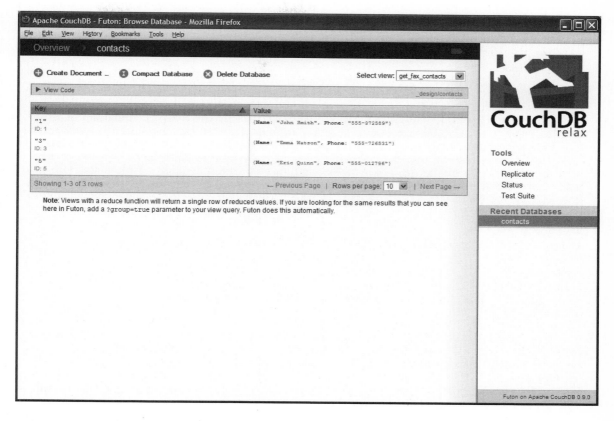

Figure 7-7. The get_fax_contacts *view in the contacts design document*

When the page refreshes, you will be viewing the page for the new permanent view, get_fax_contacts (Figure 7-7). This page is similar to the temporary view builder page. To show the code behind the view, click View Code in the box immediately above the Key/Value table. Once again, you should see the Map Function and Reduce Function columns with the Run and Save As buttons. The main differences between this page and the temporary view builder are that the "Select view" drop-down box now shows get_fax_contacts. Also, in the top right of the View Code box, you will see the name of the design document the view is stored in, _design/contacts.

Another difference between this page and the temporary view builder is that when you modify the view on this page, the buttons Revert and Save become enabled. The functionality of these buttons is exactly as you might expect—clicking Revert will undo any changes you have made since the previous save, and clicking Save persists the new view code to the design document. Let's make a change to see how this works. First, change the code to anything you like (I entered **blah**), and try the Revert button to undo it. Pretty mind-blowing stuff, eh? Next, let's make a small change to the map function so that it returns the contacts' fax numbers instead of phone numbers. Change the function to look like Listing 7-4.

Listing 7-4. Returning Fax Numbers

```
function(doc) {
        if(doc.fax)
                emit(doc._id, {Name: doc.name, Facsimile: doc.fax});
}
```

Click the Run button to make sure the view is working correctly; this time it should produce results with the Value column containing Name and Facsimile fields. If you are happy with the results, click the Save button to persist your new and improved view to the design document. When the view has been saved, you'll notice that the Revert and Save buttons are disabled once again.

Now let's create a similar view based on this view, this time returning only those contacts with an e-mail address. Rather than going back to the temporary view builder and creating the view that way, this time let's just modify the `get_fax_contacts` view instead. Change the code in the Map Function editor box to look like Listing 7-5.

Listing 7-5. Returning Only Those Contacts with E-mail Addresses

```
function(doc) {
        if(doc.email)
                emit(doc._id, {Name: doc.name, Email: doc.email});
}
```

Again, click Run to ensure that the correct results are being returned by the view. This time around, however, don't click the Save button, because that will overwrite your `get_fax_contacts` view with this new view. Instead, click the Save As button to display the Save View As dialog box. The fields will be prepopulated, with Design Document set to `_design/contacts` and View Name set to `get_fax_contacts`. Change the View Name field to `get_email_contacts`, and click the Save button to create the new view, saving it in the contacts design document.

Design Documents

As you discovered in the previous section, permanent views in CouchDB are stored in special documents called *design documents*. These documents are stored in the same way as regular documents, but they typically contain view functions rather than data. You can view all the design documents in a database by selecting "Design documents" from the "Select view" drop-down box (Figure 7-8).

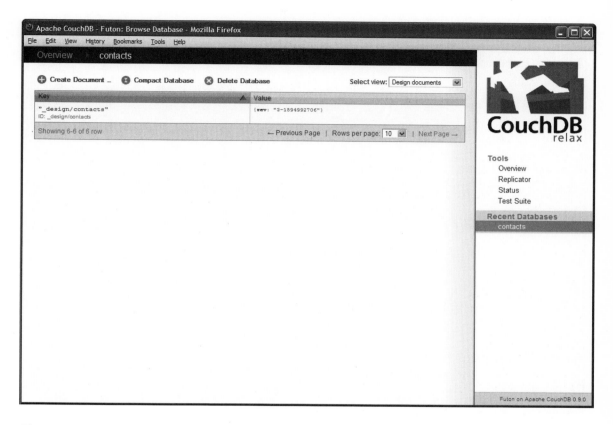

Figure 7-8. *Design documents in the contacts database*

To view a design document, click its key. In this example, the key is `_design/contacts`. The design document appears the same as a regular document—it has a document ID and a revision number, and you can save it, add fields, upload attachments, delete it, view the source code, and navigate between revisions. These special documents usually have two important fields, `language` and `views` (Figure 7-9). The `language` field denotes the language the views in the document are written in, usually `javascript` (although the latest version of CouchDB also includes an Erlang view engine). The `views` field includes the views that are contained in the document, which are themselves broken down into their map and reduce functions where available. You can expand and collapse the function code using the small icon to the left of the view name.

Figure 7-9. The contacts design document

As with regular documents, you can navigate through different revisions of the design document using the Previous Version and Next Version links. The previous revision should have only the `get_fax_contacts` view, whereas the latest version also has the `get_email_contacts` view. It is worth keeping in mind that, like regular documents, previous revisions of design documents are deleted when the database is compacted.

You can also view the source code of the design document using the Source tab at the top right of the document details. This will reveal the JSON source code the design document is made up of. Design documents are just like regular CouchDB documents, but with special features; they will also appear in the "All documents" page. Click "contacts" in the page header to go back to the contacts page, and from the "Select view" drop-down box select "All documents." You will notice that in addition to the contact documents, this table now also includes the `_design/contacts` design document.

Views and the CouchDB API

The Futon web interface makes it easy for you to create and work with the design documents and views in your databases. That said, you will often want to work with CouchDB views using the powerful RESTful API that Couch provides, allowing you to employ them in your own applications.

Let's start off with a temporary view. To execute a temporary view using the API, you send a POST request to the URI **/databasename/_temp_view**, passing the view's functions in the request body. Let's create a very simple temporary view, which has the map function shown in Listing 7-6.

Listing 7-6. A Basic Temporary View Map Function

```
function(doc) {
        emit(doc._id, doc);
}
```

Now use **curl** to make this POST request to the CouchDB server:

```
curl -X POST http://127.0.0.1:5984/contacts/_temp_view-d '{"map":"function(doc) {
emit(doc._id, doc); }"}'
```

Assuming your contacts database is configured as in the previous examples, this should bring back a result similar to that in Listing 7-7. Please note that this listing has been formatted to make it easier to read; the raw output you get from the **curl** command will not be formatted like this.

Listing 7-7. Results of the Temporary View

```
{
        "total_rows":5,"offset":0,"rows":[
                {
                        "id":"1",
                        "key":"1",
                        "value":{
                                "_id":"1",
                                "_rev":"2-1993229086",
                                "name":"John Smith",
                                "phone":"555-372589",
                                "email":"jsmith@example.com",
                                "fax":"555-372590"
                        }
        },{
                        "id":"2",
                        "key":"2",
                        "value":{
                                "_id":"2",
                                "_rev":"2-1590163054",
                                "name":"Jane Thomas",
                                "phone":"555-210897",
                                "email":"jthomas@example.com"
                        }
```

```
        },{
                "id":"3",
                "key":"3",
                "value":{
                        "_id":"3",
                        "_rev":"2-832643768",
                        "name":"Emma Watson",
                        "phone":"555-726531",
                        "email":"emma@example.com",
                        "fax":"555-726532"
                }
        },{
                "id":"4",
                "key":"4",
                "value":{
                        "_id":"4"
                        ,"_rev":"2-1539547354",
                        "name":"Charles Bing",
                        "phone":"555-821345",
                        "email":"charlesb@example.com"
                }
        },{
                "id":"5",
                "key":"5",
                "value":{
                        "_id":"5",
                        "_rev":"2-3630180106",
                        "name":"Eric Quinn",
                        "phone":"555-012796",
                        "fax":"555-098245"
                }
        }
    ]
}
```

Working with temporary views is nice and easy, but as discussed earlier in this chapter, their use is limited, and they should be avoided if possible. Before you start creating permanent views using the API, let's use the `curl` command to access the two existing views you created in your design document `/_design/contacts`. You can execute a permanent view using a GET request to the URI `/contacts/_design/contacts/_view/get_fax_contacts`, where the second `contacts` in the URI is the design document name and `get_fax_contacts` is the view name. Let's try this using `curl`:

```
curl -X GET http://127.0.0.1:5984/contacts/_design/contacts/_view/get_fax_contacts
```

All going well, you should get a result like Listing 7-8.

Listing 7-8. Result of get_fax_contacts View

```
{"total_rows":3,"offset":0,"rows":[
        {"id":"1","key":"1","value":{"Name":"John Smith","Facsimile":"555-372590"}},
        {"id":"3","key":"3","value":{"Name":"Emma Watson","Facsimile":"555-726532"}},
```

```
        {"id":"5","key":"5","value":{"Name":"Eric Quinn","Facsimile":"555-098245"}}
]}
```

Similarly, you can execute the `get_email_contacts` view the same way:

```
curl -X GET http://127.0.0.1:5984/contacts/_design/contacts/_view/get_email_contacts
```

This should return the result set shown in Listing 7-9.

Listing 7-9. Result of get_email_contacts View

```
{"total_rows":4,"offset":0,"rows":[
        {"id":"1","key":"1","value":{"Name":"John Smith","Email":"jsmith@example.com"}},
        {"id":"2","key":"2","value":{"Name":"Jane Thomas","Email":"jthomas@example.com"}},
        {"id":"3","key":"3","value":{"Name":"Emma Watson","Email":"emma@example.com"}},
        {"id":"4","key":"4","value":{"Name":"Charles Bing","Email":"charlesb@example.com"}}
]}
```

Now that you've seen how the API returns the results of a view, let's move forward and create a permanent view inside a new design document. You create a design document the same way as you create a regular CouchDB document—using a PUT HTTP request and passing the document in JSON in the request body. In this example, you are creating a new design document called `more_views`, and inside this document you have a single view called `get_email_or_fax`, which will return the name of the contact and the contact's e-mail address, fax number, or both where available.

Listing 7-10 shows the definition of the new view you are creating. Store it in a text file named `more_views.json`.

Listing 7-10. more_views.json

```
{
    "language": "javascript",
    "views": {
        "get_fax_or_email": {
            "map": "function(doc) {
                if(doc.name && doc.email && doc.fax)
                        emit(doc._id, {Name: doc.name, Email: doc.email, Fax: doc.fax});
                else if(doc.name && doc.email)
                        emit(doc._id, {Name: doc.name, Email: doc.email});
                else if(doc.name && doc.fax)
                        emit(doc._id, {Name: doc.name, Fax: doc.fax});
            }"
        }
    }
}
```

Issue the following `curl` command to create this view in the database:

```
curl -X PUT http://127.0.0.1:5984/contacts/_design/more_views -d @more_views.json
```

You should get the following response:

121

```
{"ok":true,"id":"_design/more_views","rev":"1-4096382351"}
```

Now let's test your new view by executing it using `curl`:

```
curl -X GET http://127.0.0.1:5984/contacts/_design/more_views/_view/get_fax_or_email
```

This should bring back a result like Listing 7-11.

Listing 7-11. Result of get_fax_or_email View

```
{"total_rows":5,"offset":0,"rows":[
        {"id":"1","key":"1","value":{
                "Name":"John Smith","Email":"jsmith@example.com","Fax":"555-372590"
        }},
        {"id":"2","key":"2","value":{
                "Name":"Jane Thomas","Email":"jthomas@example.com"
        }},
        {"id":"3","key":"3","value":{
                "Name":"Emma Watson","Email":"emma@example.com","Fax":"555-726532"
        }},
        {"id":"4","key":"4","value":{"
                Name":"Charles Bing","Email":"charlesb@example.com"
        }},
        {"id":"5","key":"5","value":{
                "Name":"Eric Quinn","Fax":"555-098245"
        }}
]}
```

Before finishing, let's check that your new design document and view are working as you would expect them to in Futon. Fire up the Futon interface, and navigate to the contacts database. The "Select view" drop-down box should now feature a new section called `more_views` with the new `get_fax_or_email` view available within it. Click this view to execute it, and the results will look similar to Figure 7-10.

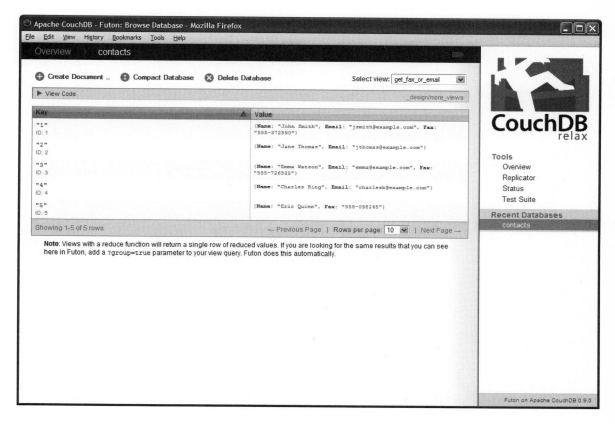

Figure 7-10. Your new get_fax_or_email view in Futon

Summary

In this chapter, you learned about CouchDB views and how they are used to aggregate and report on the data in a CouchDB database. You discovered how CouchDB uses map/reduce views instead of SQL statements to interact with data. You then learned how to create and execute temporary views using the Futon interface, before saving these views in special design documents in the CouchDB database. Finally, you learned how to use the CouchDB RESTful HTTP API to run and create views and design documents.

In the next chapter, you will explore in depth the concept of map/reduce and how it applies to CouchDB views. In Chapter 9, you will move on to some more advanced CouchDB view concepts and examples.

CHAPTER 8

■ ■ ■

Map/Reduce

In the previous chapter, you learned how to create views in CouchDB; they allow you to query your data in different ways, much like you would use SQL for in traditional relational databases. In creating these views, you may have noticed that each time you were putting your view code into something known as a *map function*. In this chapter, you will explore the concept of map functions in more detail, and you will also look at the *reduce function*. These two functions combine to form the concept of map/reduce, which CouchDB uses to determine the following:

- What data is to be retrieved

- How to filter that data

- How that data should be ordered

- How to aggregate the data

What Is Map/Reduce?

Map/reduce is a concept in software that has recently gained popularity in distributed computing. The concept is based on two functions—map and reduce—both of which are intended to be used with a list of inputs. The map function produces an output for each item in this list, while the reduce function produces a single output for the entire list. CouchDB exploits the characteristics of these two functions to provide incremental calculation of views. This means that each time a document is updated in a CouchDB database, only those documents that have been modified need to be reprocessed by the map and reduce functions.

Google use an implementation of map/reduce in its web index. Google has thousands of machines working on hundreds of terabytes of data, spread across the World Wide Web. Problems that would take a single machine months to process take a matter of hours over this distributed model. Google's MapReduce library includes features such as load balancing and disk optimization to further enhance the efficiency of the system, as well as to simplify its use. It is also built to be robust so that machine failures do not have a negative impact on solving the original problem. In fact, according to Google's publicized research on MapReduce, it once lost 1,600 out of 1,800 machines in a cluster, but the system still produced a result at the end.

Map/Reduce in CouchDB

In the previous chapter, you learned how to create CouchDB views using map functions. When creating views in CouchDB, you must create a map function. This function takes a single argument, which is the document itself, and uses the special `emit` function to produce a result. This `emit` function accepts two arguments: a key and a value. Every time the `emit` function is called, a row is added to the view. Whenever a new document is created or an existing document is updated or deleted, the rows in the view are updated automatically. Listing 8-1 shows the most basic map function (in this case, I am using the JavaScript view engine).

Listing 8-1. A Basic Map Function

```
function(doc) {
    emit(null, doc);
}
```

In this example, you can see that the map function has a single argument `doc`, which represents the CouchDB document. This particular function simply adds every document in the database to the view, with no key defined and the entire document as the value.

If the database contains documents of different types, you might use a field `type` to differentiate between different types of documents. Consider the example in Listing 8-2, where you emit only those rows that have a type `car`.

Listing 8-2. Filtering by Document Type

```
function(doc) {
    if(doc.type == "car") emit(null, { "make": doc.make, "model": doc.model, "year":
doc.year });
}
```

In this example, only those documents that have a `type` field with the value `car` will be added to the view. Again, each of these documents will be represented by a row with a `null` key and an object comprising the car's make, model, and year as the value. This type of filtering should be used only where the lookup key is fixed. Listing 8-3 provides an example that can be used for dynamic filtering.

Listing 8-3. Filtering and Sorting Documents

```
function(doc) {
    if(doc.type == "car") emit(doc.make, { "model": doc.model, "year": doc.year });
}
```

In this example, you emit a key—the make of the car. The rows in the view will be sorted by the key, so the display order of the results of the view will be based on the make of the car. Additionally, you can filter the results of the view using URL query arguments that define the key(s) that should be included in the result. In this example, you could pass the query argument `?key="Toyota"` when executing your view, and only those cars that have `"Toyota"` as the key (the `make` field) will be returned.

CouchDB views must contain a map function, and they can also optionally include a reduce function. Unlike the map function, which produces a row for each document it processes, the reduce function produces a single result for all the documents. Reduce functions are used to aggregate data. The reduce function accepts three arguments—`key`, `values`, and `reduce`. It must return a single-value result. Listing 8-4 shows the simplest example of a reduce function.

Listing 8-4. A Basic Reduce Function

```
function(key, values, rereduce) {
    return sum(values);
}
```

Assuming that the view's corresponding map function emits number values, this reduce function will return a result of the sum of the value of each row contained in the view. Depending on the amount of data being processed, the reduce operation may be broken down into smaller chunks by CouchDB. When this happens, the data will be processed by the reduce function before sending the result to the reduce function with the `rereduce` argument set to `true`.

Take Listing 8-4 as an example. Say CouchDB decides to break the data to be processed into three groups:

- *Group A*: 1, 4, 5

- *Group B*: 3, 4, 8

- *Group C*: 9, 2, 5

The view engine would first take each group individually, with `rereduce` set to `false`. This would produce three results: 10 for Group A, 15 for Group B, and 16 for Group C. These results are then sent as an array to the reduce function, with `rereduce` set to `true`. This produces a final result of 41.

Reduce functions are invoked differently based on whether `rereduce` is `true` or `false`. If `rereduce` is `false`, the keys argument will be a list of keys and IDs for each row emitted by the map function, and the `values` argument will be an array of the values emitted by the map function. If `rereduce` is `true`, however, the `keys` argument will be `null`, and the `values` argument will be an array of the results produced by the previous invocations of the reduce function.

In Listing 8-4, the type of data in the `values` argument is always the same, regardless of whether `rereduce` is `true` or `false`, and as a result, you do not need to handle `rereduce` calls separately in the reduce function. In Chapter 9, you will see an example of a reduce function where you need to take the value of `rereduce` into consideration.

Map/Reduce in Futon

In Chapter 5, you learned how to use Futon, CouchDB's web-based administration interface. In Chapter 7, you saw how you can create JavaScript views in CouchDB using Futon. Now, you'll take this knowledge a step further and learn how to create views in CouchDB that have both map and reduce functions.

In this section, you will use the same contacts database that you worked with in Chapter 7. Some of these contacts had an `email` field, some had a `fax` field, and some had both. In Chapter 7, you created views that returned rows based on whether contacts had an e-mail address or fax number. However, this type of data is more likely to be used for reporting purposes. For example, how many people have both, how many have a fax, how many have an e-mail address, and how many have neither? Using the methods described in Chapter 7, you would have to create separate views for each of these and look at the number of rows returned to find this information. Wouldn't it be much more useful if you could have just one view which did this for you? Let's find out how to create such a view.

Open Futon. (If CouchDB is installed on your local computer, you can open Futon by opening your web browser and pointing it to `http://127.0.0.1:5984/_utils`.) Assuming you created the contacts database in Chapter 7, you should be able to click that database in the CouchDB Overview page, as shown in Figure 8-1.

Figure 8-1. *CouchDB Futon Overview page*

When you navigate to the contacts database, you should be looking at the "All documents" view, as shown in Figure 8-2.

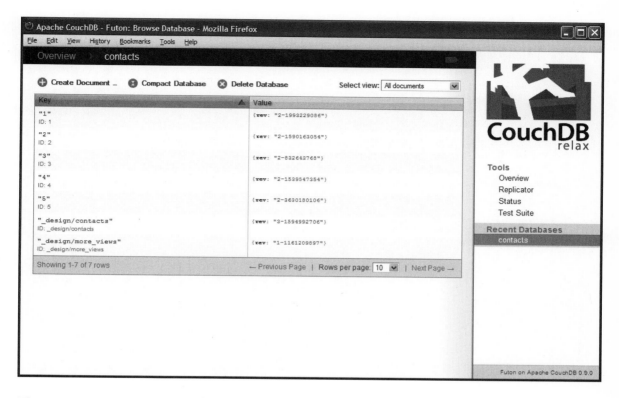

Figure 8-2. All documents in the contacts database

As you are creating a new view, open the view design page by selecting the "Temporary view" option from the "Select view" drop-down box toward the top right of the main Futon window. This should bring you to a page like the one shown in Figure 8-3.

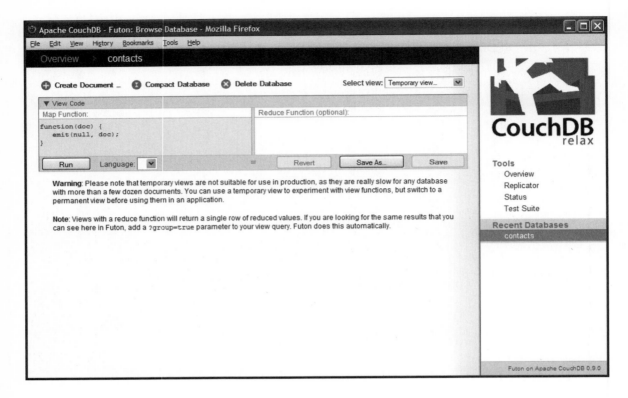

Figure 8-3. Futon view design page

On this screen, you will see two large input boxes—Map Function and Reduce Function. In the past, you have created views that required only map functions. This time around, you will be creating a reduce function also.

The view you are going to create should return the number of documents in the database that have the following properties:

- Contain **both** an e-mail address and a fax number

- Contain **only** an e-mail address

- Contain **only** a fax number

- Contain **neither** an e-mail address nor a fax number

Let's start by creating the map function. Enter the code in Listing 8-5 into the input box for the map function.

Listing 8-5. The Map Function for the Aggregate View

```
function(doc) {
    if(doc.email && doc.fax)
            emit("Both", 1);
      else if(doc.email)
            emit("Email", 1);
      else if(doc.fax)
            emit("Fax", 1);
      else
            emit("Neither", 1);
}
```

Out of interest, click the Run button, situated just below the Map Function box, and let's see what it brings back (Figure 8-4).

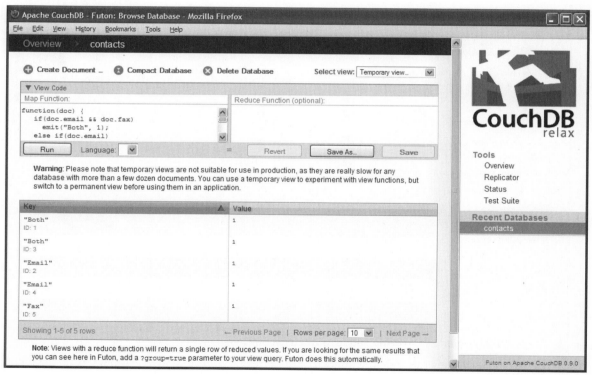

Figure 8-4. Results of the map function

As you can see, the view returns five rows. This is because the map function is testing for all possible scenarios of the presence of a fax number or e-mail address. Every document therefore is emitted by the map function, with a key of either **"Both"**, **"Email"**, **"Fax"**, or **"Neither"**, and a value of 1. Because there are only five documents in the sample database, it's fairly easy to count the number of results for each key. It would not be so simple, however, if your contacts database had hundreds or thousands of documents. So, let's see how you can aggregate this data to produce a count of the contacts for each key.

In the Reduce Function box, located to the right of the Map Function box, enter the code in Listing 8-6.

Listing 8-6. *The Reduce Function for the Aggregate View*

```
function(key, values, rereduce) {
    return sum(values);
}
```

Click the Run button once more to see the results of the view (Figure 8-5).

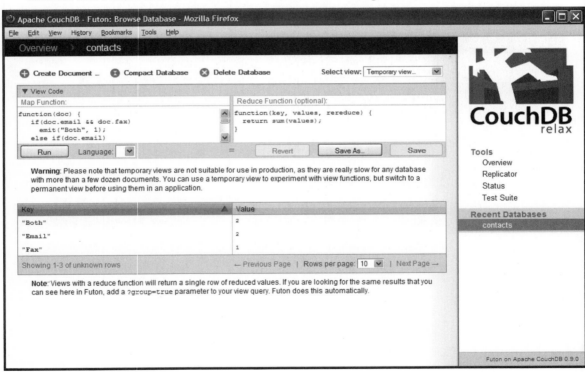

Figure 8-5. *The results of the aggregated view*

As you can see from Figure 8-5, the results are now much more readable, with the count for the number of rows for each key summed up to produce a total. As you can see, there are no documents in the database that have neither a fax number nor an e-mail address. Let's change one of the documents with both of these fields to test that the **"Neither"** feature is working correctly.

First, save your view as a permanent view in the database by clicking the Save As button, located below the Reduce Function box. In the Save View As dialog box that appears, enter **contacts** in the box for the Design Document field and **count_by_type** in the field for View Name, as shown in Figure 8-6.

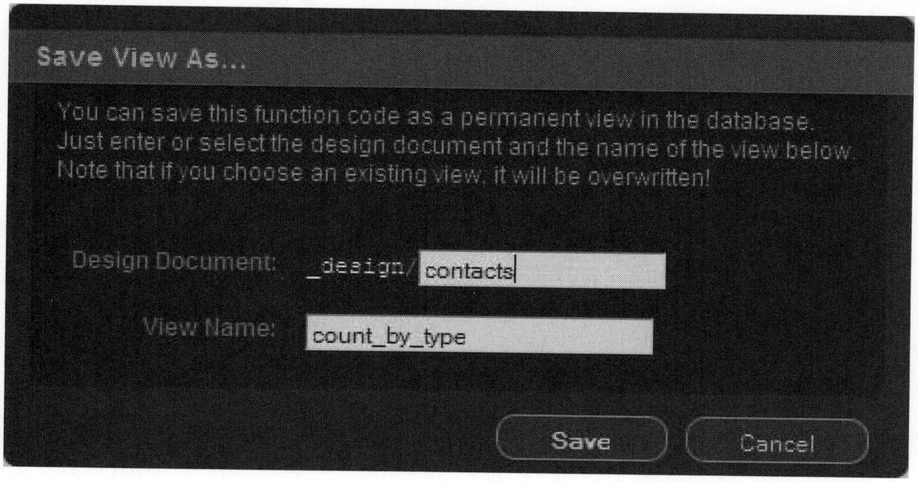

Figure 8-6. Save View As dialog box

Return to the "All documents" view of the contacts database by selecting the appropriate option from the "Select view" drop-down menu. From there, click the document with ID 1 to navigate to the document for John Smith. This document should look similar to the one in Figure 8-7.

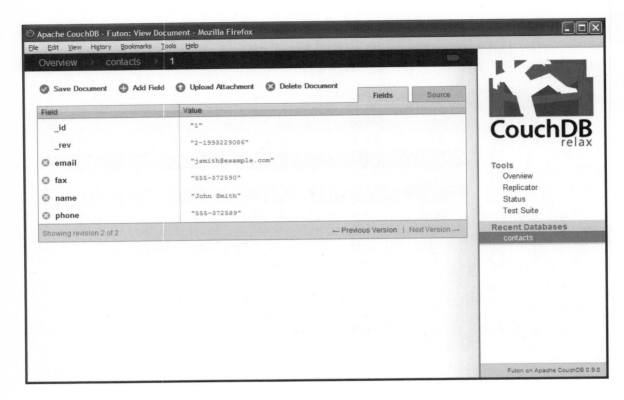

Figure 8-7. The John Smith document in the database

In this document, delete the e-mail and fax fields by clicking the small, gray *x* button to the left of the field name. The field should instantly be removed from the screen. To save these changes to the database, click the Save Document link above the Fields table. When you have saved the document, navigate to the "All documents" view of the contacts database by clicking the contacts link in the Futon header. From here, use the "Select view" drop-down box to navigate to the **count_by_type** view, located under the contacts design document (Figure 8-8).

Key	Value
"Both"	1
"Email"	2
"Fax"	1
"Neither"	1

Showing 1-4 of unknown rows ← Previous Page | Rows per page: 10 ▾ | Next Page →

*Figure 8-8. The update **count_by_type** view*

As you can see in Figure 8-8, the view results have been updated to reflect the document you just modified. Now, the database includes a single document with both email and fax fields, two documents with just an e-mail field, one document with just a fax field, and one document with neither an email nor a fax field.

Map/Reduce Views and the CouchDB API

I covered creating CouchDB views using the API in Chapter 7. You simply add a reduce function to your view's JavaScript definition to get the desired results. Listing 8-7 would create the count_by_type view from the previous section using the CouchDB RESTful HTTP API.

Listing 8-7. count_by_type.json

```
{
    "language": "javascript",
    "views": {
        "count_by_type": {
            "map": "function(doc) {
                if(doc.email && doc.fax) emit('Both', 1);
                else if(doc.email) emit('Email', 1);
                else if(doc.fax) emit('Fax', 1);
                else emit('Neither', 1);
            }",
            "reduce": "function(doc) {
                return sum(values);
            }"
        }
    }
}
```

Now let's add this view to the contacts design document in the contacts CouchDB database:

```
curl -X PUT http://127.0.0.1:5984/contacts/_design/contacts -d @count_by_type.json
```

As you can see from Listing 8-7, you simply include the reduce function alongside your map function when defining your view using JavaScript. Complex views are much easier to create using Futon, because you don't have to worry about escaping quote characters and missing braces and the like. Of course, you could always create your own application for defining views.

Let's now use curl to run the view you created in the previous section. If you saved the view in the contacts design document with the name count_by_type, you should be able to access the view using the following URL: http://127.0.0.1:5984/contacts/_design/contacts/_view/count_by_type.

```
curl -X GET http://127.0.0.1:5984/contacts/_design/contacts/_view/count_by_type
```

The results of this command should look similar to Listing 8-8.

Listing 8-8. Command-Line Results of count_by_type View

```
{"rows":[
        {"key":null,"value":5}
]}
```

That doesn't look right, does it? It's simply returning the overall count of the number of documents in the database and not grouping the aggregation based on the key. The reason for this is that you need to explicitly tell the CouchDB API to perform grouping on your view. You did not need to do this in Futon because it does it for you automatically, but using the API, this is a manual process. This time around, issue the following command:

```
cURL -X GET http://127.0.0.1:5984/contacts/_design/contacts/_view/count_by_type?group=true
```

This command should result in the code in Listing 8-9 being returned.

Listing 8-9. Grouped Results of count_by_type View

```
{"rows":[
        {"key":"Both","value":1},
        {"key":"Email","value":2},
        {"key":"Fax","value":1},
        {"key":"Neither","value":1}
]}
```

That's more like it, isn't it? As you can see, by passing the `group=true` query parameter along with your view's URI, you tell CouchDB to group the results by the view's key.

Map/Reduce vs. SQL Queries

If you come from a relational database background, the easiest way to describe how map/reduce works is to identify the components of a view based on their counterparts in a SQL query implementation. Let's take the following SQL statement:

```
SELECT id, name, email FROM contacts WHERE country = 'USA' ORDER BY name
```

In this SQL statement, you are retrieving the `id`, `name`, and `email` columns from the contacts table. You are filtering the results so that it returns only those rows in the contacts table where the `country` field is equal to the string value `"USA"`. Finally, you are requesting that the results be returned sorted by the `name` field. Now let's look at how you would retrieve results from a CouchDB database using a map function (Listing 8-10).

Listing 8-10. Using a Map Function to Filter and Sort Data

```
function(doc) {
    if(doc.type != "contact") return;
    emit([doc.country, doc.name], {name: doc.name, email: doc.email});
}
```

In the previous map function, you check that the document type is contact, and if it is, you emit a complex key made up of the country and name fields,as well as a value object with name and email fields. You can then use the startkey and endkey URI parameters to define which country you want to look up values for. Now let's compare the results from the SQL query and the map function (see Table 8-1).

Table 8-1. Results from SQL Query

id	name	email
3	Jane Smith	jane@example.com
1	Joe Lennon	joe@example.com
4	John Bloggs	john@example.com

Table 8-1 is the table of results you could expect from the SQL statement you looked at earlier. For example purposes, I'm assuming that the contact in the row with id 2 has a country value of Ireland, so they would not be returned by this query. Table 8-2 shows the results you would get from your CouchDB view using the map function defined in Listing 8-1, passing the parameter ?startkey=["USA"]&endkey=["USA",{}] to the view's URI.

Table 8-2. Results from CouchDB View

id	key	value
"3"	["USA", "Jane Smith"]	{"name":"Jane Smith","email":"jane@example.com"}
"1"	["USA", "Joe Lennon"]	{"name":"Joe Lennon","email":"joe@example.com"}
"4"	["USA", "John Bloggs"]	{"name":"John Bloggs","email":"john@example.com"}

You can see that in Table 8-2 the results are similar to those produced by the SQL statement. CouchDB views always return the document ID, a key, and a value.

But what if you want to perform aggregation on this data? For example, let's say you wanted to return a count of the number of contacts, grouped by the country field. In SQL, you would issue the following statement:

```
SELECT COUNT(*), country FROM contacts GROUP BY country
```

In the previous SQL statement, you use the COUNT function to return the number of contacts in the table, and you group these results by the country column to return the number of contacts in each country. Now let's look at how you would perform this aggregation in your CouchDB view (Listing 8-11).

Listing 8-11. Using Map and Reduce Functions to Produce Aggregated Reports on Data

```
map: function(doc) {
    emit(doc.country, 1);
}

reduce: function(key, values, rereduce) {
    return sum(values);
}
```

In Listing 8-11, you create a map function that emits the country field as the key and 1 as the value. You then create a reduce function that will aggregate the rows returned by the map function. In this instance, the reduce function simply sums the values it receives as input. Because you emit the value as 1 in the map function, it will act as a counter. When calling this view, you pass the query string parameter group=true to tell CouchDB that it should group the results by the key.

Let's take a look at the results returned by the SQL statement (Table 8-3).

Table 8-3. Results from the Aggregated SQL Query

COUNT(*)	country
1	Ireland
3	USA

As you can see, it has returned the number of rows in the contacts table, grouped by the country column. There are three contacts in the United States and a single contact in Ireland. Now let's look at what the CouchDB view returns (Table 8-4).

Table 8-4. Results from the CouchDB View

key	value
"Ireland"	1
"USA"	3

Look familiar? These results are the same as what was brought back by the SQL statement. You have calculated the number of documents in the contacts database, grouped by the country field.

Word Count Example

One of the most commonly used examples when explaining the concept of map/reduce is the word count example. Basically, you take a document of text and use map and reduce functions to return the number of times each word appears in that document. For this example, I have created a database named documents, and inside it I have created a single document, with the field **content** and its value set to the full text of U.S. President Barack Obama's 2009 inauguration speech, part of which is shown in Figure 8-9.

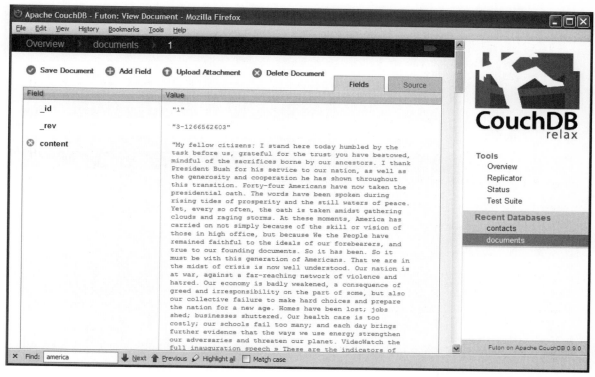

Figure 8-9. Inauguration speech in the database

Now I want to create a view that takes this speech and counts the number of times each word in the speech was mentioned. To do so, I created a new view, with the map function shown in Listing 8-12.

Listing 8-12. Map Function for Word Count View

```
function(doc) {
    var words = doc.content.toLowerCase().replace(/[^a-z]+/g, ' ').split(' ');
```

```
    for(word in words)
        emit(words[word], 1);
}
```

In the previous function, I am taking the **content** field of the document, lowering it, and replacing any nonalphabetical characters with a space, before tokenizing the document into an array of words, split by a single whitespace token. I then use a loop to iterate through each item in the words array, and I emit the word as the key and a value of 1 that will be used to count the occurrences in the reduce function, as shown in Listing 8-13.

Listing 8-13. Reduce Function for Word Count View

```
function(key, values, rereduce) {
    return sum(values);
}
```

The reduce function is the same as you saw previously when performing count aggregation on your documents. You simply take the **values** argument and return it summed up. Figure 8-10 shows a snippet of the result returned by this view.

Figure 8-10. Word count view results

You can easily produce variations of this view; for example, say you want to count the number of occurrences of words starting with each letter of the alphabet. Simply change the map function in the previous view to Listing 8-14.

Listing 8-14. Revised Map Function

```
function(doc) {
        var words = doc.content.toLowerCase().replace(/[^a-z]+/g, ' ').split(' ');
        for(word in words)
            emit(words[word].substring(0,1), 1);
}
```

This view returns the result shown in Figure 8-11.

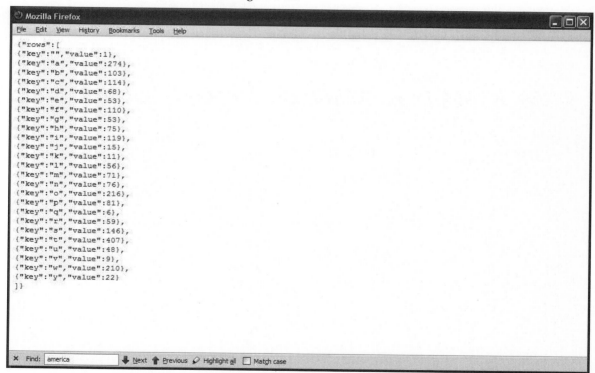

Figure 8-11. Word count by letter view results

Summary

In this chapter, you learned about map/reduce and how it is used in CouchDB views. You learned about how to map a SQL statement into its counterpart map and reduce statements, how map functions are used to define what rows and fields are to be output in the view, and how the results should be sorted. You then learned how to aggregate these results using reduce functions. You walked through the process of creating map and reduce functions in the contacts database, which groups the number of contacts that have both e-mail addresses and fax numbers, either or, and neither nor. You then saw the common map/reduce example of counting the number of occurrences of a word in a text, using the 2009 inauguration speech of U.S. President Barack Obama.

In the next chapter, you will take what you have learned in Chapters 7 and 8 to the next level by working with some advanced CouchDB views, exposing the real power behind CouchDB.

CHAPTER 9

■ ■ ■

Advanced CouchDB Views

In this chapter, you will look at more advanced areas of CouchDB views—advanced aggregation functions such as average, maximum, and minimum; ordering and filtering results using keys; and the different approaches to performing join-like operations in CouchDB.

Advanced Aggregation

For the purpose of examples in this section, I will be using a database of documents that hold employee information—their name, their salary, and the department they work in. Table 9-1 shows the contents of this database.

Table 9-1. *Tabular Representation of the Employees Database*

name	salary	department
"Jack Sawyer"	30000	"Sales"
"Kate Lynch"	45000	"Management"
"Patrick Wood"	32000	"Sales"
"John McIntyre"	19000	"Administration"
"Ann Hayes"	60000	"Management"
"Lisa Liu"	38000	"Accounts"
"David Harrington"	31000	"IT"

In the previous chapter, you learned to count grouped data. You can count the number of employees in each department with the map and reduce functions, as shown in Listing 9-1.

Listing 9-1. Counting the Number of Employees by Department

```
map: function(doc) {
    if(doc.department)
        emit(doc.department, 1);
```

```
}

reduce: function(keys, values, rereduce) {
    return sum(values);
}
```

This view will return a result like the one shown in Figure 9-1.

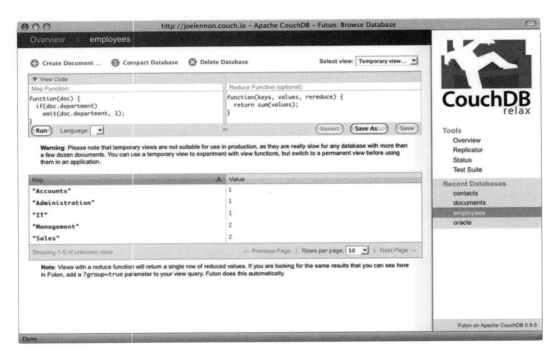

Figure 9-1. *Results of the count view*

Now let's change the view slightly so that it returns the total salary for each department. To do this, you simple emit the salary field as the value in the map function. Listing 9-2 shows the code for this sum view (with changes from Listing 9-1 in bold).

Listing 9-2. *Finding the Total Salary by Department*

```
map: function(doc) {
    if(doc.department)
        emit(doc.department, doc.salary);
}
```

```
reduce: function(keys, values, rereduce) {
    return sum(values);
}
```

The new view should return a result like the one in Figure 9-2.

Figure 9-2. *Results of the sum view*

Now let's try something a bit trickier. Let's get the average salary by department. This time, the map function can stay the same, but you need to change the reduce function, telling it to calculate the average salary instead of the total salary (Listing 9-3).

Listing 9-3. *Finding the Average Salary by Department*

```
map: function(doc) {
    if(doc.department)
        emit(doc.department, doc.salary);
}

reduce: function(keys, values, rereduce) {
    var total = sum(values);
```

```
    return Math.round((total / values.length)  *100) / 100;
}
```

In this view, you are finding the total salary for each department, and then you are finding the average by dividing this total by the number of employees in the department. In this example, you are using the `Math.round` JavaScript function to round your result to two decimal places. The result should look something like Figure 9-3.

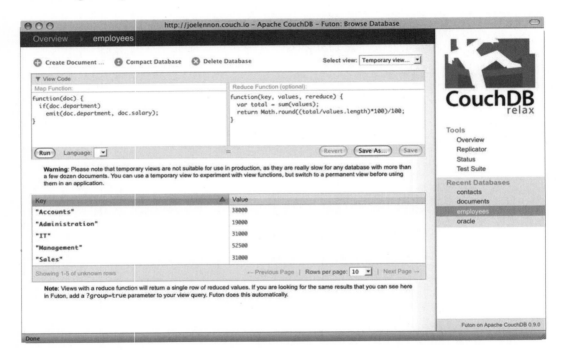

Figure 9-3. *Finding the average salary by department*

■ **Note** Futon automatically groups results on views with reduce functions. By default, however, CouchDB does not group these results. You can force this behavior by passing the parameter `?group=true` to your view's URI, however.

In all the examples so far, you have aggregated by department. But what if you want an overall result for all employees? To do this, change the key in the map function to a string label such as `"Average"`, as described in Listing 9-4.

Listing 9-4. Finding the Average Salary for All Employees

```
map: function(doc) {
    if(doc.department)
        emit("Average", doc.salary);
}

reduce: function(keys, values, rereduce) {
    var total = sum(values);
    return Math.round((total / values.length)  *100) / 100;
}
```

The two other common aggregate functions used when working with data are max and min, which, as you might expect from their names, return the maximum value and minimum values found in a resultset. In the employee database, you might want to find out what the highest and lowest salaries are. Let's find out how to do this using a CouchDB view (Listing 9-5).

Listing 9-5. Finding the Highest and Lowest Salaries

```
map: function(doc) {
    if(doc.department)
        emit("Max and Min", doc.salary);
}

reduce: function(keys, values, rereduce) {
        var max, min;
    if(rereduce == false) {
            max = values[0];
            min = values[0];

            for(item in values) {
                    if(values[item] > max) max = values[item];
                    if(values[item] < min) min = values[item];
            }
            return { "max": max, "min": min };
    } else {
            max = values[0].max;
            min = values[0].min;

            for(item in values) {
                    if(values[item].max > max) max = values[item].max;
                    if(values[item].min < min) min = values[item].min;
            }

            return { "max": max, "min": min };
    }
}
```

In Listing 9-5, you use the reduce function to initialize the max and min variables and then loop through the values sent to the reduce function to check whether the value is greater than or less than the current max and min values. You then return the max and min values.

You will notice in this example that you check to see whether the value of the **rereduce** argument is **false**. On large data sets, CouchDB breaks down the data sent to the reduce function and processes it in smaller batches. When these batches are processed, they return a value to the reduce function and set the value of **rereduce** to **true**.

In this example, if **rereduce** is **false**, the values argument will be an array of the values emitted by the map function—in this case the salary field of each document. You then process these salaries to find the maximum and minumum values and return a JSON object with two fields, **max** and **min**. If **rereduce** is **true**, the values argument will be an array of values returned by previous calls to the reduce function, in this case, the JSON objects with **max** and **min** fields. Once again, you return a JSON object with maximum and minumum values (Figure 9-4).

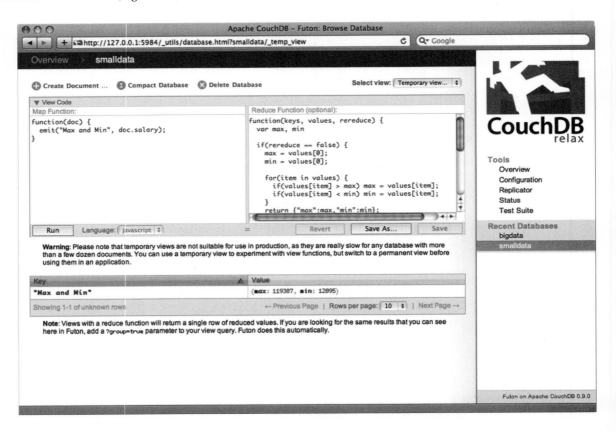

Figure 9-4. Finding the highest and lowest salaries

Of course, if you wanted the **max** and **min** values for each department, you can simply change the key in the map function to **doc.department**, and it will group the results by department accordingly. You might be wondering what good this information is to you when you don't know which employee has the maximum salary and which has the minimum salary. So, let's modify the view so that it tells you the name and salary of the highest and lowest earners (Listing 9-6).

Listing 9-6. Finding the Names and Salaries of the Highest and Lowest Earners

```
map: function(doc) {
    if(doc.department)
        emit("Max and Min", {"name": doc.name, "salary": doc.salary});
}

reduce: function(keys, values, rereduce) {
    var max, min, max_name, min_name;

    if(rereduce == false) {
        max = values[0].salary;
        min = values[0].salary;
        max_name = values[0].name;
        min_name = values[0].name;

        for(item in values) {
            if(values[item].salary > max) {
                max = values[item].salary;
                max_name = values[item].name;
            }
            if(values[item].salary < min) {
                min = values[item].salary;
                min_name = values[item].name;
            }
        }

        return {
            "max": { "name": max_name, "salary": max },
            "min": { "name": min_name, "salary": min }
        };
    } else {
        max = values[0].max.salary;
        min = values[0].min.salary;
        max_salary = values[0].max.name;
        min_salary = values[0].min.name;

        for(item in values) {
            if(values[item].max.salary > max) {
                max = values[item].max.salary;
                max_name = values[item].max.name;
            }
            if(values[item].min.salary < min) {
                min = values[item].min.salary;
                min_name = values[item].min.name;
            }
        }
    }
```

```
        return {
            "max": { "name": max_name, "salary": max },
            "min": { "name": min_name, "salary": min }
        };
    }
}
```

The main change with Listing 9-6 is that the map function emits a value of a JSON object with `name` and `salary` fields. This allows you to associate a name with each salary value when calculating the `max` and `min` values in the reduce function. You can then return a result with the name and salary of the employees with the highest and lowest salaries, as shown in Figure 9-5.

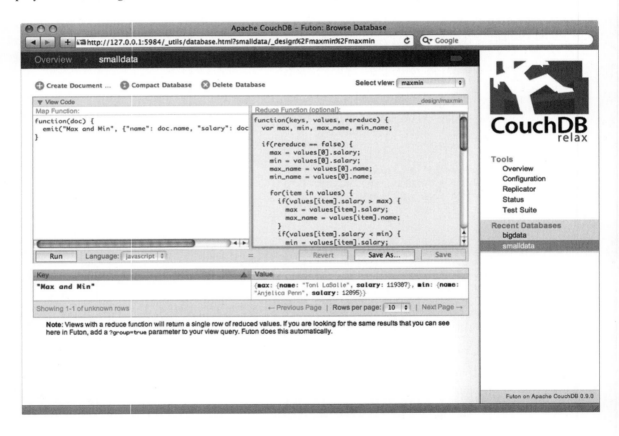

Figure 9-5. Finding the names and salaries of the highest and lowest earners

Ordering and Filtering Results

The results returned by a CouchDB view are ordered by the view's key, ascending in direction by default. Using the employees table from the previous section, let's take a look at how this works. Take the view shown in Listing 9-7 as an example.

Listing 9-7. Return All Documents, with Null as the Key

```
map: function(doc) {
    emit(null, doc);
}
```

This view simply returns all the documents in the database. It does not emit a key, and the value is the document itself. Because CouchDB automatically uses ID as part of the key in a view, the results are ordered by the document ID by default. To order by name, you'd simply use the name field of the document as the key, and CouchDB will then order the results by name (Listing 9-8).

Listing 9-8. Return All Documents, Using Name As the Key

```
map: function(doc) {
    emit(doc.name, doc);
}
```

Similarly, you can order results by the employee's salary (Listing 9-9).

Listing 9-9. Return All Documents, Using Salary as the Key

```
map: function(doc) {
    emit(doc.salary, doc);
}
```

Figure 9-6 shows the results of the last view (ordering results by salary).

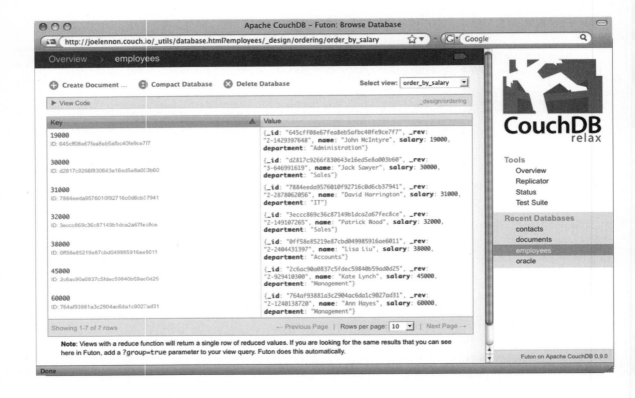

Figure 9-6. Returning all documents ordered by salary

What if you want to reverse the order the rows are displayed? In other words, what if you want the highest salary to appear first? In Futon, you can simply click the arrow in the Key column header in the results table. This will return the results in descending order. To view the results in ascending order, simply click the arrow again.

But what if you are not using Futon? If you view the raw data by navigating straight to the view's URI (or by clicking the gray tag icon in the top right of the main section of Futon), you will see that the results are brought back, ordered by salary in ascending order, with no way to change the order in which the results are displayed.

Fortunately, CouchDB provides a query parameter that you can use to change the order of results just by changing the URL. To show results in descending order, simply append `?descending=true` to the end of the URL in your browser, and CouchDB will reverse the results, as shown in Figure 9-7.

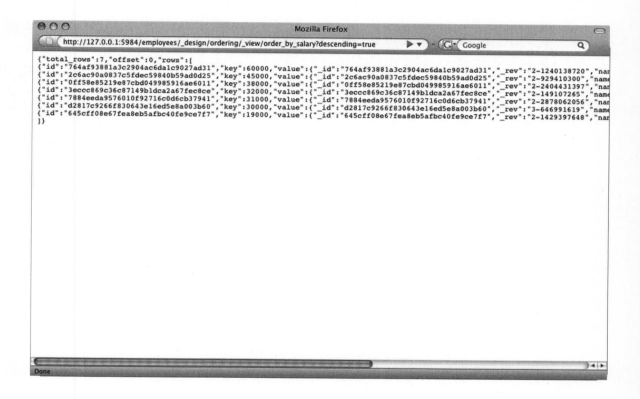

Figure 9-7. Reversing the results using `descending=true`

In addition to the `descending` option, CouchDB provides a range of URL query arguments that you can use to manipulate the resultset returned by your views. You will now look at some of the more useful arguments available.

You can search for a particular document using the `key` argument. For example, in the previous example, if you removed `?descending=true` and added `?key=45000`, you would get back only a single document—the record for Kate Lynch, whose salary is $45,000. If you changed the key to the department field and then added `?key="Sales"` to the URL, you would get back two results—the documents for Patrick Wood and Jack Sawyer, who both work in the sales department.

What if you wanted to find a range of documents? For example, say you wanted to find everyone who earned a salary between $30,000 and $40,000. You can call the view (where the key is the salary field), passing two parameters—`startkey` and `endkey`. It's important to note that you use the ? symbol only before the first argument. Each subsequent argument you pass should be prefixed with the & symbol. So, to get back the range of documents that meet the criteria of having a salary between $30,000 and $40,000, you add the string `?startkey=30000&endkey=40000` to the URL. Figure 9-8 shows the results.

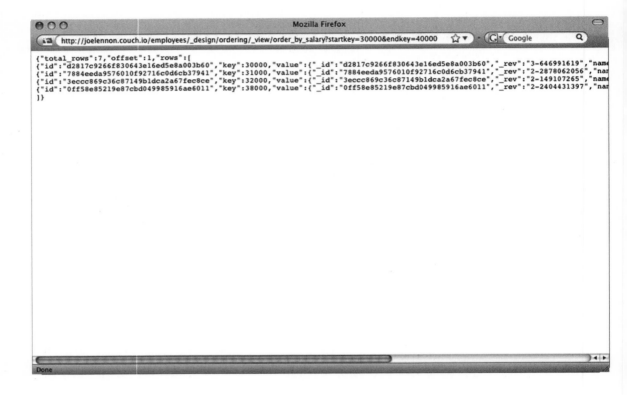

Figure 9-8. *Retrieving a range of documents*

Another useful argument is `limit`. You can use this to define a maximum number of results the query can return. If you don't want to return the first rows of the resultset, you can use the `skip` argument to define the number of rows to skip when running the query.

Working with Related Data

If you have experience with relational databases, you will be familiar with the concept of relationships. Traditionally, data is separated into different tables, and keys are used to create relationships between these tables, allowing their data to be joined using SQL. For example, an employee's payroll advice data might be stored in a separate table called *payslips*, and this table would have a reference column that indicates which employee it is stored for. You could then use SQL to join the data, retrieving the employee's name from the employees table and the dates and amounts of their payslips from the payslips table.

In CouchDB, however, there are no tables or relationships—everything is stored in self-contained documents. So, how do you store related data? One way is to store the related data in the document itself. For example, take the following employee document:

```
{
    name: "David Harrington",
    salary: 31000,
    department: "IT"
}
```

If you were to store pay advice information inside this document, it might look something like the following:

```
{
    name: "David Harrington",
    salary: 31000,
    department: "IT",
    payslips: [
        { date: "20090825", amount: 2100 },
        { date: "20090725", amount: 2100 },
        { date: "20090625", amount: 2100 }
    ]
}
```

This method is a very straightforward and simple way of storing related information. Also, because everything is kept in one document, all the data is stored together. This means that should you ever delete the document, all of the pay advice data is deleted along with the employee data. This maintains the referential integrity of the database automatically, leaving no redundant documents lying around.

Querying this data in a view is also simple. For example, if you wanted to get the total amount grouped by employee, you could create the view as described in Listing 9-10.

Listing 9-10. Getting Total Amount Paid by Employee

```
map: function(doc) {
    if(doc.payslips) {
        for(item in doc.payslips) {
            emit(doc.name, doc.payslips[item].amount);
        }
    }
}

reduce: function(keys, values, rereduce) {
    return sum(values);
}
```

Figure 9-9 shows the result of this view.

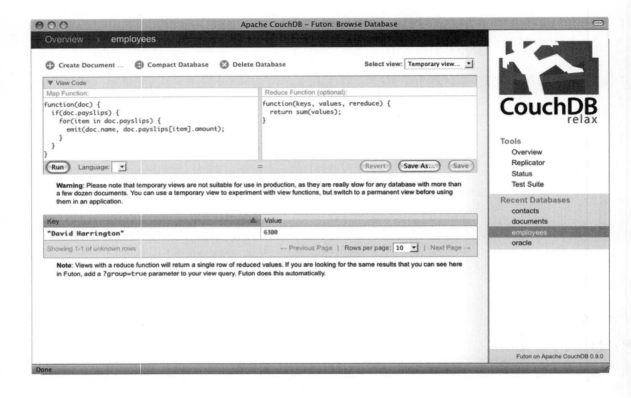

Figure 9-9. *Getting total amount paid by employee*

This method is not without its problems, however. The primary issue is that it is quite tedious to add new payslips to the document, because they would need to be inserted into the existing employee record structure. It can also lead to an increase in conflict errors. If someone tries to modify an employee's details, for example, while another user is inserting a payslip into the record, they will get a "409 Conflict" error.

An alternative method of storing related data is to store it in a separate document; in that case, each employee would have one employee document and zero or more payslip documents. To make it easy to distinguish one from the other, you might create a **type** field in each document to indicate whether it is an employee document or a payslip document. The payslip document would also need to store a reference to the employee to which it belongs.

Using this method, the employee document would look like the following:

```
{
    type: "employee",
    employee_no: 1,
    name: "David Harrington",
```

```
    salary: 31000,
    department: "IT"
}
```

It would then have three separate payslip documents:

```
{
    type: "payslip",
    employee_no: 1,
    date: "20090825",
    amount: 2100
}
{
    type: "payslip",
    employee_no: 1,
    date: "20090725",
    amount: 2100
}
{
    type: "payslip",
    employee_no: 1,
    date: "20090625",
    amount: 2100
}
```

Adding new payslips is far easier with this method, because you simply create a new document. It also doesn't suffer from concurrency issues, because the employee and payslip data are stored independent of one another—so one user can change the employee record at the same time as another user changes a payslip record.

Getting the total amount paid for each employee is simple, as shown in Listing 9-11.

Listing 9-11. Getting the Total Amount Paid by Employee

```
map: function(doc) {
    if(doc.type == "payslip")
        emit(doc.employee_no, doc.amount);
}

reduce: function(keys, values, rereduce) {
    return sum(values);
}
```

The obvious downside to this method is that you would need to use a separate view to get back the employee's information, such as their name. As a result, a separate HTTP request is required, adding load to the server. Fortunately, you can use view collation to bring back documents of different types alongside each other. So, you could bring back the employee record and then all of their associated payslip documents after it. To do this, you would use what is known as a *complex key*, using the `employee_no` field and an identifier to say which type of document should appear first. Listing 9-12 shows the code.

Listing 9-12. Using View Collation to Join Documents

```
map: function(doc) {
    if(doc.type == "employee")
        emit([doc.employee_no, 0], doc);
    else if(doc.type == "payslip")
        emit([doc.employee_no,1], doc);
}
```

This will first and foremost return the document containing the employee's information, followed by any payslip documents associated with that employee. You can see this in Figure 9-10.

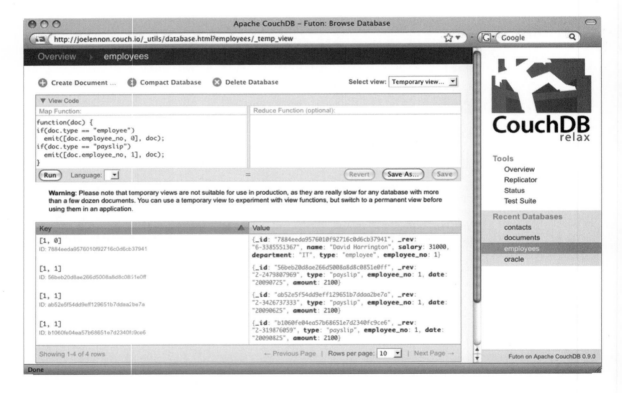

Figure 9-10. Using view collation to join documents

Which method is best really depends on the data you are working with. If your related data has many fields and requires constant additions and updates, you are probably better off storing this data in separate documents.

Summary

In this chapter, you took what you learned in Chapters 7 and 8 and brought it to the next level by looking at some of the more advanced areas of CouchDB views. You learned how to do all sorts of aggregation, filter and sort your results, and store relational data in a CouchDB database. That concludes Part 2 of the book. In Part 3, you will see how to put all of this together to create CouchDB applications using CouchApp, and you will see how you can use a CouchDB database as the back end to applications created in Python, and Ruby.

PART 3

■ ■ ■

Advanced CouchDB Topics

In this part, you will take the knowledge you gained in the previous parts of this book and apply them in a series of applications. First, you will create a full client-side web application using CouchApp. Then, you will learn how to connect to CouchDB from your Python and Ruby applications, before creating a sample application in Python using the Django web framework and the Couchdbkit library. Finally, you will explore some more advanced areas of CouchDB such as replication, compaction, load balancing, security, and more.

CHAPTER 10

Developing CouchDB Applications with CouchApp

In this part of the book, you will leverage the skills you learned in the first two parts of this book to create some CouchApps. If you have experience with server-side web application development, you may be familiar with the process of creating a database in the vein of MySQL, Oracle, or another relational database management system and then developing your application using a programming language such as Python or Ruby.

You'll learn how to develop CouchDB applications in these languages later. First you will investigate *CouchApp*—a set of scripts that allow complete, stand-alone CouchDB applications to be built using just HTML and JavaScript. These applications are housed in the CouchDB database, meaning that when the database is replicated, any applications stored in that database are also replicated.

Installing CouchApp

CouchApp is a Python module and requires Python to be installed on your system to work. If you are using Linux or Mac OS X, it is most likely that Python came preinstalled with your operating system. To check, open a Terminal or shell window, and type the following command:

```
python -V
```

If Python is installed, you should see a response like the following:

```
Python 2.6.2
```

If Python is not installed, you might get the following:

```
bash: python: command not found
```

■ **Note** Installing Python is outside the scope of this book. If you need assistance setting up Python on your system, refer to the Python documentation, available at (http://www.python.org/download/).

Now you need to install **python-setuptools**. You can use a package manager like **apt-get** if you want, but for the sake of platform independence, I will install it manually. First download the **.egg** file using **wget**:

wget http://pypi.python.org/packages/2.5/s/setuptools/setuptools-0.6c9-py2.5.egg

When the download has completed and you are returned to the shell, issue the following command to install setuptools:

Sudo sh setuptools-0.6c9-py2.5.egg

If all has gone according to plan, the script should install setuptools, and you will see messages similar to those shown in Figure 10-1.

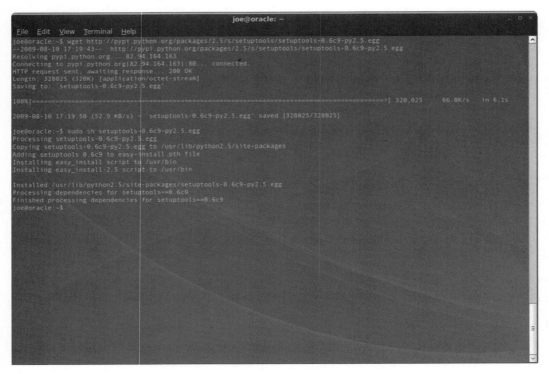

Figure 10-1. Installing python-setuptools

Now that you have installed python-setuptools, you can use `easy_install` to install the CouchDB, SimpleJSON, and CouchApp Python modules (Listing 10-1).

Listing 10-1. Installing CouchApp and Dependencies Using python-setuptools

```
easy_install couchdb
easy_install simplejson
easy_install couchapp
```

That's it—CouchApp is now installed, and you can begin writing CouchDB applications using nothing but HTML and JavaScript! In the next section, you'll look at getting up and running with CouchApp.

Your First CouchApp

Now that you have installed CouchApp, you can start developing CouchApps right away. The first thing to do is create a directory where you will store your CouchApps. I usually create a subdirectory called `couchapps` below my home directory, as shown in Listing 10-2.

Listing 10-2. Creating a CouchApps Directory

```
mkdir ~/couchapps
cd ~/couchapps
```

From here, you use the following command to generate a new CouchApp:

```
couchapp generate test
```

This should generate a response like this:

```
[INFO] Generating a new CouchApp in /home/joe/couchapps/test
```

Now you need to push your CouchApp to your CouchDB installation. Assuming that your CouchDB server is installed on your local machine and you have not set up authentication, you should be able to push your CouchApp using the following command:

```
couchapp push test http://127.0.0.1:5984/testapp
```

If that worked correctly, you should see a message like this:

```
[INFO] Visit your CouchApp here: http://127.0.0.1:5984/testapp/_design/test/index.html
```

Copy and paste this URL into your favorite web browser, and you should see a screen similar to Figure 10-2.

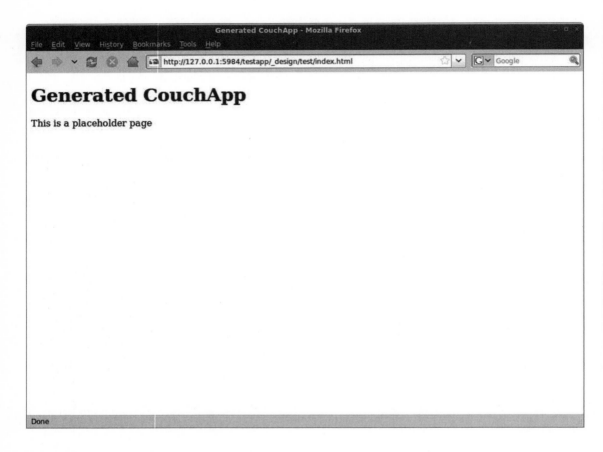

Figure 10-2. The first CouchApp up and running

Let's make a few changes to the first CouchApp before you move on to a more advanced example. In your shell, navigate to the directory where you store your CouchApps, such as ~/couchapps. From here, enter the directory for the test CouchApp you just created and list its contents using the following commands:

```
cd test
ls
```

You should see five directories: _attachments, lists, shows, vendors, and views, as well as a single couchapp.json file. I'll discuss these in more detail in the next section, but for now let's just go into the _attachments directory and list its contents using this:

```
cd _attachments
ls
```

In this directory is a file **index.html** and a folder **style**. Style sheets for the application are usually stored in the **style** directory. Let's worry about changing the styles later; for now let's just make some rudimentary changes to the application's content by modifying the **index.html** file. Open this file in your favorite text editor (I like **nano**). Its contents should look like Figure 10-3.

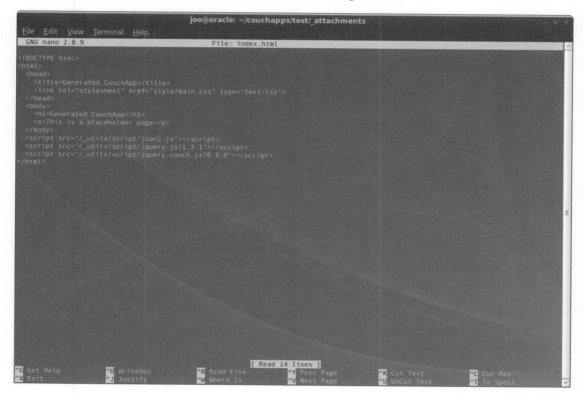

Figure 10-3. CouchApp index.html *file*

Change the code between the **<title>** and **</title>** tags to something else. I decided to be hyperbolic and name my app Super CouchApp. Also, change the text between the **<h1>** and **</h1>** tags to the same, and change the text between the **<p>** and **</p>** tags to something along the lines of This ain't no placeholder page no more! Your final code should look somewhat along the lines of Listing 10-3.

Listing 10-3. The Newly Updated index.html File

```
<!DOCTYPE html>
<html>
    <head>
        <title>Super CouchApp</title>
        <link rel="stylesheet" href="style/main.css" type="text/css">
    </head>
    <body>
        <h1>Super CouchApp</h1>
        <p>This ain't no placeholder page no more!</p>
    </body>
    <script src="/_utils/script/json2.js"></script>
    <script src="/_utils/script/jquery.js?1.3.1"></script>
    <script src="/_utils/script/jquery.couch.js?0.9.0"></script>
</html>
```

When you have finished making changes, save the index.html file, and reload your CouchApp browser window. Hmmm, nothing has changed, has it? That's because you need to push the CouchApp to CouchDB once again. You will need to do this every time you make changes to your CouchApp's files. Use the following command to push the CouchApp from the current directory:

```
couchapp push . http://127.0.0.1:5984/testapp
```

Once again you should get a message telling you the URL where you can visit your CouchApp. Now head back to your browser window and try that URL once more. This time you should see a more satisfying result, like the one in Figure 10-4.

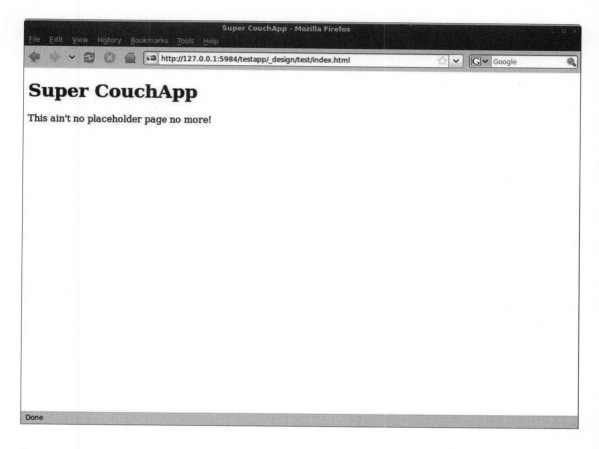

Figure 10-4. The new and improved CouchApp

As you can see, working with CouchApps is very straightforward. You simply edit the source files on the disk and push the app to CouchDB when you want to test your changes. In the next section, you'll start creating a more useful application.

Creating CouchTasks: A Simple Task Manager

In this section, you'll use HTML, JavaScript, and some CSS styling to create a simple task manager. By the end of this chapter, you will have developed a CouchApp that allows you to create a new task and delete existing tasks. It will also display any existing tasks when it loads. The application will use the jQuery JavaScript library that comes with CouchApp, as well as some CouchApp extensions to this library that neatly wrap the Ajax requests to the CouchDB database for you.

The end result should look something like Figure 10-5.

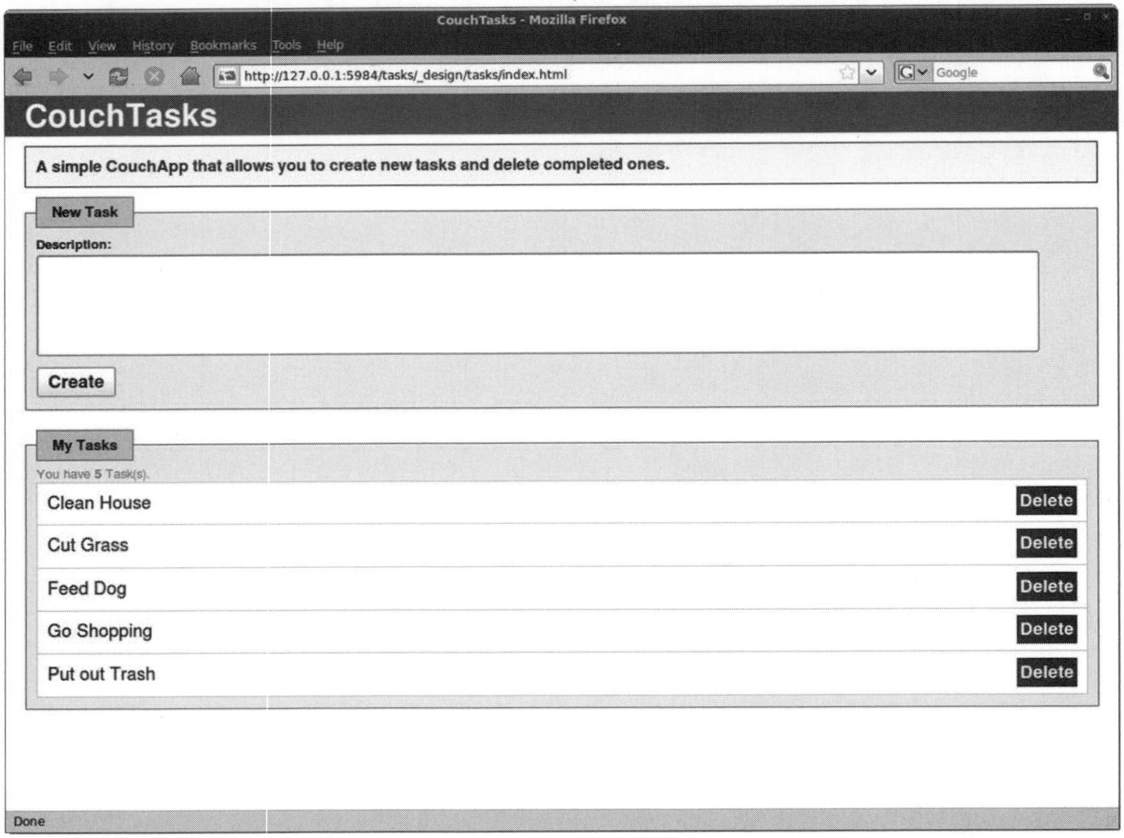

Figure 10-5. The final CouchTasks application

The first thing you need to do is generate a new CouchApp. Open a Terminal window, and navigate to your CouchApps folder (mine is `~/couchapps`). From here, issue the following command to generate the **couchtasks** CouchApp folder:

```
couchapp generate couchtasks
```

This will create a new directory in your CouchApps folder named **couchtasks**. Enter this directory, and navigate to the **_attachments** subdirectory using the following command:

```
cd couchtasks/_attachments
```

As you saw in the previous section, CouchApp automatically creates an `index.html` file and a `main.css` file within the **style** subdirectory. The first thing you are going to do is edit your `index.html` file to house the frame for your CouchTasks application. Open the file in your favorite text editor, and replace the contents of the file with the code in Listing 10-4.

Listing 10-4. index.html

```
<!DOCTYPE html>
<html>
    <head>
        <title>CouchTasks</title>
        <link rel="stylesheet" href="style/main.css" type="text/css">
    </head>
    <body>
        <h1>CouchTasks</h1>
        <p>A simple CouchApp that allows you to create new tasks
            and delete completed ones.</p>
        <form name="add_task" id="add_task">
            <fieldset>
                <legend>New Task</legend>
                <label for="desc">Description:</label><br />
                <textarea id="desc" name="desc"></textarea><br />
                <input type="submit" id="create" value="Create" />
            </fieldset>
        </form>

        <form name="tasks" id="tasks">
            <fieldset>
                <legend>My Tasks</legend>
                <div id="task_count">You have <span>0</span> Task(s).</div>
                <ul id="my_tasks"></ul>
            </fieldset>
        </form>
    </body>
    <script src="/_utils/script/json2.js"></script>
    <script src="/_utils/script/jquery.js?1.3.1"></script>
    <script src="/_utils/script/jquery.couch.js?0.9.0"></script>
    <script src="vendor/couchapp/jquery.couchapp.js"></script>
</html>
```

Let's push the progress to CouchDB so you can see what this HTML has produced. In your Terminal window, navigate to the main CouchTasks application directory (~/couchapps/couchtasks), and run the following command:

```
couchapp push . http://127.0.0.1:5984/couchtasks
```

If everything works as expected, you should see a message informing you that you can visit your CouchApp at the URL `http://127.0.0.1:5984/couchtasks/_design/couchtasks/index.html`. Enter this URL into your web browser, and you should see a page similar to the one shown in Figure 10-6.

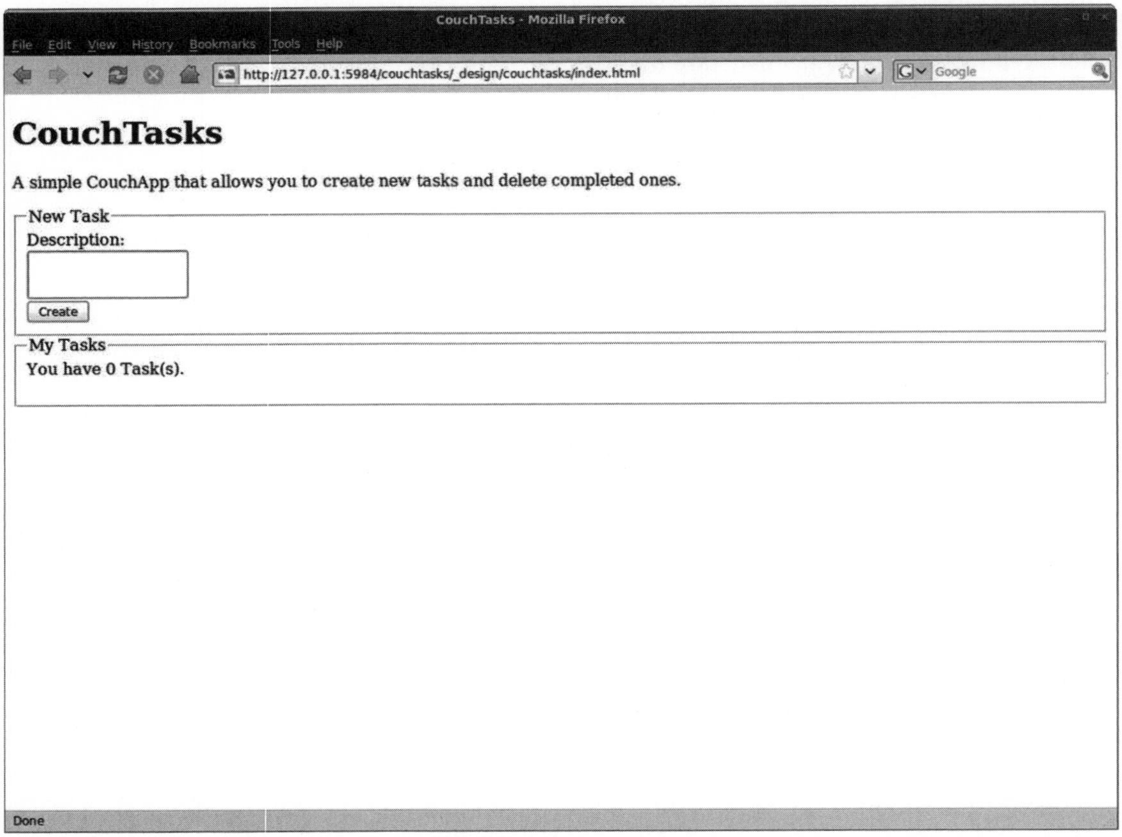

Figure 10-6. The frame of your CouchTasks application

The bare bones of the application are now there, but it looks a bit dreary, doesn't it? Let's spruce it up somewhat by adding a splash of color. To do this, you will modify the `main.css` file that CouchApp kindly created for you when it generated your CouchTasks app. This file is in `_attachments/style`—again, open it in your text editor. This time, replace the contents with the CSS code in Listing 10-5.

Listing 10-5. main.css

```
* {
  font-family: Helvetica, Arial, sans-serif;
}

body {
  margin: 0px; padding: 0px;
}

h1 {
  margin:0;
  padding: 0px 0px 0px 20px;
  background-color: #336699;
  color: #fff;
}

p {
  border: 1px solid #342c03;
  color: #342c03;
  background-color: #f0ffc2;
  padding: 10px;
  margin: 10px 20px 10px 20px;
  font-weight: bold;
}

fieldset {
  border: 1px solid #666;
  margin: 0px 20px 20px 20px;
  background-color: #eee;
}

legend {
  padding: 5px 15px 5px 15px;
  background-color: #ccc;
  border: 1px solid #666;
  font-weight: bold;
  font-size: 0.9em;
}

label {
  font-weight: bold;
  font-size: 0.8em;
```

```
}

textarea {
  width: 95%;
  height: 100px;
  margin-bottom: 10px;
}

input[type=submit] {
  font-size: 1.1em;
  font-weight: bold;
}

div#task_count {
    font-size: 0.8em;
    color: #888;
}

div#task_count span {
    font-weight: bold;
}
```

Save this file, and make sure you're in the main CouchTasks directory in your Terminal window. Now push the application to CouchDB once again using this:

```
couchapp push . http://127.0.0.1:5984/couchtasks
```

Now reload your CouchTasks browser window, and you should see a much more attractive user interface, as shown in Figure 10-7.

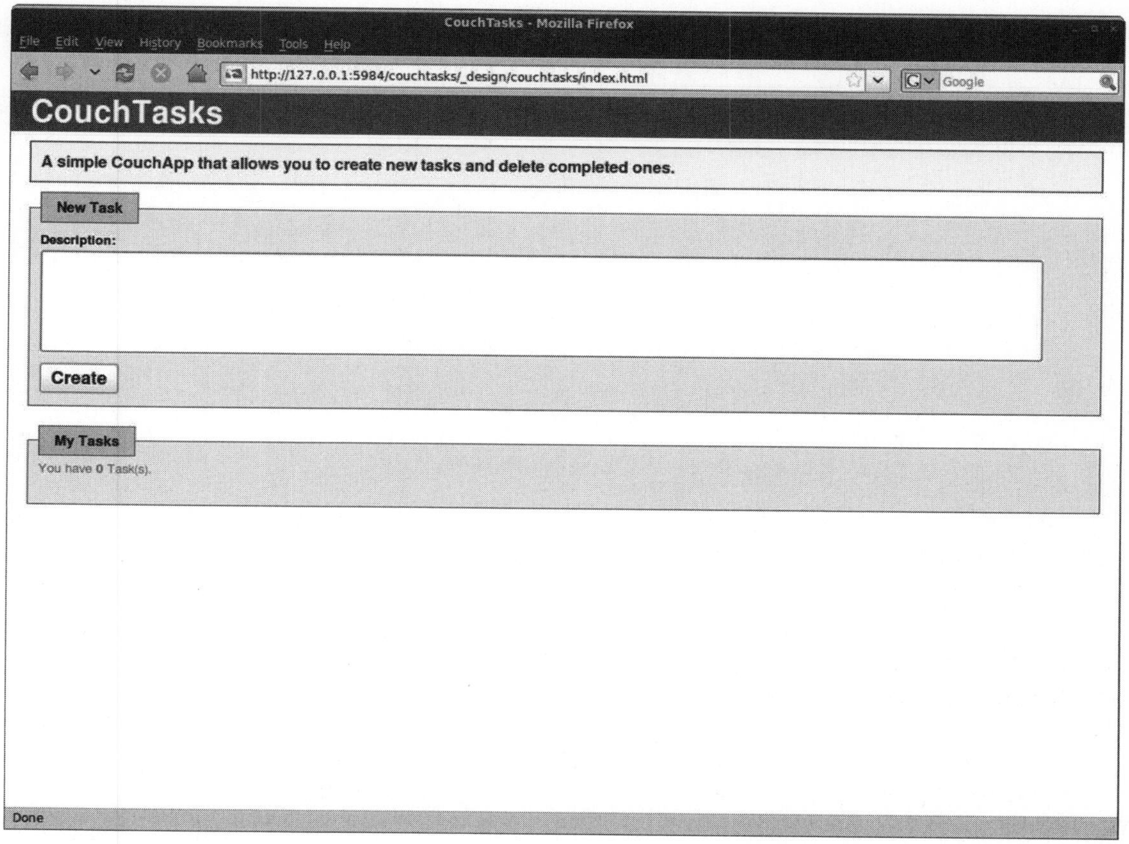

Figure 10-7. The restyled CouchTasks interface

So, now the application looks pretty, but you'll notice that it still doesn't actually do anything. Let's implement the New Task form so that it creates new task documents in the CouchDB database. To do this, you need to create some JavaScript code. You could insert this directly into the index.html file, but to keep your code manageable, you'll create a separate JavaScript file and link to that from the index.html file. In your terminal or shell, navigate to the _attachments subdirectory within your couchtasks folder. Currently, there should be just the index.html file and style subdirectory in this location. Let's create a second subdirectory called script and create a file named main.js inside it:

```
mkdir script
cd script
touch main.js
```

Now open this main.js file, and add the code from Listing 10-6 to it.

Listing 10-6. `main.js`

```
$.CouchApp(function(app) {
    $('form#add_task').submit(function(e) {
        e.preventDefault();
        var newTask = {
            desc: $('#desc').val()
        }
        if(newTask.desc.length > 0) {
            app.db.saveDoc(newTask, { success: function(resp) {
                $('ul#my_tasks').append('<li>'+newTask.desc+'</li>');
                $('ul#my_tasks li:last').hide().fadeIn(1500);
                $('#desc').val('');
                var task_count = parseInt('#task_count span').html(), 10);
                task_count++;
                $('#task_count span').html(task_count);
            }});
        } else {
            alert('You must enter a description to create a new task!');
        }
    });
});
```

Let's briefly walk through what this code does. First you are opening an instance of CouchApp, which will automatically set up the database and design document variables for you. Within this, you are capturing the `submit` event of the form with the ID `add_task`. In this function, you first prevent the default action from being performed (in this case the form being submitted). You then build up your new task's document in JSON format, using the value of the Description `textarea` field for the value of the `desc` field.

Next, you check that the user has actually entered something in the Description field, displaying an error message if not. If all appears fine, you save the document to the CouchDB database. When CouchDB returns and confirms that the document was saved correctly, you add your new task to the My Tasks section of the page. You then clear the description `textarea` value and increase the task count above your list of tasks.

Before you push the application to CouchDB, you need to make a small modification to the `index.html` file to tell it to read your new JavaScript file. The new line is highlighted in bold in Listing 10-7.

Listing 10-7. index.html

```
<!DOCTYPE html>
<html>
    <head>
        <title>CouchTasks</title>
        <link rel="stylesheet" href="style/main.css" type="text/css">
    </head>
    <body>
        <h1>CouchTasks</h1>
        <p>A simple CouchApp that allows you to create
                    new tasks and delete completed ones.</p>
        <form name="add_task" id="add_task">
            <fieldset>
                <legend>New Task</legend>
                <label for="desc">Description:</label><br />
                <textarea id="desc" name="desc"></textarea><br />
                <input type="submit" id="create" value="Create" />
            </fieldset>
        </form>

        <form name="tasks" id="tasks">
            <fieldset>
                <legend>My Tasks</legend>
                <div id="task_count">You have <span>0</span> Task(s).</div>
                <ul id="my_tasks"></ul>
            </fieldset>
        </form>
    </body>
    <script src="/_utils/script/json2.js"></script>
    <script src="/_utils/script/jquery.js?1.3.1"></script>
    <script src="/_utils/script/jquery.couch.js?0.9.0"></script>
    <script src="vendor/couchapp/jquery.couchapp.js"></script>
    <script src="script/main.js"></script>
</html>
```

Now you are ready to push your application once again. Again, making sure you are in the main couchtasks directory, issue the following command:

```
couchapp push . http://127.0.0.1:5984/couchtasks
```

Now reload your CouchTasks browser window, and this time add a description and click the Create button. You should see the Buy Milk list item fade in, and the task counter should update to 1, as shown in Figure 10-8.

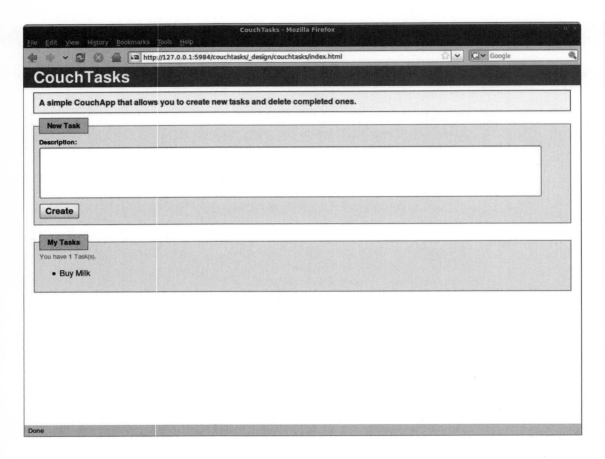

Figure 10-8. Creating new tasks with CouchTasks

Feel free to check that the document was indeed saved to the database in Futon. It will be saved in the `couchtasks` database.

Unfortunately, however, the application is not maintaining state between sessions. If you refresh the CouchTasks browser window, you will notice that no tasks are displaying, and the counter is showing zero results. That is because you have not told your application to bring back data from the CouchDB database yet. To do so, you need to create a view and tell your CouchApp to read data from this view.

To create a view in your CouchApp, you need to define it in the special `views` subdirectory in the `couchtasks` directory. If you store your CouchApps in `~/couchapps`, you should find this in `~/couchapps/couchtasks/views`. The `views` directory is structured into subdirectories, each of which is the name of the view. Within each of these subdirectories, you create a `map.js` file for your map function and an optional `reduce.js` file for reduce functions if required.

For this application, you need to retrieve the tasks that are currently stored in the database when the application first loads. To do this, you need a simple view that you shall call get_tasks. Open your shell window, and navigate to your couchtasks directory. From here, issue the following commands to set up your view file structure:

```
mkdir views/get_tasks
touch views/get_tasks/map.js
```

Now open the map.js file in your text editor, and add the code in Listing 10-8 to it.

Listing 10-8. map.js

```
function(doc) {
    emit(doc.desc, doc);
}
```

Save your changes to the map.js file before continuing. Next, you need to modify your main.js file (in the couchtasks/_attachments/script directory) to tell your application to load existing data on launch. The new content of main.js is shown in Listing 10-9.

Listing 10-9. main.js

```
$.CouchApp(function(app) {
    $('form#add_task').submit(function(e) {
        e.preventDefault();
        var newTask = {
            desc: $('#desc').val()
        }
        if(newTask.desc.length > 0) {
            app.db.saveDoc(newTask, { success: function(resp) {
                $('ul#my_tasks').append('<li>'+newTask.desc+'</li>');
                $('ul#my_tasks li:last').hide().fadeIn(1500);
                $('#desc').val('');
                var task_count = parseInt($('#task_count span').html(), 10);
                task_count++;
                $('#task_count span').html(task_count);
            }});
        } else {
            alert('You must enter a description to create a new task!');
        }
    });

    app.view("get_tasks", { success: function(json) {
        json.rows.map(function(row) {
```

```
        $('ul#my_tasks').append('<li>'+row.key+'</li>');
    });
    $('#task_count span').html(json.rows.length);
}});
});
```

When you have saved `main.js`, push your application to CouchDB again using this:

```
couchapp push . http://127.0.0.1:5984/couchtasks
```

Now when you open CouchTasks in your web browser, you should see the task you previously entered. Next, let's make the list of tasks look a bit prettier with some padding and borders, and also let's add a delete button next to each task so that the user can delete the task from the database. First let's modify the `main.css` file (located in `couchtasks/_attachments/style/main.css`), adding some style sheet rules for the tasks list and the delete buttons you are going to create. Add the code in Listing 10-10 to the end of the `main.css` file.

Listing 10-10. Code to Append to main.css

```css
ul#my_tasks {
    list-style: none;
    margin: 0; padding: 0;
    border: 1px solid #ccc;
    border-top: none;
}

ul#my_tasks li {
    list-style: none;
    display: block;
    padding: 10px;
    background-color: #fff;
    border-top: 1px solid #ccc;
}

ul#my_tasks div.desc {
    width: 80%;
    float: left;
    font-size: 1.1em;
}

ul#my_tasks li div.link {
    width: 20%;
    float: left;
    text-align: right;
}
```

```
ul#my_tasks li div.clear {
    clear: both;
}

ul#my_tasks li a {
    background-color: maroon;
    color: #fff;
    padding: 2px;
    font-size: 1.1em;
    border: 1px solid #000;
    font-weight: bold;
    text-decoration: none;
}

ul#my_tasks li a:hover {
    background-color: red;
}
```

Now you need to modify the `main.js` file to take care of two scenarios—first adding delete buttons to links generated when a user adds a new task and second adding delete buttons to links generated when the application launches. Change the content of the `main.js` to match the code in Listing 10-11.

Listing 10-11. main.js

```
$.CouchApp(function(app) {
    $('form#add_task').submit(function(e) {
        e.preventDefault();
        var newTask = {
            desc: $('#desc').val()
        }
        if(newTask.desc.length > 0) {
            app.db.saveDoc(newTask, { success: function(resp) {
                $('ul#my_tasks').append('<li id="'+newTask._id+'">'
                    +'<div class="desc">'+newTask.desc+'</div>'
                    +'<div class="link">'
                    +'<a href="#" onclick="return false;"'
                    +'  id="'+newTask._rev+'">Delete</a>'
                    +'</div>'
                    +'<div class="clear"></clear>'
                    +'</li>');
                $('#'+newTask._rev).click(function() {
                    if(confirm("Are you sure you want to delete this task?")) {
                        var delTask = {
```

```
                                    _id: newTask._id,
                                    _rev: newTask._rev
                                }
                            app.db.removeDoc(delTask, {});
                            $('#'+newTask._id).show().fadeOut(2000);
                            var del_count = parseInt($('#task_count span').html(), 10);
                            del_count--;
                            $('#task_count span').html(del_count);
                            return false;
                        }
                    });
                    $('ul#my_tasks li:last').hide().fadeIn(1500);
                    $('#desc').val('');
                    var task_count = parseInt($('#task_count span').html(), 10);
                    task_count++;
                    $('#task_count span').html(task_count);
                }});
            } else {
                alert('You must enter a description to create a new task!');
            }
        });


        app.view("get_tasks", { success: function(json) {
            json.rows.map(function(row) {
                $('ul#my_tasks').append('<li id="'+row.value._id+'">'
                    +'<div class="desc">'+row.key+'</div>'
                    +'<div class="link">'
                    +'<a href="#" onclick="return false;"'
                    +'  id="'+row.value._rev+'">Delete</a>'
                    +'</div>'
                    +'<div class="clear"></clear>'
                    +'</li>');
                $('#'+row.value._rev).click(function() {
                    if(confirm("Are you sure you want to delete this task?")) {
                        var delTask = {
                            _id: row.value._id,
                            _rev: row.value._rev
                        }
                        app.db.removeDoc(delTask, {});
                        $('#'+row.value._id).show().fadeOut(2000);
                        var del_count = parseInt($('#task_count span').html(), 10);
                        del_count--;
                        $('#task_count span').html(del_count);
                        return false;
```

```
                }
            });
        });
        $('#task_count span').html(json.rows.length);
    }});
});
```

Save this file, and push the application to CouchDB again. When you refresh your CouchTasks browser window, you will notice that the task list items now appear in a nicer format, and each of them has a red delete button on the right side. If you click the delete button, you will be asked for confirmation that you want to delete the task (Figure 10-9), and if you click OK, it will be deleted from the database.

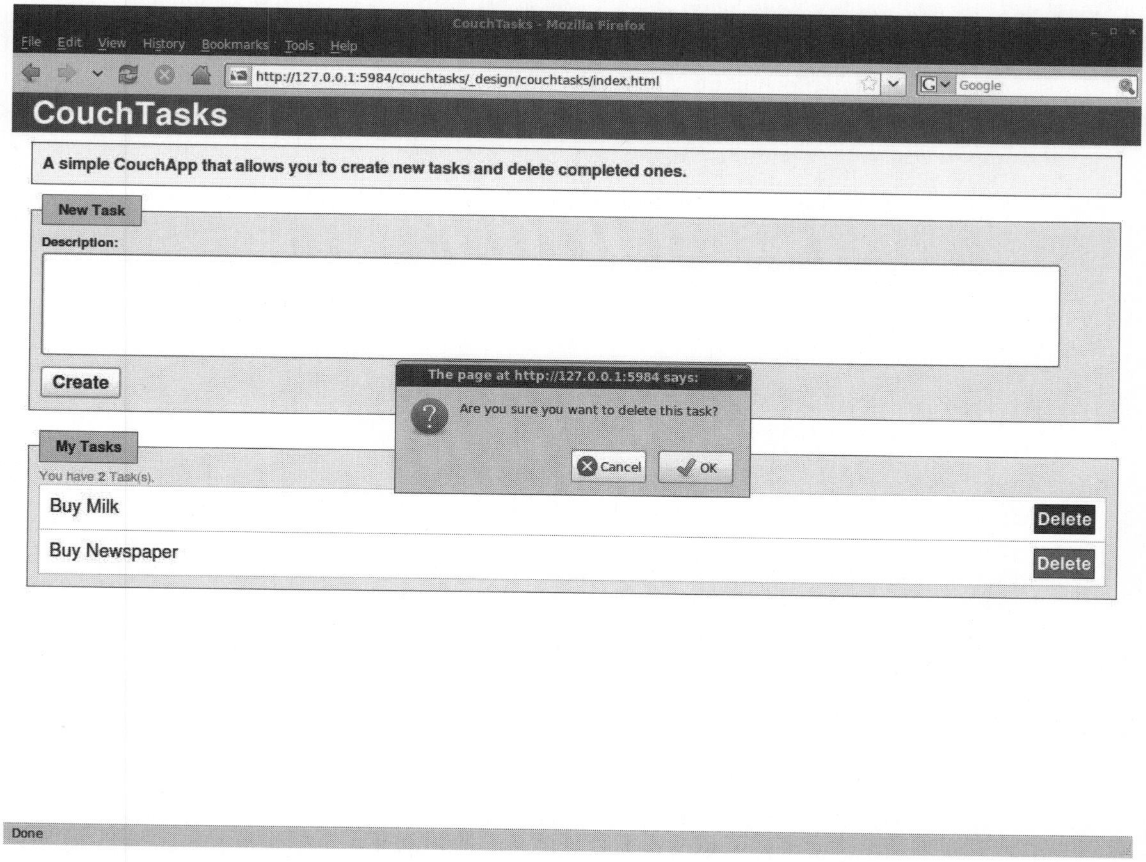

Figure 10-9. Delete task confirmation dialog box

Now the application is performing the functions outlined earlier in this section. You can add tasks to the database using the form your application provides. This application is displaying the tasks that already exist in the database using a CouchDB view, and you can delete existing and newly created tasks in the My Tasks list.

Suggested Improvements

Obviously, the CouchTasks application is simple in its current form, but with a little knowledge of JavaScript and the jQuery framework, you can build on this sample application and create a powerful task management application. Some features you could quite easily add to the application include the following:

- More detailed task documents. Add fields like Due Date, Priority, Category, and more.

- Instead of deleting tasks, allow the user to mark them as completed and then provide a view of previously completed tasks.

- Allow the user to edit tasks.

- Allow the user to rearrange the display order of tasks.

Summary

In this chapter, you learned how to create fully functional web application using CouchApp—a development framework that allows you to build applications in HTML, CSS, and JavaScript that can interact with a CouchDB database. You learned that the advantages that a 100 percent client-side application can offer in terms of flexibility and portability. Finally, you put all of this into practice by creating a task management CouchApp.

In the next chapter, you will look at using CouchDB as a traditional database back end to a server-side application developed in Python.

CHAPTER 11

∎∎∎

Developing Applications with CouchDB

In this chapter, you will learn how to develop software applications that are powered by a CouchDB database. First you will look at the libraries available that allow you to connect to CouchDB from two programming languages: Python and Ruby. In both cases, I will show how to use a software library to connect to a CouchDB server from the programming language. You will then use this library to interact with CouchDB by creating and working with databases and documents. Once I have walked you through the basics, you will develop a sample application using Python and the Django web application development framework, with the data stored in a CouchDB database.

Developing in Python with Couchdbkit

A number of CouchDB libraries are available for the Python programming language, and in this section you will use the Couchdbkit library to connect to CouchDB from your Python applications. At the time of writing, Couchdbkit requires the following:

- CouchDB 0.9.0 or newer.

- Python 2.5 or 2.6. Couchdbkit does not work with Python 3.0.

∎ **Note** Many UNIX-based systems, including Linux distributions and Mac OS X, come with a version of Python preinstalled. You can check whether Python is installed on your system (and which version you have) by issuing the command `python -version` at the shell prompt or in a Terminal window. If Python is not installed, or the version installed is not compatible with Couchdbkit, visit `http://www.python.org/download` to download a suitable version for your operating system.

With the prerequisites installed, you are almost ready to install Couchdbkit. The easiest way to do so is using `easy_install`, which requires that a recent version of `setuptools` be installed. If it is not (or you are not sure), issue the following commands in your shell or Terminal window:

```
curl -O http://peak.telecommunity.com/dist/ez_setup.py
sudo python ez_setup.py -U setuptools
```

With `easy_install` available, you can now proceed to install `pycurl` by issuing this command:

```
sudo easy_install -U pycurl
```

With `pycurl` installed, you are now ready to install Couchdbkit. This is as simple as entering the following command:

```
sudo easy_install -U Couchdbkit
```

This will download Couchdbkit and its dependencies (`simplejson`, `restclient`, and `httplib`) and install them for you automatically. When it's finished, you're ready to start developing CouchDB applications in Python!

Open the Python interpreter by issuing the following command in your shell or Terminal window:

```
python
```

Now let's start using Python to work with the CouchDB server. First things first, let's create a CouchDB database. At the Python interpreter prompt (usually denoted by >>>), enter the code in Listing 11-1 to create a CouchDB database.

Listing 11-1. Creating a CouchDB Database in Python

```
from couchdbkit.client import Server
server = Server()
server.create_db("python_test")
```

When you finish entering the third line from Listing 11-1, you should get a result like this:

```
<Database python_test>
```

Let's be skeptics in this case, however, and verify that the database has been created. Open your favorite web browser, and visit the Futon administration interface for your CouchDB server at `http://127.0.0.1:5984/_utils`. If the database was successfully created, you should see it in all its glory, as shown in Figure 11-1.

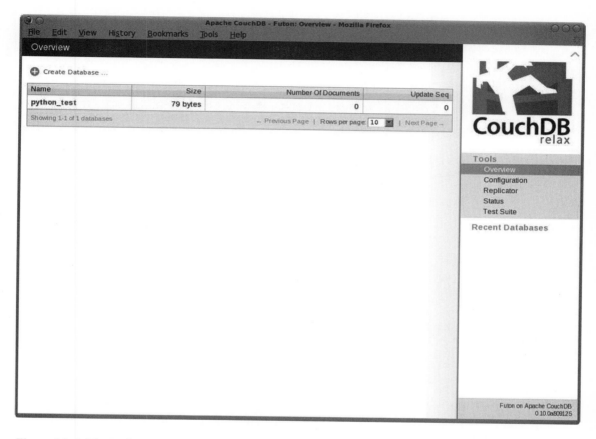

Figure 11-1. *The Python-created database in Futon*

Next, let's take things a step further by creating a CouchDB document using Couchdbkit. First, let's move from entering code at the interactive prompt to using source code files. Create a directory in your home folder called **python_couch**. Now use your favorite text editor to create a new file in this folder, named **Bookmark.py**. Add the code in Listing 11-2 to **Bookmark.py**.

Listing 11-2. Bookmark.py

```
from couchdbkit.schema import Document
from couchdbkit.schema.properties import *

class Bookmark(Document):
    url = StringProperty()
    title = StringProperty()
    date_added = DateTimeProperty()
```

Now, try running this source code by issuing the following command:

```
python Bookmark.py
```

If you don't see any error messages, your class was evaluated successfully. Now let's create some code to utilize this class to create and save CouchDB documents. Create a new file in the python_couch folder. Name this one BookmarksApp.py. This file should contain the code in Listing 11-3.

Listing 11-3. BookmarksApp.py

```
from datetime import datetime
from Bookmark import Bookmark
from couchdbkit.client import Server
from couchdbkit.session import create_session

server = Server()
db = create_session(server, "python_test")
bmark = Bookmark(
    url="http://couchdb.apache.org",
    title="Official Apache CouchDB project website",
    date_added=datetime.utcnow()
)

print('Saving CouchDB document')
db(bmark).save()
print('Document Saved.')
```

Now run this source code by issuing the following command:

```
python BookmarksApp.py
```

You should see the messages "Saving CouchDB document" and "Document Saved"—but once again, let's not take the application's word for it. If you take a quick look in Futon, you can see that your python_test database now has a document, with the values from the previous code stored. If you run the code again, you'll see that a second document has been created.

It's unlikely you'd want to store the data to be added to CouchDB in your source code, of course. You'd probably want to allow the user to enter the URL and title of the bookmark. Let's make a few simple changes to the application to allow for user input. Modify the BookmarksApp.py file, making the changes highlighted in Listing 11-4.

Listing 11-4. Updated Version of BookmarksApp.py

```
from datetime import datetime
from Bookmark import Bookmark
from couchdbkit.client import Server
from couchdbkit.session import create_session

server = Server()
db = create_session(server, "python_test")

the_url = raw_input('Enter website URL: ')
```

```python
the_title = raw_input('Enter website title: ')

bmark = Bookmark(
    url=the_url,
    title=the_title,
    date_added=datetime.utcnow()
)

print('Saving CouchDB document')
db(bmark).save()
print('Document Saved.')
```

Now run your application again by entering this command:

```
python BookmarksApp.py
```

This time around, you should be prompted for a URL and a title, as shown in Figure 11-2.

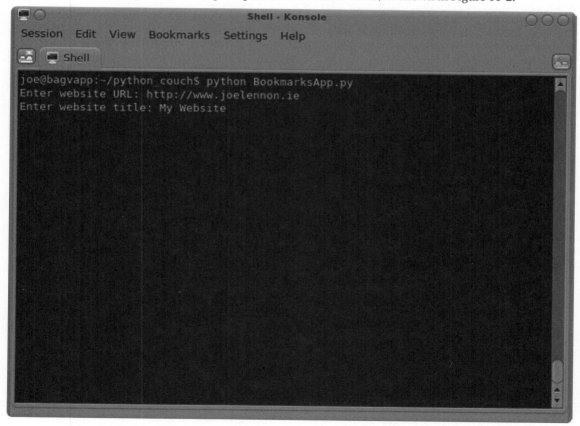

Figure 11-2. Prompting for user input

It's great that you can create CouchDB documents from Python, but what if you wanted to use Python to execute CouchDB views? You'd need to create a view. Of course, you could use Futon or the CouchDB API to create this view, but you can also use Couchdbkit for this. The first thing you need to do is create a valid directory structure for your view's design document. In your python_couch directory, create a subdirectory called views/_design/bookmark/views/all using the following command:

```
mkdir -p views/_design/bookmark/views/all
```

Now create a file in the all subdirectory named map.js. The contents of this file should match Listing 11-5.

Listing 11-5. map.js

```
function(doc) {
    if(doc.doc_type == "Bookmark")
        emit(doc._id, doc);
}
```

Now you need to use the "loaders" feature of Couchdbkit to load this view and insert it into the CouchDB database. Back in your python_couch directory (where you saved Bookmark.py and BookmarksApp.py earlier), create a new file named BookmarksView.py, and add the code in Listing 11-6 to it.

Listing 11-6. BookmarksView.py

```
from Bookmark import Bookmark
from couchdbkit.client import Server
from couchdbkit.session import create_session
from couchdbkit.loaders import FileSystemDocsLoader

server = Server()
db = create_session(server, "python_test")

Bookmark = db(Bookmark)

loader = FileSystemDocsLoader('/home/joe/python_couch/views/_design')
loader.sync(db, verbose=True)

bmarks = Bookmark.view('bookmark/all')
print(str(bmarks.count()) + ' bookmark(s) in database.')
```

This code will take the view you defined in Listing 11-5 and load it into CouchDB in a design document. You then execute the view, which returns a ViewResults object. You then use the count instance method of this object to print the number of bookmarks currently stored in the database.

As you have seen, Couchdbkit provides you with many utilities for working with CouchDB databases in your Python projects. In fact, there is quite a bit more to Couchdbkit than the small sections we touched on in this section.

If you want to learn more about Couchdbkit, visit the project's API at http://www.couchdbkit.org/docs/api/.

In the next section, you will look at using the CouchRest Ruby library in the same way as you used Couchdbkit in this section. You will then use the skills you learned in this section to develop a Django application that is powered by a CouchDB database.

Developing in Ruby with CouchRest

If you worked through the previous section, you saw how simple it is to use Python to create applications that store data in CouchDB. In this section, you will learn about how CouchRest offers the same simplicity to Ruby developers. The requirements for CouchRest, at the time of writing, are as follows:

- CouchDB 0.9.0 or newer installed

- Ruby installed (I have tested on version 1.8.7, but other versions should work)

- RubyGems installed

■ **Note** If you do not have Ruby installed, take a trip to `http://rubyonrails.org`, and follow the instructions there. You will need to install Ruby and RubyGems for this section. You do not need to install Rails, but if you are planning on developing Ruby on Rails applications in the future, you may as well install it now also.

Before installing CouchRest, you'll need to make sure that your RubyGems install is up-to-date. If you have just installed RubyGems, you should be fine, but if not (or you want to be sure), simply issue the following command in a shell or Terminal window:

```
sudo gem update -system
```

With RubyGems up-to-date, you can install CouchRest using RubyGems. Simply enter the following command:

```
sudo gem install couchrest
```

This will use the RubyGems package manager to download CouchRest and any dependency packages, before automatically installing them. With CouchRest installed, let's hop into the Ruby interpreter and perform a quick test to see that CouchRest is working. Issue the following command to open the Ruby interpreter:

```
irb
```

At the Ruby interpreter prompt (denoted by `>>` or `irb(main):001:0>`), enter the following line:

```
require 'couchrest'
```

Unless you have previously installed the JSON gem, you will more than likely get an error like the one shown in Figure 11-3.

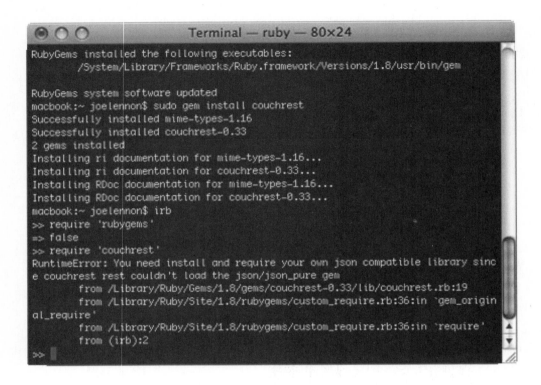

Figure 11-3. No JSON-compatible library is installed.

Exit the Ruby interpreter by entering **exit** at the Ruby prompt. This will return you to your system shell. From here, enter the following command to install the JSON RubyGem:

```
sudo gem install json
```

Now open the Ruby interpreter once again, and this time, enter the lines of code in Listing 11-7.

Listing 11-7. Testing CouchRest

```
require 'rubygems'
require 'couchrest'
SERVER = CouchRest.new
DB = SERVER.database!('ruby_test')
```

If the code worked correctly, you should see some fairly cryptic messages, which, if you read them carefully, reveal information about the ruby_test database you just created, as shown in Figure 11-4.

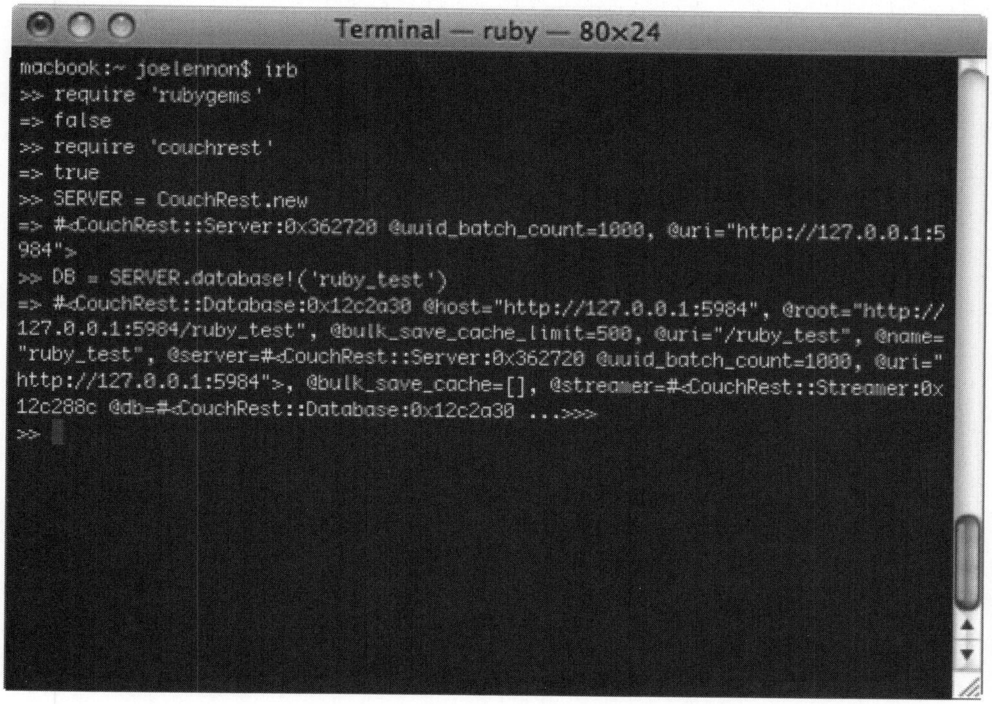

Figure 11-4. Creating CouchDB databases in Ruby with CouchRest

Let's remain skeptical, however, and head into Futon to check that it did indeed create a database. Open your favorite web browser, and enter the URL http://127.0.0.1:5984/_utils. If it worked, you should see the new ruby_test database in the list of databases, as shown in Figure 11-5.

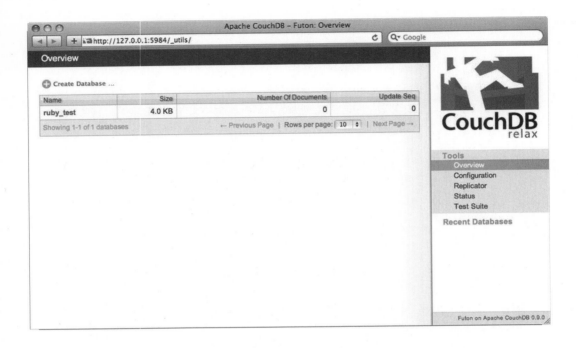

Figure 11-5. The CouchRest-created `ruby_test` *database in Futon*

In the previous section of this chapter, you learned how to work with documents in Python using the example of storing bookmarks in the CouchDB database. I will use the same example in this section, except the application will be developed in Ruby using CouchRest.

In your home directory, create a subdirectory named `ruby_couch`. In it, create a new file called `Bookmark.rb`, and enter the code in Listing 11-8 in it.

Listing 11-8. Bookmark.rb

```ruby
require 'rubygems'
require 'couchrest'

SERVER = CouchRest.new
DB = SERVER.database('ruby_test')

class Bookmark < CouchRest::ExtendedDocument
    use_database DB

    property :url
    property :title
```

```
timestamps!

view_by :title
```

```
end
```

Now it's time to compile the `Bookmark` class using the Ruby compiler. In your Terminal window, navigate to the `ruby_couch` directory in your home folder, and run the following command:

```
ruby Bookmark.rb
```

Now let's create a Ruby application that uses this class. Create a new file called `BookmarksApp.rb`, and save it in the same location as the `Bookmark.rb` file. Edit its contents so it is the same as the code in Listing 11-9.

Listing 11-9. BookmarksApp.rb

```
require 'Bookmark'

bmark = Bookmark.new(
    :url => 'http://couchdb.apache.org',
    :title => 'Official Apache CouchDB project website'
)

puts "Saving bookmark: #{bmark.inspect}"
bmark.save
puts "Bookmark Saved."
```

Now, compile this code using the following command at your shell prompt (not the Ruby prompt):

```
ruby BookmarksApp.rb
```

This should return with the JSON representation of the document that is being created and the message "Bookmark Saved," as shown in Figure 11-6.

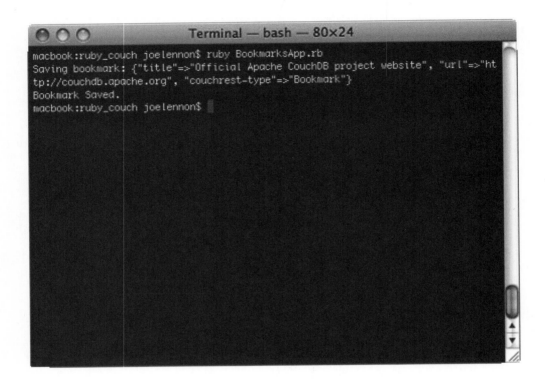

Figure 11-6. *The CouchDB document created in Ruby using CouchRest*

Ever the skeptics, let's double-check that it worked in Futon. If you can find the document, which looks like in Figure 11-7, it worked!

Figure 11-7. The CouchRest-created document in Futon

Running the application again and again re-creates the same document. Of course, it would be much nicer if you could define the URL and title you want to add to the database at runtime. Modify the BookmarksApp.rb file, making the changes highlighted in bold in Listing 11-10.

Listing 11-10. Updated Version of BookmarksApp.rb

```
require 'Bookmark'

puts "Enter website URL: "
STDOUT.flush
the_url = gets.chomp

puts "Enter website title: "
STDOUT.flush
the_title = gets.chomp

bmark = Bookmark.new(
    :url => the_url,
    :title => the_title
```

```
)

puts "Saving bookmark: #{bmark.inspect}"
bmark.save
puts "Bookmark Saved."
```

Rerun the application by issuing the following command:

```
ruby BookmarksApp.rb
```

This time, you should be prompted for a website URL and title, and the values you enter here will be used to form the document that is saved in the database. You can see the output returned by Ruby in Figure 11-8.

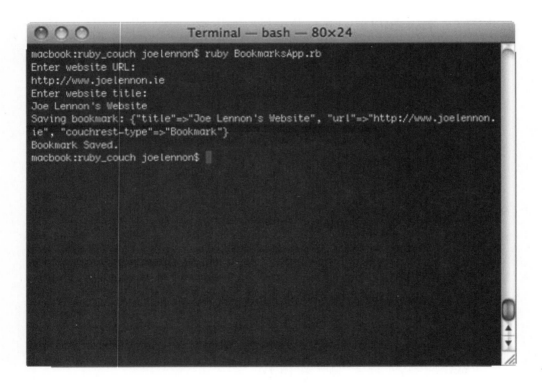

Figure 11-8. Saving custom documents using Ruby and CouchRest

Up until this point, working with CouchDB in Python using Couchdbkit and in Ruby using CouchRest has been quite similar, albeit with differing syntax. The following method of creating

CouchDB views is quite different from the method used in Couchdbkit. Create a new file named BookmarksView.rb, and save it in the same location as the other two Ruby source files you have created. Add the code in Listing 11-11 to this file.

Listing 11-11. BookmarksView.rb

```
require 'Bookmark'

all_view = {
    :map = 'function(doc) { if(doc["couchrest-type"] == "Bookmark") emit(doc._id, doc); }'
}

DB.delete_doc DB.get("_design/bookmark") rescue nil

DB.save_doc({
    "_id" => "_design/bookmark",
    :views => {
        :all => all_view
    }
})

puts DB.view('bookmark/all')['rows'].inspect
```

Now run this file using the following command:

```
ruby BookmarksView.rb
```

The output should be each "Bookmark" document stored in your CouchDB database, as shown in Figure 11-9.

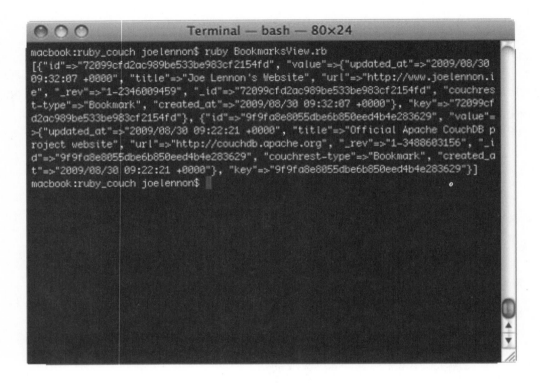

Figure 11-9. Results of `BookmarksView.rb`

In the next section, you will develop a web application using Python and Django that uses CouchDB to store its data. If you want to learn more about CouchRest, visit `http://github.com/jchris/couchrest/tree/master`.

Creating a Bookmarks Application with CouchDB and Django

In this section, you will create a sample bookmark application that is deployed as a web application using the Python-based Django framework. Luckily, the Couchdbkit framework you used earlier in this chapter has Django extensions built into it, making it simple to build Django applications that use CouchDB to store data.

■ **Note** In this section, you are using `wget` to download Django. If you are using Linux, this should be already installed on your system, but if you are using Mac OS X, you probably don't have `wget`. If you followed the instructions for installing CouchDB on Mac OS X in Chapter 3, you will have MacPorts installed on your system. You can use this to download and install `wget` by issuing the following command in a Terminal window: `sudo port install wget`. You will be asked to enter your administrator password, and once you do, MacPorts will download and install `wget` on your system automatically. You can then use `wget` to download Django.

The first thing you need to do is install Django. From your home directory, issue the following command to download and install Django 1.1 (the latest release version available at the time of writing):

```
wget http://www.djangoproject.com/download/1.1/tarball/
tar xzvf Django-1.1.tar.gz
cd Django-1.1
sudo python setup.py install
```

That's it! Django is now installed and ready to use! Let's move on and create the Django project. Make sure you are in your home directory, and issue the following command:

```
django-admin.py startproject myproject
```

This will create a new Django project called *myproject*, automatically creating a directory of the same name beneath the directory you ran the command from. Enter this directory by issuing the following:

```
cd myproject
```

Now, let's create the Django application:

```
python manage.py startapp bookmarks
```

This will create a new directory called **bookmarks** beneath the **myproject** directory. Now let's start to build the Django application. The first thing you need to do is make a few changes to your project's **settings.py** file, found in the **myproject** folder. Open this file in your favorite text editor, and change it so that it matches Listing 11-12 (changes from the standard file are highlighted in bold).

Listing 11-12. settings.py

```
import os, platform
PROJECT_PATH = os.path.dirname(os.path.abspath(__file__))
DEBUG = True
TEMPLATE_DEBUG = DEBUG

ADMINS = (
    ('Joe Lennon', 'joe@joelennon.ie'),
)
MANAGERS = ADMINS
```

```
DATABASE_ENGINE = 'sqlite3'
DATABASE_NAME = 'dummy.db'

COUCHDB_DATABASES = (
    ('myproject.bookmarks', 'http://127.0.0.1:5984/bookmarks'),
)

TIME_ZONE = 'Europe/Dublin'
LANGUAGE_CODE = 'en-us'
SITE_ID = 1
USE_I18N = True
MEDIA_ROOT = os.path.join(PROJECT_PATH, 'static')
MEDIA_URL = '/media'
ADMIN_MEDIA_PREFIX = '/media/admin/'

SECRET_KEY = 'fsdg43sdfgu5tfgjfhdgsd554ergf54yhdsgeghdgghgfd56ytr'

TEMPLATE_LOADERS = (
    'django.template.loaders.filesystem.load_template_source',
    'django.template.loaders.app_directories.load_template_source',
)

MIDDLEWARE_CLASSES = (
    'django.middleware.common.CommonMiddleware',
    'django.contrib.sessions.middleware.SessionMiddleware',
    'django.contrib.auth.middleware.AuthenticationMiddleware',
)

ROOT_URLCONF = 'myproject.urls'

TEMPLATE_DIRS = (
    os.path.join(PROJECT_PATH, 'templates'),
)

INSTALLED_APPS = (
    'django.contrib.auth',
    'django.contrib.contenttypes',
    'django.contrib.sessions',
    'django.contrib.sites',
    'couchdbkit.ext.django',
    'myproject.bookmarks',
)
```

Next, you need to change your urls.py file to tell Django what views to point what URLs to. Modify this file in your favorite text editor so it matches the code in Listing 11-13.

Listing 11-13. urls.py

```
from django.conf.urls.defaults import *

urlpatterns = patterns('',
    (r'^$', 'bookmarks.views.index'),
)
```

Next, let's create the application models. In the bookmarks directory, edit the models.py file, and modify it so that it reflects the code shown in Listing 11-14.

Listing 11-14. models.py

```
from datetime import datetime
from django.db import models
from couchdbkit.ext.django.schema import *

class Bookmark(Document):
    url = StringProperty(required=True)
    title = StringProperty(required=True)
    date_added = DateTimeProperty(default=datetime.utcnow)
```

Now, modify the views.py file. This is where you will create the index view, which the main Django application URL will access. Listing 11-15 shows the contents of this file.

Listing 11-15. views.py

```
from datetime import datetime
from django.shortcuts import render_to_response
from django.template import RequestContext, loader, Context
from couchdbkit.ext.django.forms import DocumentForm
from myproject.bookmarks.models import Bookmark

class BookmarkForm(DocumentForm):
    class Meta:
        document = Bookmark
        exclude = ('date_added',)

def index(request):
    bookmark = None

    if request.POST:
        form = BookmarkForm(request.POST)
        if form.is_valid():
            bookmark = form.save()
    else:
        form = BookmarkForm()
```

```
bookmarks = Bookmark.view('bookmarks/all', descending=True)

return render_to_response("index.html", {
    "form": form,
    "bookmark": bookmark,
    "bookmarks": bookmarks
}, context_instance=RequestContext(request))
```

You may have noticed in Listing 11-15 that you are returning the bookmarks stored in the database using a CouchDB view: bookmarks/all. This view does not exist, however, so you need to create it. In the bookmarks directory, create a nested directory structure as follows:

```
_design
    views
        all
```

You can create this by issuing the command (assuming you are in the bookmarks directory):

```
mkdir -p _design/views/all
```

Now you need to create a new file at the bottom of this structure (in other words, in the all subdirectory) called map.js, which will house your view's map function. This view will simply return a list of all documents in the database that have a doc_type field with the value Bookmark. This allows you to display only data documents from your database (whereas the _all_docs view would include design documents also). Listing 11-16 shows the map.js file source code.

Listing 11-16. map.js

```
function(doc) {
    if(doc.doc_type == "Bookmark")
        emit(doc._id, doc);
}
```

The final thing you need to do is create the template index.html file that is used by the Django view. In the main project directory (myproject), create a new directory named templates as follows:

```
mkdir templates
```

In this directory, create a new file named index.html, with the code in Listing 11-17.

Listing 11-17. index.html

```
{% load i18n %}

<html>
<head>
<title>Bookmarks Application</title>
<style type="text/css">
* { font-family: Helvetica, Verdana, sans-serif; }
body { margin: 0; padding: 0; }
```

```
h1 { background-color: #336699; color: #fff; font-size: 1.3em; margin: 0; padding: 10px; }
fieldset { margin: 20px; border: 1px solid #ccc; }
legend {
  border: 1px solid #ccc; background-color: #eee; padding: 4px; font-weight: bold; font-
size: 0.8em;
}
form table { margin: 10px; }
form table th { text-align: left; }
form table th label[for="id_url"] { text-transform: uppercase; }
h2 { margin: 20px; padding: 10px; background-color: #eee; border: 1px solid #ccc; font-size:
1.1em; }
table.results {
  width: 95%; margin: 20px; border: 1px solid #ccc; border-bottom: none; border-righ: none;
}
table.results th {
  text-align: left; background-color: #eee; border-bottom: 1px solid #ccc; border-right: 1px
solid #ccc;
}
table.results td { border-bottom: 1px solid #ccc; border-right: 1px solid #ccc; }
p { margin: 20px; color: green; font-weight: bold; }
</style>
</head>

<body>
<h1>Bookmarks Application</h1>
<form method="post">
<fieldset><legend>Create New Bookmark</legend>
<table>
{{ form.as_table }}
<tr><td colspan="2" align="center">
<input type="submit" id="submit" value="Create Bookmark" />
</td></tr></table></fieldset></form>

{% if bookmark %}
<p>{{ bookmark.title }} was added.</p>
{% endif %}

<h2>View Bookmarks</h2>
<table class="results" cellspacing="0" cellpadding="4">
<tr><th>Link</th><th>Date Added</th></tr>
{% for b in bookmarks %}
<tr>
<td><a href="{{ b.url }}">{{ b.title }}</a></td>
<td>{{ b.date_added|date:"D d M Y @ H:i:s" }}</td>
</tr>
{% endfor %}
</table>
</body>
</html>
```

That's it; your Django + CouchDB application is ready to be tested! Navigate to the main project directory (`myproject`), and issue the following command:

```
python manage.py syncdb
```

This will start creating some tables in the SQLite database for some preinstalled Django modules. You may be asked to create a superuser; feel free to do so by answering the questions when prompted. When your superuser has been created, you will notice the message "sync 'myproject.bookmarks' in CouchDB" before some messages about installing indexes. Does this mean that the bookmarks database has been created in CouchDB? Let's check in Futon by visiting `http://127.0.0.1:5984/_utils` in a web browser. You should see a positive result, as shown in Figure 11-10.

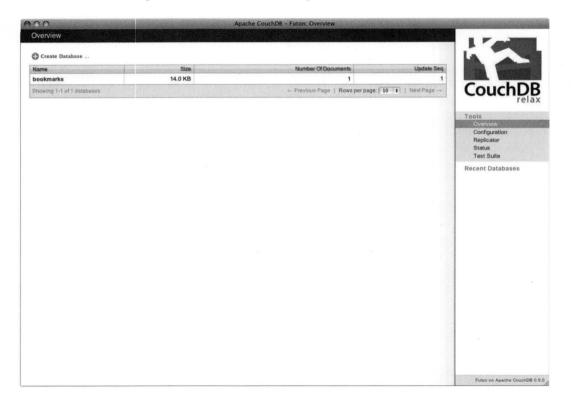

Figure 11-10. *The bookmarks database, automatically created by Django*

But that's nothing that you couldn't do with some simple Python code yourself. How about an actual Django web application? Head back to your shell prompt or Terminal window, and from the `myproject` directory, issue the following command:

```
python manage.py runserver
```

This will validate your Django models and launch Django's built-in development web server on port 8000. You should see a message like the one shown in Figure 11-11.

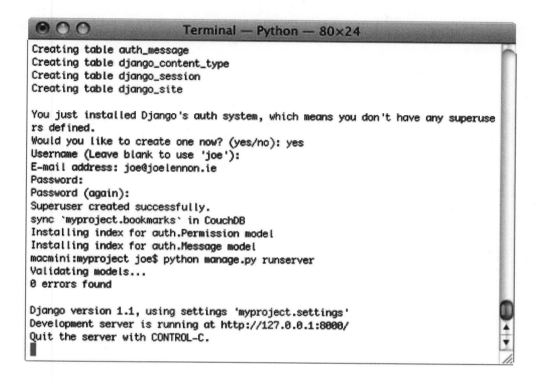

Figure 11-11. *Running the Django development web server*

As instructed, visit the URL http://127.0.0.1:8000 in your web browser. You should now be able to add new bookmarks, which will be retrieved from CouchDB and displayed in the table at the bottom of the page. The end product should look something like Figure 11-12.

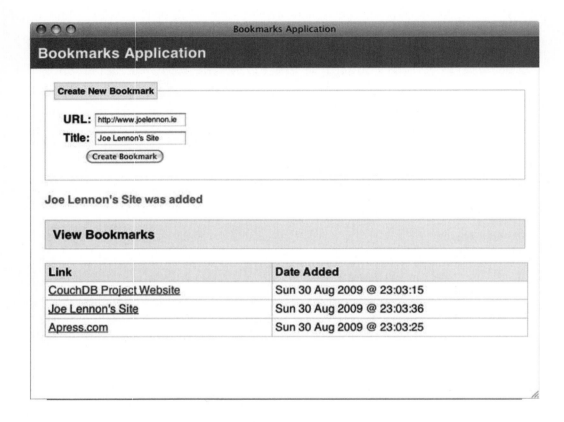

Figure 11-12. The bookmark Django + CouchDB application

Congratulations, you have developed a bookmark web application in Python using the Django web application development framework that uses CouchDB to store its data. Of course, this sample application barely scratches the surface in terms of potential features. However, with some basic knowledge of Python, Django, and Couchdbkit, you can take the sample application you have developed here and turn it into a full-blown CouchDB-driven application. Some suggestions for feature enhancements include the following:

- Allow bookmarks to be edited and deleted

- Add more fields to the application, such as tags, description, rating, and so on

- Separate the application into multiple views

- Create more CouchDB views to give multiple representations of the data, such as tag clouds, sorting by fields, pagination, and so on

- Use JavaScript to allow bookmarks to be sorted using drag and drop

- Allow bookmarks to be organized into categories

The possibilities for this application are truly endless.

Summary

In this chapter, you learned how to work with CouchDB databases using two modern programming languages: Python and Ruby. With Python, you learned how to leverage the Couchdbkit library to create and work with CouchDB databases and views. You then saw how to do the same in Ruby using CouchRest. Finally, you developed a basic bookmark storage web application using the Django framework for Python, with your data stored in CouchDB, of course.

In the next chapter, you will learn about some of the more advanced aspects of CouchDB, such as replication, compaction and working with documents in bulk.

■ ■ □

CHAPTER 12

Advanced CouchDB Topics

In this chapter, you will learn about some of the more advanced aspects of CouchDB. First, you will see how a CouchDB database can be replicated—to another database on the local CouchDB server and to a database on a remote CouchDB instance. Then, you'll learn about database compaction and how it reduces the size of the database file, as well as its impact on previous revisions of documents. Next, you will learn how to fetch and write documents from and to the database in bulk. Finally, you will see how show functions allow you to represent CouchDB data in different formats.

Replication

CouchDB is designed to allow bidirectional replication in an efficient and reliable manner. It does this through an incremental replication model, where only those documents that have changed since the last replication are processed. By design, CouchDB's replication system allows a failed replication process to pick up from the last saved checkpoint.

In addition to regular CouchDB documents that store data, the design documents that house CouchDB views are also replicated, as well as any document's attachments. This means that entire CouchDB applications can enjoy the benefits of this replication feature, not just the data.

Let's take a look at how to perform replication in CouchDB. The first method is using Futon, the web-based administration interface that comes with every CouchDB installation. Open your web browser, and visit the URL `http://127.0.0.1:5984/_utils` (assuming CouchDB is installed on your local computer). In Futon, create two databases—one called *futon-one* and the other called *futon-two*. In the futon-one database, create three documents (you don't need to worry about creating any fields because the aim is merely to get replication working). When viewing Futon's Overview page, you should see your two databases, similar to Figure 12-1. Note that futon-one has three documents and futon-two has zero documents.

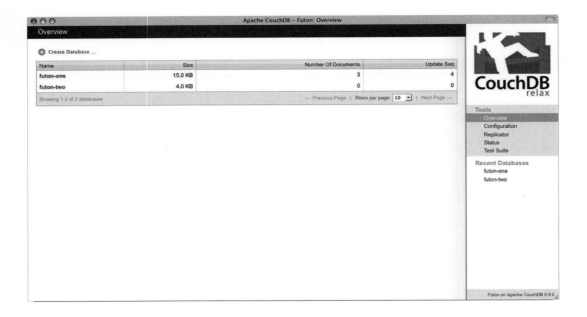

Figure 12-1. The futon-one and futon-two databases

Now, in the main menu of Futon on the right side, click the Replicator link to navigate to the Futon replication tool. This page should look like the one shown in Figure 12-2.

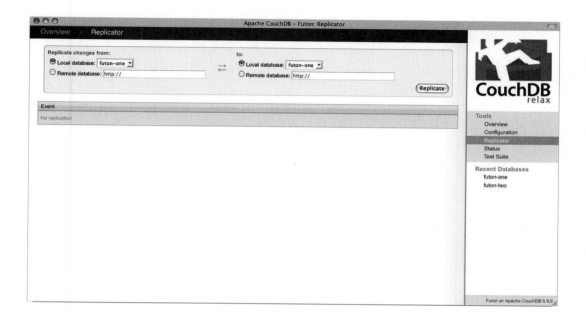

Figure 12-2. *Futon replication tool*

At the top of this page you will see two sides, one with the heading "Replicate changes from" and the other with the heading "to." Under each you will see two options—"Local database" and "Remote database." For this example, you will be replicating your local database futon-one to another local database, futon-two. Make sure that under "Replicate changes from," the "Local database" option is selected and that the futon-one database is selected. Ensure that under "to" that "Local database" is also selected but that here the futon-two database is selected. When you are ready to replicate the database, click the Replicate button. The replication process will start and should finish almost immediately, because the database is very small. When it is done, you will see a message in the Event area like the one shown in Figure 12-3.

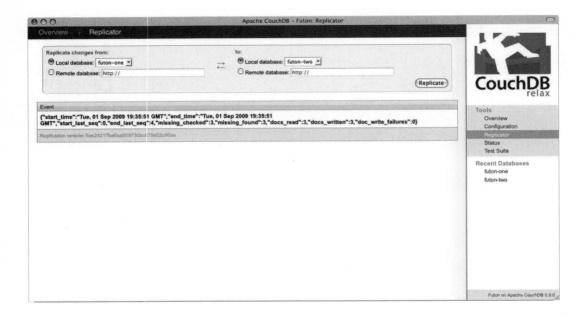

Figure 12-3. *Futon replication result*

The message in the Event area is a JSON object with details about the replication and its results. You can see in Figure 12-3 that, in my case, the replication took less than a second to complete, checked three documents to see whether they were missing, found that all three were missing, read the three of them, wrote them to the other database, and encountered zero failures.

Now let's return to the Overview page of Futon, where you can see that the futon-two database now contains three documents, just as futon-one does (Figure 12-4).

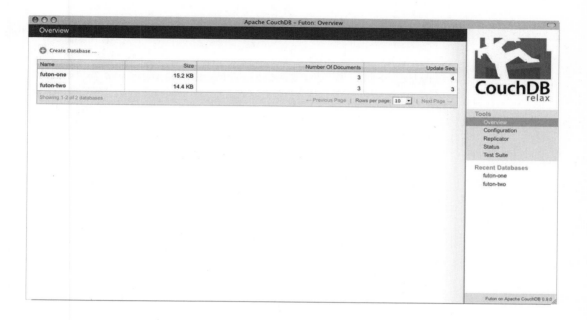

Figure 12-4. Futon's Overview page after replication

Next, let's investigate how the incremental replication works. From Futon's Overview page, open the futon-two database, and create two new documents. Again, you don't need to create any real data, unless you feel a burning desire to do so, of course! Your databases should now look something like Figure 12-5, with futon-one containing three documents and futon-two containing five documents.

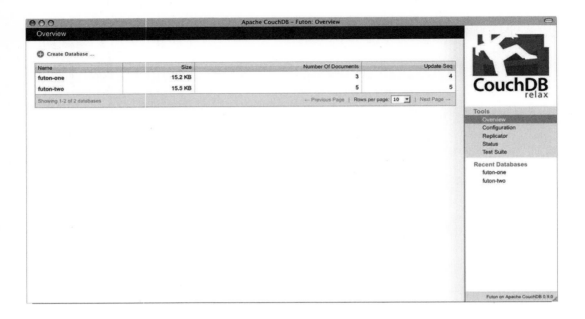

Figure 12-5. Getting ready for incremental replication

Head back over to the Replicator tool; this time select futon-two under the "Replicate changes from" heading, and select the futon-one database below the "to" heading. Click the Replicate button to commence replication. The results will again show in the Event section, as shown in Figure 12-6.

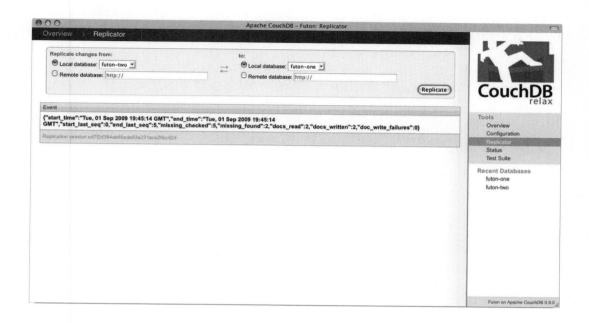

Figure 12-6. *Result of incremental replication*

If you read through the JSON result object, you will see that this time around it checked five documents to see whether any were missing from the target database, and it found that two were missing (the two we just created). It then read these two documents from the source database and wrote them to the target database. Now let's examine replicating across different CouchDB instances.

For the purposes of this example, I will assume that you have CouchDB installed on two separate computers that are connected to the same network. If you don't have two machines, you can try installing two instances of CouchDB on the same computer, or of course you can create a virtual machine and install CouchDB there. In my case, my CouchDB instances are installed on my Mac mini computer, which has an IP address of 192.168.1.8, and on my MacBook, which has an IP address of 192.168.1.14. Be sure to replace these IP addresses with the addresses for your own computers.

■ **Caution** Before trying to replicate databases between CouchDB instances, it's a good idea to test that the computers can find each other. Open a shell or Terminal window on each machine, and use the `ping` command to see whether it can find the other. For example, on my Mac mini I issued the command `ping 192.168.1.14`, and on my MacBook I issued `ping 192.168.1.8`. If you fail to receive a response from the other computer, you will need to resolve this issue before you can try replicating CouchDB databases.

By default, CouchDB is configured to listen on port 5984, binding to the IP address 127.0.0.1. As a result, it will not be discoverable by other computers in your network. To see what I mean, try to visit the CouchDB front page on machine B using your browser on machine A. You should get a result like the one shown in Figure 12-7.

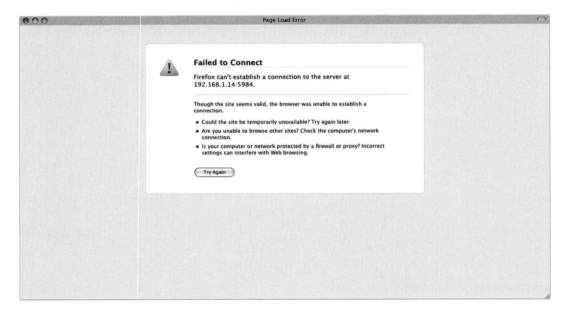

Figure 12-7. CouchDB only listens to local connections by default.

To resolve this issue, you will need to modify CouchDB's configuration file. Fortunately, Futon provides an easy way to do this. On each machine, visit the Futon page for the local instance of CouchDB at `http://127.0.0.1:5984/_utils`. Click the Configuration link in the menu on the right to visit the CouchDB Configuration options page. You should see an array of different configuration options here, but you are interested only in the "bind_address" option in the "httpd" section, as shown in Figure 12-8. By default, this is set to 127.0.0.1, but by changing it to 0.0.0.0 you can tell CouchDB to bind to all available addresses for incoming connections. Double-click the "127.0.0.1" text, and an editable text box will open. Enter **0.0.0.0**, and click the green check icon to the right of the field to save the configuration. Repeat this process on your other computer.

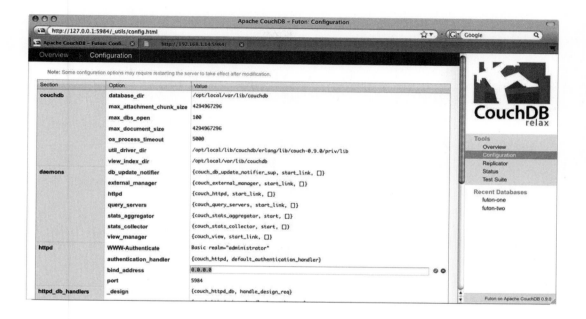

Figure 12-8. *Futon configuration tool*

With this configuration completed, try to connect to CouchDB on the remote machine once again. This time you should have more success, as shown in Figure 12-9.

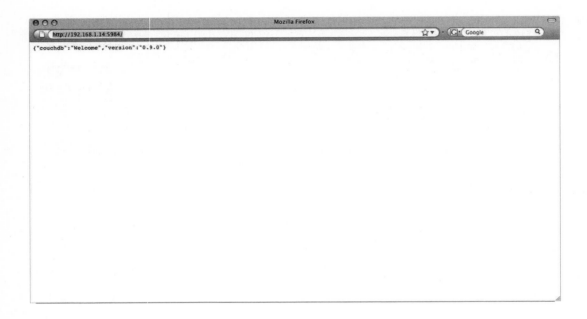

Figure 12-9. Accessing CouchDB remotely

Now let's replicate the futon-one database from the machine you created it on earlier to the machine that doesn't have the database. First create a new database on the target instance called futon-copy. Your target machine's Futon interface should show this database with zero documents, as shown in Figure 12-10.

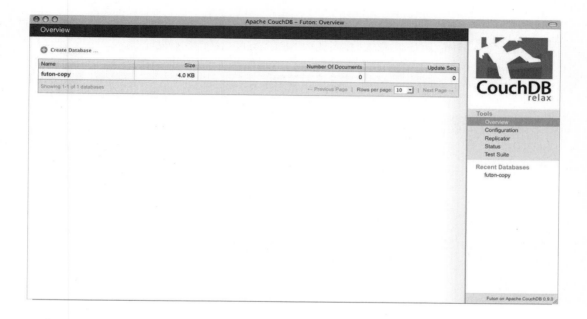

Figure 12-10. *Setting up the target database for replication*

Now open the Futon page for your source instance, and navigate to the Replicator tool. Under the "Replicate changes from" heading, select the "Local database" option, and make sure futon-one is chosen in the drop-down list. Under the "to" heading, select the "Remote database" option, and in the text box enter the URL **http://192.168.1.14:5984/futon-copy**. Then click the Replicate button. If all goes well, you should see an outcome like Figure 12-11.

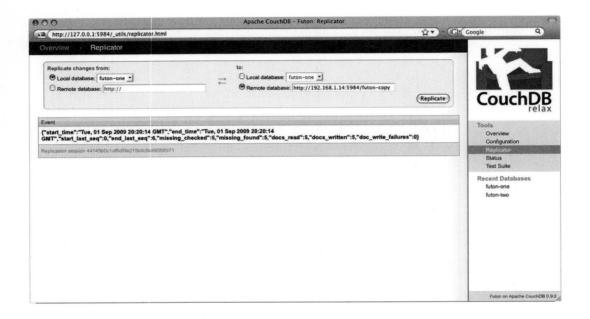

Figure 12-11. Result of remote replication

■ **Caution** Be sure to replace the IP address in this URL with the IP address of the machine you are working with, or it will not work!

If the JSON response in the Event section looks like it's in order, head over to the Futon interface for the target instance, and check that the database replicated as expected. If it did, you should now see that the futon-copy database contains five documents, the five that were replicated from the futon-one database on the other machine (Figure 12-12). CouchDB replication really is that simple.

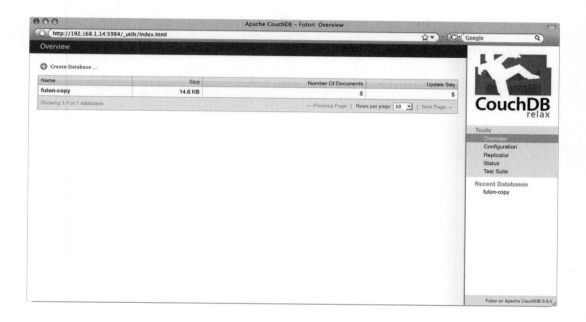

Figure 12-12. Replicated data in the remote target database

Although Futon does a really good job at implementing CouchDB's replication features, you will probably want to trigger database replication from your own applications. This is also very simple to perform, thanks to CouchDB's RESTful Replication API. Before you investigate interacting with this API using `curl`, let's create a new database that we will replicate data into. On the same machine that you created the futon-copy database, create a new database called *futon-copy-two*. Now open a shell or Terminal window on the machine that contains your source database, in this instance, the futon-two database.

At the prompt, enter the following command (replacing the IP address with the IP of the target instance):

```
curl http://192.168.1.14:5984
```

This will test that `curl` is installed and that you can access the remote CouchDB server. If you get a response with a JSON object containing a welcome message and version number, you're ready to replicate using the API. Enter the following command to replicate the local futon-two database to the remote futon-copy-two database:

```
curl -X POST -d "{\"source\":\"futon-two\",\"target\":\"http://192.168.1.14:5984/futon-copy-two\"}" http://127.0.0.1:5984/_replicate
```

When you press Enter, the futon-two database in the local instance will be replicated to the futon-copy-town database in the remote instance (on 192.168.1.14 in my case). The result is similar to the one you received in Futon earlier, as shown in Figure 12-13.

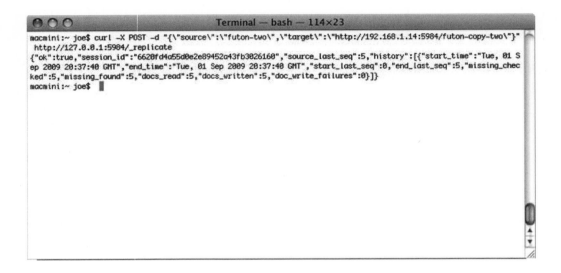

Figure 12-13. Result of Replication API call

In this command, we are making a POST request to the URI `http://127.0.0.1:5984/_replicate`, which is the location of the CouchDB Replication API. You are passing in a JSON object in the message body, with two properties—**source** and **target**. If either of these two properties represents a database on the local machine, you merely specify the database name, but if it resides on a remote database, you must give the full URL to that database.

Compaction

One of the features of CouchDB is that each time a document is modified, it does not overwrite the old document but rather creates a new revision of it. The new revision will have the same `_id` value as the old version, but it will have a new `_rev` value. This system is used by CouchDB to implement optimistic concurrency control—which basically means that if you edit an old revision of a document (that is, a new revision has been created between the time you started to edit the document and the time you saved it), a conflict error will be raised. Although this is very useful, it requires that system resources (specifically disk space) need to be reclaimed periodically.

To counter this problem, CouchDB provides a compaction feature, which is used to purge old revisions of documents from the database. When the database is compacted, the database file is rewritten, with out-of-date revisions and previously deleted documents permanently removed from the database. It is an irreversible operation, so once you compact the database, there is no way to retrieve those purged documents.

Performing database compaction is very simple using the Futon interface. For example, I have a database named *my-database* with four documents currently stored in it. I earlier deleted a document from this database, which had some sizable attachments, and as you can see in Figure 12-14, despite this documents being deleted, my meager four-document database still takes up 28.8MB of disk space.

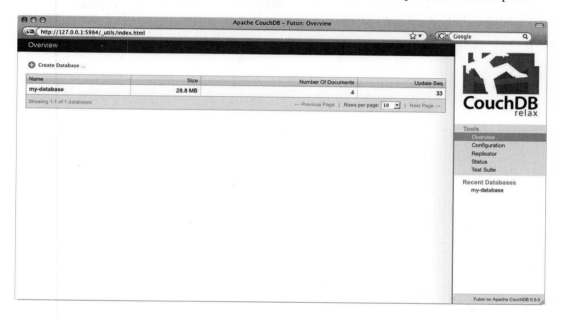

Figure 12-14. A database in need of compaction

Now I'm going to use compaction to reclaim some of that lost space. Click the database name to navigate to the database's page. From the menu near the top of the page, select the Compact Database option, which will open a confirmation dialog box, as in Figure 12-15.

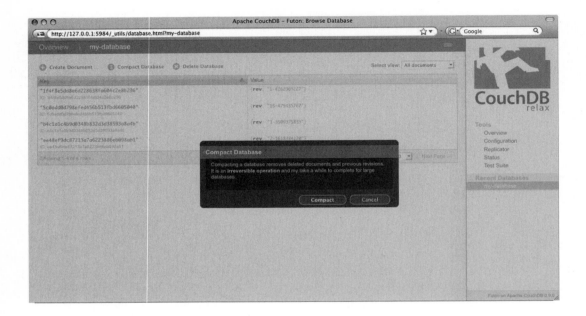

Figure 12-15. Confirm database compaction

Click Compact to confirm, and when the page reloads, navigate to the Overview page to check the database size. As you can see in Figure 12-16, my database has been shaved down to just 0.6MB, thanks to the deletion of those old documents with heavy attachments that I previously deleted.

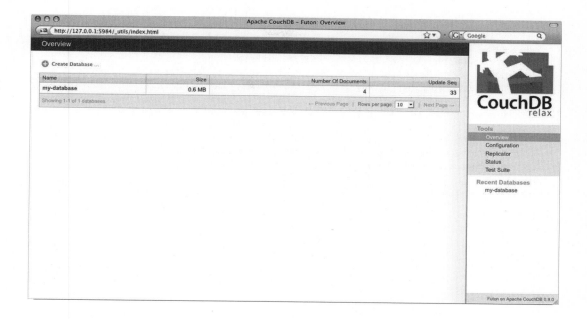

Figure 12-16. *My post-diet database*

Once again, Futon makes this process so easy—but it is likely that you won't always use it to perform these operations. You will probably want to build compaction into your applications—and this is also very simple—using the Compaction API.

Open your shell or Terminal window. In this example, I am once again shaving down a database that contains a deleted document with a large attachment. First, let's see the current size of the database using the following command:

```
curl http://127.0.0.1:5984/my-database
```

Make a note of the `disk_size` field value (in my case it's 30,011,574 bytes, which equates to 28.6MB). Now issue the following command to compact the database:

```
curl -X POST http://127.0.0.1:5984/my-database/_compact
```

You should receive a response telling you that all went OK. Let's check that out by rerunning the earlier command:

```
curl http://127.0.0.1:5984/my-database
```

This time, the `disk_size` value should be smaller (assuming you had previous revisions or deleted documents when you ran compaction, of course!). For example, my disk size is now 587,342 bytes, or 0.6MB. You can see the results of these three commands on my machine in Figure 12-17.

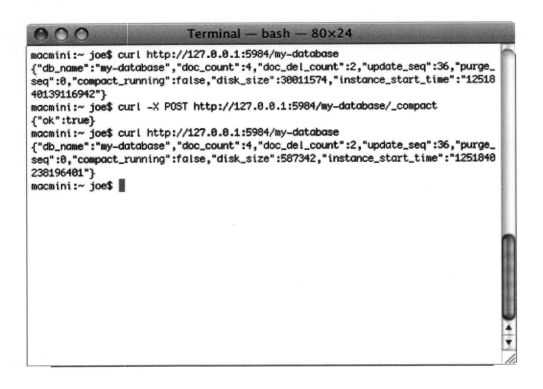

Figure 12-17. Compaction with the CouchDB API

■ **Note** Because CouchDB databases can (and should) be compacted in this manner, the document revisions in the database itself should never be used as the basis for version control of documents in your applications.

At the time of writing, compacting CouchDB databases can be performed manually only, one database at a time. Future versions of CouchDB may include more advanced compaction features such as queuing compactions and processing multiple compactions with one API call.

Fetching Documents in Bulk

CouchDB allows multiple documents to be fetched with a single HTTP request. To do this, you make a POST request to the /[databasename]/_all_docs URI, with the message body containing a JSON array object with the document IDs you want to retrieve. For example, take the following example database called *people*. As you can see in Figure 12-18, I have six documents in this database, with each person's first name as the document ID. It's not a very practical system, but let's keep things simple!

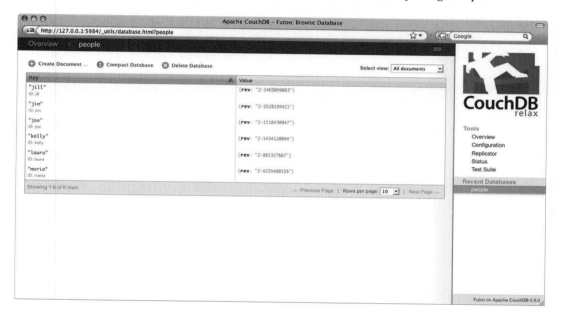

Figure 12-18. *My people database*

Now, I open my Terminal window and issue the following command:

```
curl http://127.0.0.1:5984/people/_all_docs
```

This brings back all the documents in the database, as you might expect (Figure 12-19).

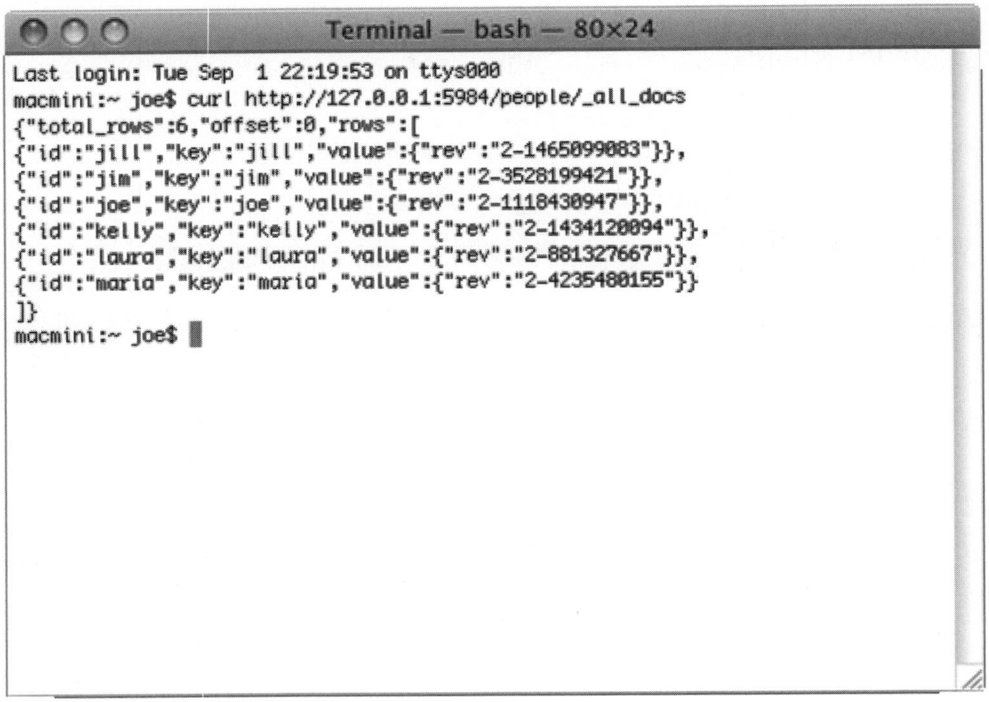

```
⬤ ⬤ ⬤                  Terminal — bash — 80×24
Last login: Tue Sep  1 22:19:53 on ttys000
macmini:~ joe$ curl http://127.0.0.1:5984/people/_all_docs
{"total_rows":6,"offset":0,"rows":[
{"id":"jill","key":"jill","value":{"rev":"2-1465099083"}},
{"id":"jim","key":"jim","value":{"rev":"2-3528199421"}},
{"id":"joe","key":"joe","value":{"rev":"2-1118430947"}},
{"id":"kelly","key":"kelly","value":{"rev":"2-1434120094"}},
{"id":"laura","key":"laura","value":{"rev":"2-881327667"}},
{"id":"maria","key":"maria","value":{"rev":"2-4235480155"}}
]}
macmini:~ joe$ ▮
```

Figure 12-19. Returning all documents

This time, I'm going to make a POST request to this URI, passing a JSON array of the document IDs I want to bring back (in this case `jill`, `kelly`, `laura`, and `maria`) as the request message:

```
curl -X POST -d '{"keys":["jill","kelly","laura","maria"]}'
http://127.0.0.1:5984/people/_all_docs
```

As you can see in Figure 12-20, this time around only those documents that match the document IDs I supplied are returned in the response.

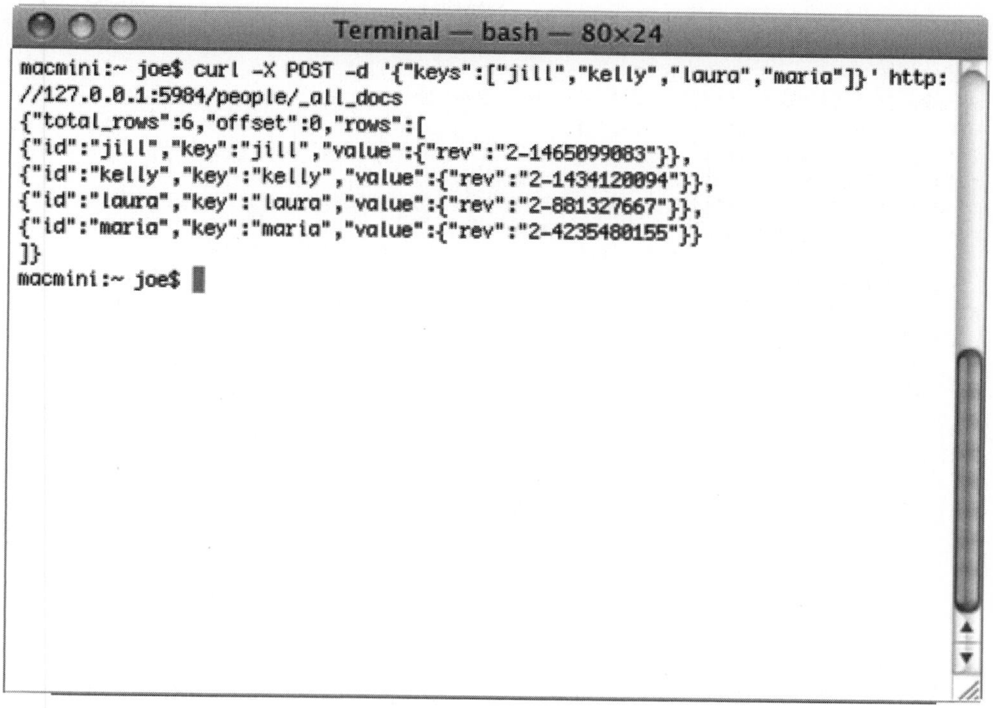

```
macmini:~ joe$ curl -X POST -d '{"keys":["jill","kelly","laura","maria"]}' http:
//127.0.0.1:5984/people/_all_docs
{"total_rows":6,"offset":0,"rows":[
{"id":"jill","key":"jill","value":{"rev":"2-1465099083"}},
{"id":"kelly","key":"kelly","value":{"rev":"2-1434120094"}},
{"id":"laura","key":"laura","value":{"rev":"2-881327667"}},
{"id":"maria","key":"maria","value":{"rev":"2-4235480155"}}
]}
macmini:~ joe$
```

Figure 12-20. Returning all documents matching set of supplied document IDs

You may have noticed in the previous example that only the _id and _rev fields were returned from the document itself. What if you want to get back the documents? In my example, I have given each document a name field with the person's full name. I use the query parameter ?include_docs=true at the end of the URI in my HTTP request to tell CouchDB to include the documents in the response:

```
curl -X POST -d '{"keys":[" jill","kelly","laura","maria"]}'
http://127.0.0.1:5984/people/_all_docs?include_docs=true
```

The result is shown in Figure 12-21—notice that each row has a doc field with the actual document inside.

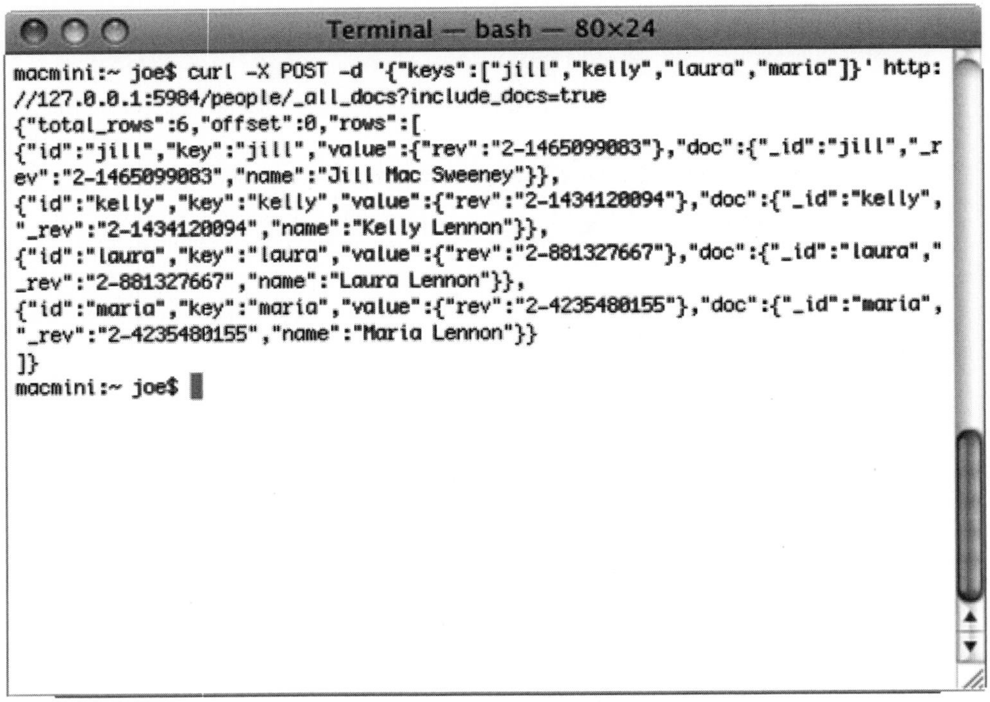

```
  ○ ○ ○                    Terminal — bash — 80×24
macmini:~ joe$ curl -X POST -d '{"keys":["jill","kelly","laura","maria"]}' http:
//127.0.0.1:5984/people/_all_docs?include_docs=true
{"total_rows":6,"offset":0,"rows":[
{"id":"jill","key":"jill","value":{"rev":"2-1465099083"},"doc":{"_id":"jill","_r
ev":"2-1465099083","name":"Jill Mac Sweeney"}},
{"id":"kelly","key":"kelly","value":{"rev":"2-1434120094"},"doc":{"_id":"kelly",
"_rev":"2-1434120094","name":"Kelly Lennon"}},
{"id":"laura","key":"laura","value":{"rev":"2-881327667"},"doc":{"_id":"laura","
_rev":"2-881327667","name":"Laura Lennon"}},
{"id":"maria","key":"maria","value":{"rev":"2-4235480155"},"doc":{"_id":"maria",
"_rev":"2-4235480155","name":"Maria Lennon"}}
]}
macmini:~ joe$ ▌
```

Figure 12-21. Including documents in bulk read calls

Writing Documents in Bulk

What about writing multiple documents into the CouchDB database with a single call to the API? Once again, this is very simple—you simply make a POST request to the /[databasename]/_bulk_docs URI with the documents you want to write to the database in the request body. This makes it much easier to import data into CouchDB from external data sources. For example, take the contents of Listing 12-1, which I have saved in a file named new_people.json.

Listing 12-1. new_people.json

```
{
    "docs": [
        {"_id": "patrick", "name": "Patrick Mac Sweeney"},
```

```
        {"_id": "susie", "name": "Susan Mac Sweeney"},
        {"_id": "sarah": "name": "Sarah Mac Sweeney"}
    ]
}
```

I can now use the Bulk Document API to load this JSON file into the database, creating the three new documents specified:

```
curl -X POST -d @new_people.json http://127.0.0.1:5984/people/_bulk_docs
```

The CouchDB server returns a response with the document IDs and revision numbers, which looks pretty positive. I also make a call to `_all_docs` to make sure the new documents were created, as shown in Figure 12-22.

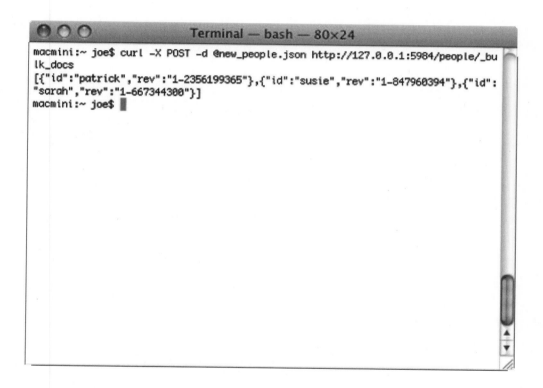

Figure 12-22. Loading bulk documents into the database

Pretty sweet, huh? In this example, I specified a document ID for my new documents. If you omit the `_id` field, Couch will automatically assign the document a UUID. If you want to modify existing documents, simply include the _id and _rev fields of the latest revision of the document you want to update. Want to delete a document? Pass in the _deleted field with a value of true. For example, if I wanted to modify the documents for Jill and Jim and delete the document for Joe, I would use the JSON code in Listing 12-2.

Listing 12-2. change_people.json

```
{
    "docs": [
        {"_id":"jill","_rev":"2-1465099083","name":"Jillian Mac Sweeney"},
        {"_id":"jim","_rev":"2-3528199421","name":"James Lennon"},
        {"_id":"joe","_rev":"2-1118430947","_deleted":true}
    ]
}
```

As you can see from the temporary view shown in Figure 12-23, the jill and jim documents have been updated accordingly, and the joe document has been deleted from the database.

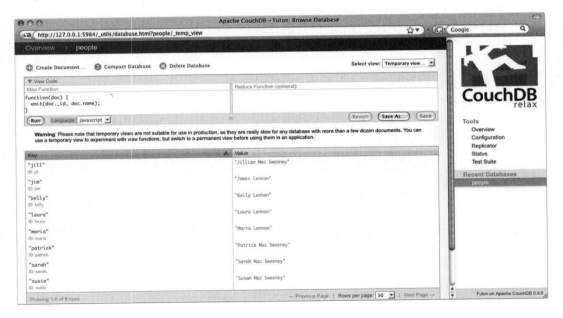

Figure 12-23. Result of bulk modification

The default behavior of Bulk Document updates in CouchDB 0.9.0 and newer is that updates are *nonatomic*; that is, some of the document updates may have failed, while others may have succeeded, with documents that succeeded/failed clearly indicated in the response. The most common reason for a document not updating is a conflict error. This behavior ensures that just because one document fails to update does not mean the entire bulk update will fail.

An alternative behavior is "all-or-nothing"—where if any document fails to update, none of the changes to any of the documents will be committed. Additionally, with this method there is no conflict detection; documents are committed regardless, even if you supply an invalid revision number when trying to update a document. The conflicting documents will not be overwritten, but rather you will have two documents with the same document ID after the bulk update.

If you want to perform an "all-or-nothing" bulk update, you simply pass the `all_or_nothing` field with a value of true alongside your `docs` array, as shown in Listing 12-3.

Listing 12-3. change_people.json

```
{
    "all_or_nothing":"true",
    "docs": [
        {"_id":"jill","_rev":"2-1465099083","name":"Jillian Mac Sweeney"},
        {"_id":"jim","_rev":"2-3528199421","name":"James Lennon"},
        {"_id":"joe","_rev":"2-1118430947","_deleted":true}
    ]
}
```

Show Functions

From version 0.9.0 of CouchDB on, you can store *show* functions in your design documents, which will present your JSON documents in a non-JSON format. Each document is processed individually for efficiency, and the functions are designed to be cacheable. These functions can be used only to represent JSON data in other document formats, and they cannot make HTTP requests.

These functions are stored in design documents, in the `shows` and `lists` keys, respectively. I'm going to use Futon to create a new design document and modify it to include these keys with a sample of each type of function. First, let's create a show function.

For this example I'm using the same database I used in the previous section (the people database). In Futon, I navigate to the people database, and from there I select "Temporary view…" from the "Select view" drop-down list. I don't modify the map and reduce functions for the view and simply choose Save As to save the design document. This opens the dialog box shown in Figure 12-24.

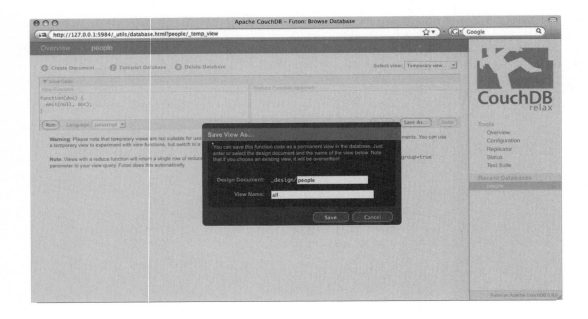

Figure 12-24. Creating a design document

I name my design document _design/people; the view name is irrelevant in this case. Now from the "Select view" drop-down I select Design Documents, which shows my newly created design document. Clicking this allows me to modify this document's keys and values. To create my show functions, I add a new field named shows and add the JSON object shown in Figure 12-25 as its value. I then save the design document.

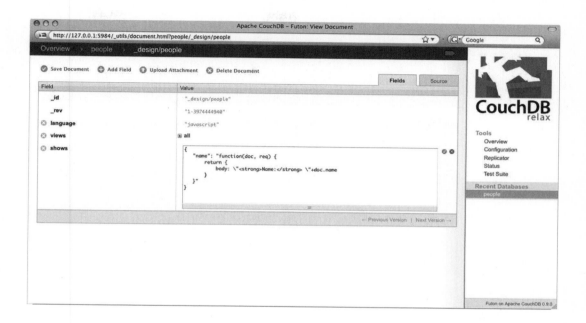

Figure 12-25. *My Shows function—name*

Now I can have a look at my function in action by visiting the following URL in my browser: `http://127.0.0.1:5984/people/_design/people/_show/name/jill`. Figure 12-26 shows the result.

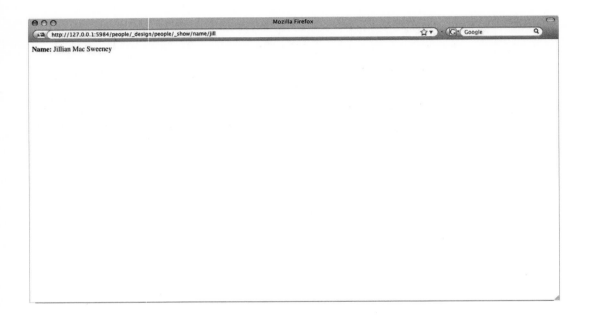

Figure 12-26. Show function in action

Impressive, eh? If you use your imagination, I'm sure you can see the potential this offers. In the previous URL, if I change the `jill` portion (the document ID) to another document ID, that person's name will be displayed.

As well as show functions, CouchDB supports *list* functions, which can be used to format the results returned by a CouchDB view. For example, if I have a view, which returns all rows in my people database sorted by the `name` key, I can use a list function to format this in pretty HTML, with links to a show function for each item in the list. Unfortunately, the support for list functions is experimental in version 0.9.0, although drastic improvements are available in the trunk development version. The API for list functions is volatile at present, so check the CouchDB wiki for the syntax to use for these functions. They are saved the same way as show functions and are called using the following URL syntax: `http://127.0.0.1:5984/[db_name]/_design/[design_doc_name]/[list_name]/[view_name]`.

Summary

In this chapter, you saw some of the more advanced features of the CouchDB database such as how to replicate databases either locally or remotely across CouchDB servers. You learned how to replicate databases using the Futon administration interface and using the raw CouchDB API. Similarly, you saw how to use the Compaction API to remove old revisions and deleted documents from the database, freeing up valuable resources. Again, you used both Futon and the API to do so. Then you learned how to retrieve more than one document at a time using a single HTTP request. You then used the `_bulk_docs` API to create, update, and delete multiple documents in the same request. Finally, you saw how recent versions of CouchDB include show and list functions, allowing users to format their JSON data in different ways that are more meaningful to the user.

In the next and final chapter, I'll cover some of the issues surrounding the deployment of CouchDB in a production environment, including topics such as security, configuration, load balancing, clustering, backup, and reverse proxies.

■■■

Mechanics of CouchDB Deployment

In this chapter, you will learn some of the key areas of ensuring your CouchDB installation is configured correctly for deployment to a production environment. At the time of writing, CouchDB is in beta and has been used in production by a number of organizations. In fact, the latest version of Ubuntu Linux, 9.10 Karmic Koala, includes a copy of CouchDB by default. With that in mind, it is worth remembering that CouchDB is still beta software, and the API for new and existing features may change between versions. Some older versions of CouchDB will also require a dump/load cycle of data as the database formats change.

Measuring Performance

CouchDB 0.9.0 and newer includes a runtime statistics feature that allows you to measure your CouchDB installation's performance. To see all the statistics available, issue an HTTP GET request to the URI /_stats. If you have CouchDB installed on your local machine, either you can use the following curl command:

```
curl http://127.0.0.1:5984/_stats
```

or you can simply visit the URL http://127.0.0.1:5984/_stats in your web browser. You should see a response similar to the one shown in Listing 13-1. Please note that I have formatted this JSON response to make it easier to read.

Listing 13-1. CouchDB Runtime Statistics Sample Response

```
{
    "httpd_status_codes": {
        "200": {
            "current":25,
            "count":58,
            "mean":0.4310344827586207,
            "min":0,
            "max":6,
            "stddev":1.2192715316025617,
            "description":"number of HTTP 200 OK responses"
        }, "404": {
            "current":4,
```

```
            "count":58,
            "mean":0.06896551724137934,
            "min":0,"max":2,
            "stddev":0.3649312153192539,
            "description":"number of HTTP 404 Not Found responses"
        }
    }, "httpd_request_methods" : {
        "GET": {
            "current":57,
            "count":60,
            "mean":0.9499999999999996,
            "min":0,
            "max":17,
            "stddev":2.8660367524975436,
            "description":"number of HTTP GET requests"
        }
    }, "httpd": {
        "requests": {
            "current":57,
            "count":60,
            "mean":0.9499999999999996,
            "min":0,
            "max":17,
            "stddev":2.8660367524975436,
            "description":"number of HTTP requests"
        }
    }, "couchdb": {
        "open_databases": {
            "current":2,
            "count":53,
            "mean":0.03773584905660379,
            "min":0,
            "max":2,
            "stddev":0.2721170773935086,
            "description":"number of open databases"
        }, "open_os_files": {
            "current":2,
            "count":53,
            "mean":0.03773584905660379,
            "min":0,
            "max":2,
            "stddev":0.2721170773935086,
            "description":"number of file descriptors CouchDB has open"
        }, "request_time": {
            "current":0,
            "count":57,
            "mean":1.5789473684210524,
            "min":0,
            "max":10,
            "stddev":3.646422752776584,
            "description":"length of a request inside CouchDB without MochiWeb"
```

```
        }
    }
}
```

The statistics produced here are broken into different groups representing different areas of CouchDB: couchdb, httpd, httpd_request_methods, and http_status_codes. Each of these areas are further broken down into keys; for example, the http_status_codes has a key for the various HTTP status codes that are sent as responses to API requests (for example, 200, 403, 404, 500). In Listing 13-1, you will notice that there are keys for the status codes 200 and 404 only. This is because there were no responses of other HTTP status codes generated by my CouchDB install since I started the CouchDB server.

Every key in the response contains the same metrics: current, count, mean, max, min, stddev, and description. The description provides a useful English description of what the metric actually measures.

By default, these statistics produce results that measure the interaction with the server since it was started. You can also choose to view results for the last minute, the last five minutes, and the last fifteen minutes if you so wish. To do this, you simply append the following string:

```
?range=n
```

where n is the number of seconds you want to query. So, for example, if you would like results for the past 15 minutes, you would issue a GET request to the URI /_stats?range=900. The only valid values for this parameter are 60, 300, and 900.

You can also request only those statistics for a particular key if you want. To do so, you simply issue a GET request to the URI /_stats/group/key. For example, to view the statistics for the GET key in the httpd_request_methods group, you issue your request to the URI /_stats/httpd_request_methods/GET. Listing 13-2 show a sample result from this request, which I have formatted to make it easier to read.

Listing 13-2. CouchDB Runtime Statistics by Key

```
{
    "httpd_request_methods": {
        "GET": {
            "current":8,
            "count":3206,
            "mean":0.0024953212726138586,
            "min":0,
            "max":7,
            "stddev":0.12485804469709988,
            "description":"number of HTTP GET requests"
        }
    }
}
```

As you can see, this request only returned the metric for the GET key of the httpd_request_methods group.

Configuring CouchDB

When you first build or install CouchDB on your system, there is zero configuration required to start creating CouchDB databases. That does not mean there are not any configuration options, however. CouchDB's configuration file includes many options for customizing your CouchDB installation.

There are two primary ways of modifying the CouchDB configuration file. The first is to manually edit the file itself. You can find this in the directory /usr/local/etc/couchdb or /opt/local/etc/couchdb, depending on your operating system. The configuration file is one of the areas of CouchDB that has changed significantly over recent releases. At the time of writing, the latest version of CouchDB provides two configuration files, default.ini and local.ini. The default.ini file includes the standard CouchDB configuration options and is overwritten when you upgrade CouchDB. As a result, any modifications you make to default.ini will be lost when you upgrade. For that reason, any changes to the CouchDB configuration should be made in local.ini, which will not be overwritten in an upgrade.

The second, and easier way of changing configuration options, is to use the Futon web-based administration interface, which includes a utility for modifying CouchDB's configuration file. If CouchDB is installed on your local computer, you can open the Futon configuration utility by pointing your web browser to the address http://127.0.0.1:5984/_utils/config.html. See Figure 13-1 for an example of this utility in action.

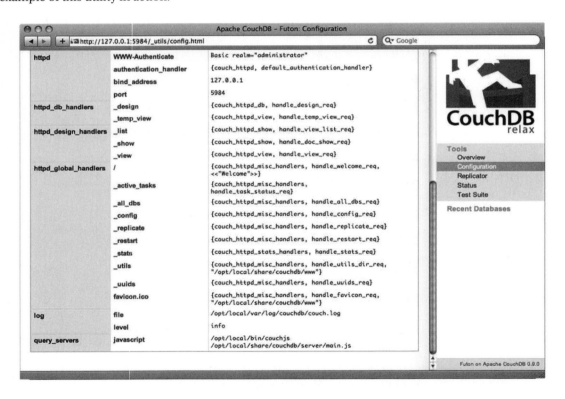

Figure 13-1. *The Futon configuration utility*

To change a particular option using this utility, you double-click the current value, which will switch that option's value column to an editor field, as shown in Figure 13-2. You can then modify the text of the option, and either use the green accept icon to save the change or click the red reject icon to cancel the change. Some changes will take effect immediately, but others may not have an impact until CouchDB is restarted.

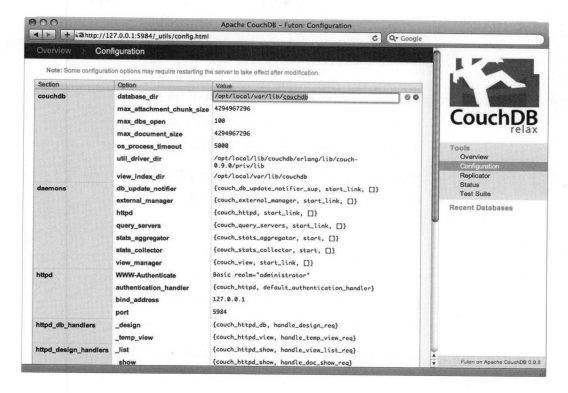

Figure 13-2. *Changing a configuration option*

The CouchDB configuration options are split into several sections: couchdb, daemons, httpd, httpd_db_handlers, httpd_design_handlers, httpd_global_handlers, log, and query_servers. An example of an option you may want to change is the bind_address option, which by default tells CouchDB to listen only on the local loopback IP address 127.0.0.1. This means that remote computers cannot access the CouchDB server. To make CouchDB listen to incoming connections on all available IP addresses, simply change the value of the bind_address option to 0.0.0.0.

A common question is how to make the Futon administration interface display when the user visits the root URI, in other words, http://127.0.0.1:5984/. By default this responds with a CouchDB welcome message and the version number of the CouchDB server that is installed on the machine. To change this to redirect to the Futon interface, you simply change the option / under httpd_global_handlers to the following value:

```
{couch_httpd, send_redirect, "/_utils"}
```

■ **Note** Configuration changes made using the Futon administration utility may take several minutes to take effect.

Newer versions of CouchDB also facilitate working with the configuration file using the `_config` API. You will see an example of this later when I cover how to implement security in CouchDB.

Conflict Resolution

When CouchDB encounters a conflict in a document during the replication process, it adds a special field to that document called `_conflicts`. To see all the conflicts that have occurred in your database, you can create a CouchDB view with the map function as defined in Listing 13-3.

Listing 13-3. Finding Conflicts in the Database

```
function(doc) {
    if(doc._conflicts) {
        emit(doc._conflicts, null);
    }
}
```

If there are no conflicts in the database, the response you will receive from the view should look something like this:

```
{"total_rows":0,"rows":[]}
```

If a conflict is found, the result may look something like the following:

```
{"total_rows":1,"offset":0,"rows":[
{"id":"my-document","key":["3-1185264872"],"value":null}
]}
```

This response tells you that one document has had a conflict; also, the ID of that document was my-document, and the revision 3-1185264872 of the version that lost the conflict. To find the revision number of the winning version, you simply request the document itself by issuing a GET request to the URI /[db_name]/[document_id]. Alternatively, you could modify the view in Listing 13-3 along the lines of the function in Listing 13-4.

Listing 13-4. Returning the Current Revision First

```
function(doc) {
    if(doc._conflicts) {
        emit([doc._rev].concat(doc._conflicts)], null);
    }
}
```

This way, the current revision is returned first, with any conflicts following. This saves you from making a second HTTP request to figure out which revision has won the conflict.

Security

Security is an important issue for any database management system. Data should be protected by security mechanisms such as authentication, authorization, encryption, and validation to ensure that the integrity of the data in the database is maintained and to keep sensitive data hidden from prying eyes.

CouchDB is still in the alpha stage of development, and as a result its security features are incomplete and constantly evolving. At the time of writing, CouchDB has relatively mature support for basic HTTP authentication, which allows administrator accounts to be set up in the CouchDB configuration file.

To create an administrator account, edit your CouchDB installation's `local.ini` configuration file with your favorite text editor. You will see the following lines at the bottom of this file:

```
;[admins]
;admin = mysecretpassword
```

Uncomment these two lines by removing the semicolons at the beginning of each line. Then change the value `mysecretpassword` to a more secure password. This will automatically be hashed into an encrypted string when you restart the CouchDB server. With this authentication enabled, you will be required to log in to complete certain operations such as creating or deleting a database or triggering database compaction. You can see an example of how this authentication is implemented in Figure 13-3.

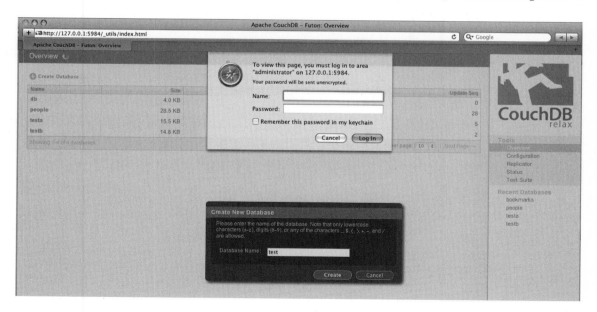

Figure 13-3. Login dialog box for restricted features

An obvious problem with this is that the connection is not secure, and an attacker could potentially intercept the authentication credentials if the CouchDB server is exposed to remote connections. Unfortunately, CouchDB does not support SSL at the time of writing. A workaround would be to create an SSL proxy using nginx or Apache and `mod_proxy`.

Another issue is that this form of authentication is quite antiquated and will not be familiar to many users. It is implemented via unfamiliar pop-up login dialog boxes like the one shown in Figure 13-3, rather than integrated login boxes in the application itself. Recent developments in the trunk version of CouchDB include support for cookie authentication and OAuth authentication, which should allow for a much more streamlined security solution than the basic HTTP authentication option. These solutions are not yet finalized, however, and may have changed dramatically by the time this book goes to print.

Authorization is an important security concept and refers to the concept of who can see or modify what data. Unfortunately, CouchDB currently supports only a single role, which caters to administrators. This means that it is not currently possible to restrict read access to the database, and as a result, anybody who can communicate with the database server can read the data within it.

The fact that CouchDB supports only a single role also makes it difficult to define "who has access to what." For example, user A can modify documents 1, 2, and 3, and user B can modify documents 4 and 5. A basic workaround (albeit easy to circumvent) is to create a `validate_doc_update` function in your design documents. By specifying the owner of the document in a field in the document itself, you can match this up with the login name of the user currently logged in before an update of that document is processed. Listing 13-5 shows an example of such a function.

Listing 13-5. Validating Document Owner Against Logged-in User

```
function(newDoc, oldDoc, userCtx) {
    if(newDoc.owner && newDoc.owner != userCtx.name)
        throw({"error": "You do not own this document!"});
}
```

CouchDB's security features are being constantly developed, and by the time the application reaches version 1.0, a strong security model should be in place. Until then, basic controls like the ones provided and using reverse proxies such as nginx and Apache/`mod_proxy` provide you with ample options for securing your CouchDB databases.

Backup

It goes without saying that it is a good policy to regularly back up your database and its associated data. Individual CouchDB databases can be backed up to remote computers using replication. For more information on this, see Chapter 12 of this book where CouchDB replication is described in more detail.

It is also good practice to regularly back up the CouchDB-related files on the file system. The important files to back up are the database, configuration, and log files. The directories you need to back up are as follows:

- *Database files*: `${PREFIX}/var/lib/couchdb`

- *Configuration files*: `${PREFIX}/etc/couchdb`

- *Log files*: `${PREFIX}/var/log/couchdb`

The value of `${PREFIX}` depends on your operating system. On a Linux system, this is usually `/usr/local`, and on Mac OS X it is typically `/opt/local`.

■ **Caution** Because CouchDB is beta software, certain features may be added, modified, or removed between versions. Also, some new configuration options may be added with each release. Before a final release version of CouchDB is available, you should ensure that when restoring a backed-up CouchDB database file and configuration file, you restore it to a CouchDB instance that is the same version as the one you backed up from.

If you have backed up a CouchDB database by replicating it to another CouchDB server and you need to restore that backup, simply create a new database on the primary CouchDB server and replicate the backed-up database to it.

Fault Tolerance and Load Balancing

In the previous section, you learned that you could use replication to back up a CouchDB database to an off-site CouchDB database. Every computer system suffers from faults at some point in the system. You might have a second hard disk installed in a RAID 1 configuration so that if your primary disk fails, the secondary one can take over. You can have a similar setup with CouchDB—simply set up a second server in a location separate from your primary CouchDB server, and make sure that changes are replicated across to it. One way of doing this would be to set up a cron job that runs at a frequent interval, calling a script that uses `curl` to replicate your primary database to a database on your backup server.

The primary issue with the cron job is that, unless your cron job runs every second (which could lead to some serious performance issues), there may be a period of time during which your two servers are not in sync. An alternative and less-resource-wasteful method is to use the `update_notification` section of the CouchDB configuration file. With this method, you can use the same script that the cron job calls, but the script will get called only when a document is modified.

To set this up, open the `local.ini` configuration file, and find the following lines:

```
[update_notification]
;unique notifier name=/full/path/to/exe -with "cmd line arg"
```

Change the second line to the following:

```
backup_db=/path/to/script
```

where `/path/to/script` is the full system path to your script that replicates the database. All that's left is to test that the script is working by adding a new document or modifying an existing document in your primary database and checking that it has successfully replicated across to the backup database. This script would typically trigger replication in intervals of updates or seconds. The CouchDB wiki features an example of a script that updates views for every tenth update or at most once a second.

You will now need to set up a failover system so that in the event of the primary server crashing, requests are redirected to the secondary server.

Clustering

Fault tolerance accounts for situations where a server actually fails, but what about a scenario where the performance of a server is suffering under a heavy load? As your database requirements grow, you'll quickly realize that a single server is not sufficient to process transactions on its own. Sure, you could upgrade your server or purchase a new, more powerful server, but eventually this will also be insufficient.

A solution to this issue would be to set up a cluster of servers that share the load generated by the database between them. Clustering features are not built in to CouchDB itself but are available through a third-party proxy-based partitioning/clustering framework known as couchdb-lounge. At the time of writing, this framework only supports CouchDB 0.9.0 and is in a very early stage of development. For more information, visit the project web site at `http://code.google.com/p/couchdb-lounge/`.

Summary

In this chapter, you learned about various topics that are relevant when readying your CouchDB installation for deployment to a production environment. You learned how to view CouchDB runtime statistics to measure your instance's performance. I then showed you how to configure the installation to your requirements using the CouchDB configuration file. Next, you saw how to identify any conflicts that have occurred after replication and how you can resolve them. You then learned about security in CouchDB and the options currently available and those that are currently under development in trunk versions of the database. Finally, you discovered how to ensure that your data is kept safe and consistent by backing up your databases and CouchDB-related files, how to automate replication to ensure a failover for fault tolerance, and the options that are available to you to ensure your CouchDB server keeps running smoothly under heavy loads.

APPENDIX A

CouchDB API Reference

This appendix is an overview of the API calls you can make to the CouchDB server.

Server APIs

Server Information

Request Method:	GET
Request URI:	/
Request Headers:	None
Request Body:	Empty
Request Parameters:	None
Description:	Returns a welcome message and the CouchDB version number
Sample Request URI:	http://127.0.0.1:5984/

The following is a sample response:

```
{"couchdb":"Welcome","version":"0.9.1"}
```

Current Configuration

Request Method:	GET
Request URI:	/_config
Request Headers:	None
Request Body:	Empty
Request Parameters:	None
Description:	Returns all of CouchDB's configuration options and their current values
Sample Request URI:	http://127.0.0.1:5984/_config

The following is a sample response:

```
{"httpd_design_handlers":{"_list":"{couch_httpd_show,
handle_view_list_req}","_show":"{couch_httpd_show,
handle_doc_show_req}","_view":"{couch_httpd_view,
handle_view_req}"},"httpd_global_handlers":{"/":"{couch_httpd_misc_handlers,
handle_welcome_req, <<\"Welcome\">>}","_active_tasks":"{couch_httpd_misc_handlers,
handle_task_status_req}","_all_dbs":"{couch_httpd_misc_handlers,
handle_all_dbs_req}","_config":"{couch_httpd_misc_handlers,
handle_config_req}","_replicate":"{couch_httpd_misc_handlers,
handle_replicate_req}","_restart":"{couch_httpd_misc_handlers,
handle_restart_req}","_stats":"{couch_httpd_stats_handlers,
handle_stats_req}","_utils":"{couch_httpd_misc_handlers, handle_utils_dir_req,
\"/usr/local/share/couchdb/www\"}","_uuids":"{couch_httpd_misc_handlers,
handle_uuids_req}","favicon.ico":"{couch_httpd_misc_handlers, handle_favicon_req,
\"/usr/local/share/couchdb/www\"}"},"log":{"file":"/usr/local/var/log/couchdb/couch.log","le
vel":"info"},"query_servers":{"javascript":"/usr/local/bin/couchjs
/usr/local/share/couchdb/server/main.js"},"daemons":{"db_update_notifier":"{couch_db_update_
notifier_sup, start_link, []}","external_manager":"{couch_external_manager, start_link,
[]}","httpd":"{couch_httpd, start_link, []}","query_servers":"{couch_query_servers,
start_link, []}","stats_aggregator":"{couch_stats_aggregator, start,
[]}","stats_collector":"{couch_stats_collector, start, []}","view_manager":"{couch_view,
start_link, []}"},"httpd":{"WWW-Authenticate":"Basic
realm=\"administrator\"","authentication_handler":"{couch_httpd,
default_authentication_handler}","bind_address":"127.0.0.1","port":"5984"},"httpd_db_handler
s":{"_design":"{couch_httpd_db, handle_design_req}","_temp_view":"{couch_httpd_view,
handle_temp_view_req}"},"test":{"foo":"bar"},"couchdb":{"database_dir":"/usr/local/var/lib/c
ouchdb","max_attachment_chunk_size":"4294967296","max_dbs_open":"100","max_document_size":"4
294967296","os_process_timeout":"5000","util_driver_dir":"/usr/local/lib/couchdb/erlang/lib/
couch-0.9.1/priv/lib","view_index_dir":"/usr/local/var/lib/couchdb"}}
```

Runtime Statistics

Request Method:	GET
Request URI:	/_stats
Request Headers:	None
Request Body:	Empty
Request Parameters:	range (integer, time period for which to retrieve stats, default 0) Valid values: 0 (since the server booted), 60, 300, 900
Description:	Returns a set of CouchDB runtime statistics
Sample Request URI:	http://127.0.0.1:5984/_stats

The following is a sample response:

```
{"httpd_status_codes":{"200":{"current":152,"count":9466,"mean":0.016057468835833463,"min":0
,"max":22,"stddev":0.2956761553416581,"description":"number of HTTP 200 OK
responses"},"201":{"current":78,"count":9465,"mean":0.0082408874801902,"min":0,"max":21,"std
dev":0.25164166969889457,"description":"number of HTTP 201 Created
responses"},"202":{"current":2,"count":9414,"mean":0.00021244954323348223,"min":0,"max":1,"s
tddev":0.0145741006043276,"description":"number of HTTP 202 Accepted
responses"},"304":{"current":1,"count":9414,"mean":0.00010622477161674126,"min":0,"max":1,"s
tddev":0.0103059928155727,"description":"number of HTTP 304 Not Modified
responses"},"400":{"current":1,"count":2416,"mean":0.0004139072847682145,"min":0,"max":1,"st
ddev":0.02034050062136692,"description":"number of HTTP 400 Bad Request
responses"},"404":{"current":12,"count":9465,"mean":0.001267828843106181,"min":0,"max":6,"st
ddev":0.06660175343709973,"description":"number of HTTP 404 Not Found
responses"},"405":{"current":2,"count":9442,"mean":0.00021181952976064448,"min":0,"max":1,"s
tddev":0.014552479591033817,"description":"number of HTTP 405 Method Not Allowed
responses"},"409":{"current":1,"count":595,"mean":0.0016806722689075649,"min":0,"max":1,"std
dev":0.0409615381746351,"description":"number of HTTP 409 Conflict
responses"},"500":{"current":1,"count":4887,"mean":0.00020462451401678002,"min":0,"max":1,"s
tddev":0.014303238892818738,"description":"number of HTTP 500 Internal Server Error
responses"}},"httpd_request_methods":{"COPY":{"current":2,"count":9432,"mean":0.000212044105
17387668,"min":0,"max":1,"stddev":0.01456019033087608,"description":"number of HTTP COPY
requests"},"DELETE":{"current":42,"count":9465,"mean":0.00443740095087166,"min":0,"max":6,"s
tddev":0.10472898092881516,"description":"number of HTTP DELETE
requests"},"GET":{"current":113,"count":9466,"mean":0.011937460384534125,"min":0,"max":21,"s
tddev":0.24915896286993675,"description":"number of HTTP GET
requests"},"POST":{"current":14,"count":9450,"mean":0.0014814814814814847,"min":0,"max":3,"s
```

tddev":0.04598051031711314,"description":"number of HTTP POST
requests"},"PUT":{"current":78,"count":9466,"mean":0.008240016902598794,"min":0,"max":22,"st
ddev":0.26029556220645184,"description":"number of HTTP PUT
requests"}},"httpd":{"bulk_requests":{"current":1,"count":9430,"mean":0.00010604453870625688
,"min":0,"max":1,"stddev":0.010297246877785696,"description":"number of bulk
requests"},"requests":{"current":250,"count":9466,"mean":0.02641031058525249,"min":0,"max":3
2,"stddev":0.5274422956827197,"description":"number of HTTP
requests"},"temporary_view_reads":{"current":2,"count":9450,"mean":0.0002116402116402122,"mi
n":0,"max":1,"stddev":0.014546319811589058,"description":"number of temporary view
reads"},"view_reads":{"current":2,"count":9454,"mean":0.00021155066638459967,"min":0,"max":1
,"stddev":0.014543242853646884,"description":"number of view
reads"}},"couchdb":{"database_reads":{"current":42,"count":9460,"mean":0.004439746300211437,
"min":0,"max":10,"stddev":0.1446047067385059,"description":"number of times a document was
read from a
database"},"database_writes":{"current":66,"count":9461,"mean":0.0069760067646126005,"min":0
,"max":22,"stddev":0.27500988894664896,"description":"number of times a database was
changed"},"open_databases":{"current":3,"count":9465,"mean":0.0003169572107765436,"min":-
5,"max":5,"stddev":0.0815843181281427,"description":"number of open
databases"},"open_os_files":{"current":3,"count":9465,"mean":0.0003169572107765436,"min":-
5,"max":5,"stddev":0.08660958488049343,"description":"number of file descriptors CouchDB has
open"},"request_time":{"current":2,"count":250,"mean":6.872,"min":0,"max":1093,"stddev":68.9
0938699480645,"description":"length of a request inside CouchDB without MochiWeb"}}}

Get UUIDs

Request Method:	GET
Request URI:	/_uuids
Request Headers:	None
Request Body:	Empty
Request Parameters:	count (integer, the number of UUIDs to return, default 1)
Description:	Returns a list of UUIDs
Sample Request URI:	http://127.0.0.1:5984/_uuids?count=3

The following is a sample response:

```
{"uuids":["1beb354da53d6581efb552fd18d30694","e5b2e7d2866af47d114676fb8fc813b","d2cac24e8b22
1a8f2481ce6990731e71"]}
```

Database APIs

Create Database

Request Method:	PUT
Request URI:	/[db_name]
Request Headers:	None
Request Body:	Empty
Request Parameters:	None
Description:	Creates a new database
Sample Request URI:	http://127.0.0.1:5984/employees

The following is a sample response:

```
{"ok":true}
```

Delete Database

Request Method:	DELETE
Request URI:	/[db_name]
Request Headers:	None
Request Body:	Empty
Request Parameters:	None
Description:	Deletes (drops) an existing database
Sample Request URI:	http://127.0.0.1:5984/employees

The following is a sample response:

```
{"ok":true}
```

List Databases

Request Method:	GET
Request URI:	/_all_dbs
Request Headers:	None
Request Body:	Empty
Request Parameters:	None
Description:	Returns an array with the names of all databases on the server
Sample Request URI:	http://127.0.0.1:5984/_all_dbs

The following is a sample response:

```
["my_db","employees","contacts","customers"]
```

Database Information

Request Method:	GET
Request URI:	/[db_name]
Request Headers:	None
Request Body:	Empty
Request Parameters:	None
Description:	Returns basic information about a CouchDB database
Sample Request URI:	http://127.0.0.1:5984/employees

The following is a sample response:

```
{"db_name":"employees","doc_count":125,"doc_del_count":3,"update_seq":190,"purge_seq":10,"compact_running":false,"disk_size":192847,"instance_start_time":"1254437520141551"}
```

Replicate Database

Request Method:	POST
Request URI:	`/_replicate`
Request Headers:	None
Request Body:	JSON object with two fields, source and target, each represented by a database name (if local) or the URL (if remote)
Request Parameters:	None
Description:	Replicates a source database to a target database
Sample Request URI:	`http://127.0.0.1:5984/_replicate`

The following is a sample response:

{"ok":true,"session_id":"95896d0cb2f59ae4b5717f128300697","source_last_seq":1,"history":[{"start_time":"Thu, 01 Oct 2009 22:45:29 GMT","end_time":"Thu, Oct 01 2009 22:45:29 GMT","start_last_seq":0,"end_last_seq":1,"missing_checked":1,"missing_found":1,"docs_read":1,"docs_written":1,"doc_write_failures":0}]}

Compact Database

Request Method:	POST
Request URI:	/[db_name]/_compact
Request Headers:	None
Request Body:	Empty
Request Parameters:	None
Description:	Deletes documents marked as deleted and old revisions of documents
Sample Request URI:	http://127.0.0.1:5984/employees/_compact

The following is a sample response:

```
{"ok":true}
```

Document APIs

Create New Document (Use UUID-Generated Document ID)

Request Method:	POST
Request URI:	/[db_name]
Request Headers:	None
Request Body:	The document itself as a JSON object
Request Parameters:	None
Description:	Creates a new document in the database, with the document ID automatically generated by the server
Sample Request URI:	http://127.0.0.1:5984/employees

The following is a sample response:

```
{"ok":true,"id":"89107b443aadb405dc871efbec5073ad","rev":"1-2286301188"}
```

Create New Document (User Specified Document ID)

Request Method:	PUT
Request URI:	/[db_name]/[doc_id]
Request Headers:	None
Request Body:	The document as a JSON object
Request Parameters:	None
Description:	Creates a new document in the database, with the specified document ID
Sample Request URI:	http://127.0.0.1:5984/employees/126

The following is a sample response:

```
{"ok":true,"id":"126","rev":"1-2833850875"}
```

Update Existing Document

Request Method:	PUT
Request URI:	/[db_name]/[doc_id]
Request Headers:	X-Couch-Full-Commit: true (optional). Ensure that the document has synced to disk before returning success.
Request Body:	The document itself as a JSON object. It must include the _rev property, with the revision number of the document the update is based on as the value.
Request Parameters:	None
Description:	Updates an existing document and replaces it with a new revision
Sample Request URI:	http://127.0.0.1:5984/employees/126

The following is a sample response:

```
{"ok":true,"id":126,"rev":"2-4058198378"}
```

Delete Document

Request Method:	DELETE
Request URI:	/[db_name]/[doc_id]
Request Headers:	None
Request Body:	Empty
Request Parameters:	**rev** (String, required, revision number of document to be deleted)
Description:	Deletes a document from the database by creating a new revision of the document, which is marked as deleted. The document will be removed permanently from the database the next time it is compacted.
Sample Request URI:	http://127.0.0.1:5984/employees/126

The following is a sample response:

```
{"ok":true,"id":"126","3-2206761782"}
```

Copy Document

Request Method:	COPY
Request URI:	`/[db_name]/[doc_id]`
Request Headers:	`Destination: [destination_doc_id]`
Request Body:	Empty
Request Parameters:	None
Description:	Copies a document to the document ID specified in the destination header. If overwriting an existing document, you need to specify the revision being overwritten using the rev parameter in the Destination header (such as `Destination: 126?rev=2-345345345345`).
Sample Request URI:	`http://127.0.0.1:5984/employees/126`

The following is a sample response:

```
{"rev":"1-1950429145"}
```

List Documents

Request Method:	GET
Request URI:	`/[db_name]/_all_docs`
Request Headers:	None
Request Body:	Empty
Request Parameters:	`descending` (Boolean, reverses order of results, default `false`) `include_docs` (Boolean, include full document, default `false`) `limit` (Number, restrict number of results) `startkey` (String, start key to return documents in a range) `endkey` (String, end key to return documents in a range) `startkey_docid` (String, start document ID of range) `endkey_docid` (String, end document ID of range) `key` (String, only display document that matches key) `stale` (String=ok, don't refresh views for quicker results) `skip` (Number, skip the defined number of documents) `group` (Boolean, results should be grouped, default `false`) `group_level` (Number, oevel at which documents should be grouped) `reduce` (Boolean; if exists, display result of reduce function; default `true`)
Description:	Returns every document in a database
Sample Request URI:	`http://127.0.0.1:5984/employees/_all_docs`

The following is a sample response:

```
{"total_rows":125,"offset":0,"rows":[
{"id":"001","key":"001","value":{"rev":"1-4228106699"}},
…
{"id:"125","key":"125","value":{"rev":"2-3453483473}}
]}
```

List Documents Specifying a Key Set

Request Method:	GET
Request URI:	/[db_name]/_all_docs
Request Headers:	None
Request Body:	{"keys":["docid1","docid2",...,"docidN"]}
Request Parameters:	descending (Boolean, reverses order of results, default false) include_docs (Boolean, include full document, default false) limit (Number, restrict number of results) startkey (String, start key to return documents in a range) endkey (String, end key to return documents in a range) startkey_docid (String, start document ID of range) endkey_docid (String, end document ID of range) key (String, only display document that matches key) stale (String=ok, don't refresh views for quicker results) skip (Number, skip the defined number of documents) group (Boolean, results should be grouped, default false) group_level (Number, level at which documents should be grouped) reduce (Boolean; if exists, display result of reduce function; default true)
Description:	Returns every document in a database
Sample Request URI:	http://127.0.0.1:5984/employees/_all_docs

The following is a sample response:

```
{"total_rows":125,"offset":0,"rows":[
{"id":"docid1","key":"001","value":{"rev":"1-4228106699"}},
{"id":"125","key":"125","value":{"rev":"2-3453483473}},
...
]}
```

List Modified Documents

Request Method:	GET
Request URI:	/[db_name]/_all_docs_by_seq
Request Headers:	None
Request Body:	Empty
Request Parameters:	descending (Boolean, reverses order of results, default false) include_docs (Boolean, include full document, default false) limit (Number, restrict number of results) startkey (String, start key to return documents in a range) endkey (String, end key to return documents in a range) startkey_docid (String, start document ID of range) endkey_docid (String, end document ID of range) key (String, only display document that matches key) stale (String=ok, don't refresh views for quicker results) skip (Number, skip the defined number of documents) group (Boolean, results should be grouped, default false) group_level (Number, level at which documents should be grouped) reduce (Boolean; if exists, display result of reduce function; default true)
Description:	Returns documents that have been updated or deleted
Sample Request URI:	http://127.0.0.1:5984/employees/_all_docs_by_seq

The following is a sample response:

```
{"total_rows":1,"offset":0,"rows":[
{"id":"001","key:1,"value":{"rev":"1-4228106699"}},
{"id":"126","key":4,"value":{"rev":"3-2206761782","deleted":true}}
]}
```

List Modified Documents Specifying a Key Set

Request Method:	GET
Request URI:	`/[db_name]/_all_docs_by_seq`
Request Headers:	None
Request Body:	`{"keys":["docid1","docid2",...,"docidN"]}`
Request Parameters:	`descending` (Boolean, reverses order of results, default `false`)
	`include_docs` (Boolean, include full document, default `false`)
	`limit` (Number, restrict number of results)
	`startkey` (String, start key to return documents in a range)
	`endkey` (String, end key to return documents in a range)
	`startkey_docid` (String, start document ID of range)
	`endkey_docid` (String, end document ID of range)
	`key` (String, only display document that matches key)
	`stale` (String=ok, don't refresh views for quicker results)
	`skip` (Number, skip the defined number of documents)
	`group` (Boolean, results should be grouped, default `false`)
	`group_level` (Number, level at which documents should be grouped)
	`reduce` (Boolean; if exists, display result of reduce function; default `true`)
Description:	Returns documents that have been updated or deleted.
Sample Request URI:	`http://127.0.0.1:5984/employees/_all_docs_by_seq`

The following is a sample response:

```
{"total_rows":1,"offset":0,"rows":[
{"id":"docid1","key:1,"value":{"rev":"1-4228106699"}},
{"id":"docid2","key":4,"value":{"rev":"3-2206761782","deleted":true}},
…
]}
```

View Document

Request Method:	GET
Request URI:	/[db_name]/[doc_id]
Request Headers:	None
Request Body:	Empty
Request Parameters:	`full` (Boolean, return full documents including metadata, default `false`) `revs` (Boolean, return a list of previous revisions, default `false`) `rev` (String, set a specific revision number) `attachments` (Boolean, get attachments in Base64, default `false`)
Description:	Returns a document from a CouchDB database
Sample Request URI:	`http://127.0.0.1:5984/employees/025`

The following is a sample response:

```
{"_id":"025","_rev":"1-4546452541","name":"Joe Lennon","location":"Cork"}
```

Create/Update Attachment

Request Method:	PUT
Request URI:	`/[db_name]/[doc_id]/[attachment_filename]`
Request Headers:	`Content-Type: [mime_type]` `Content-Length: [file_size]`
Request Body:	The attachment file data itself
Request Parameters:	**rev** (String, revision number of document, omit to create new doc)
Description:	Attaches a file to a document
Sample Request URI:	`http://127.0.0.1:5984/employees/126/photo.jpg`

The following is a sample response:

```
{"ok":true,"id":"45fd4543543g43432ab342","rev":"1-2489366227"}
```

Delete Attachment

Request Method:	DELETE
Request URI:	/[db_name]/[doc_id]/[attachment_filename]
Request Headers:	None
Request Body:	Empty
Request Parameters:	**rev** (String, required, revision number of document)
Description:	Deletes an attachment from a document
Sample Request URI:	http://127.0.0.1:5984/employees/126/photo.jpg?rev=1-2489366227

The following is a sample response:

```
{"ok":true,"id":"126","rev":"2-130046133"}
```

Get Attachment

Request Method:	GET
Request URI:	/[db_name]/[doc_id]/[attachment_filename]
Request Headers:	None
Request Body:	Empty
Request Parameters:	None
Description:	Retrieves an attachment from a document
Sample Request URI:	http://127.0.0.1:5984/employees/126/photo.jpg

The response is the actual file attachment (in this example, a JPEG photo).

Managing Bulk Documents

Request Method:	POST
Request URI:	`/[db_name]/_bulk_docs`
Request Headers:	`X-Couch-Full-Commit:` **true** (optional). Ensure that the document has synced to disk before returning success.
Request Body:	JSON object with **docs** field containing array of documents
Request Parameters:	None
Description:	Creates, updates and deletes documents in bulk. Documents that are to be updated or deleted must contain the **_rev** field, specifying the revision number to be deleted as the value. To delete a document, it should include the field `"_deleted":`**true**.
Sample Request URI:	`http://127.0.0.1:5984/employees/_bulk_docs`

The following is a sample response:

```
[{"id":"2d32010cc35bdeb92dac487274662809","rev":"1-
2530238890"},{"id":"e24d6da28466cf136242b150f38e2dcb","rev":"1-879513885"}]
```

View API

Create Design Document

Request Method:	PUT
Request URI:	/[db_name]/_design/[design_doc_name]
Request Headers:	None
Request Body:	JSON document with **views** field for storing permanent views, **shows** field for storing show functions, and **lists** field for storing list functions
Request Parameters:	None
Description:	Creates a design document to store permanent CouchDB views, show functions, and list functions
Sample Request URI:	http://127.0.0.1:5984/employees/_design/myviews

The following is a sample response:

```
{"ok":true,"id":"_design/myviews","rev":"1-1907630304"}
```

Query Temporary View

Request Method:	POST
Request URI:	`/[db_name]/_temp_view`
Request Headers:	`Content-type: application/json`
Request Body:	Map function (required) and Reduce function (optional) of view
Request Parameters:	`descending` (Boolean, Reverses order of results, default `false`) `include_docs` (Boolean, include full document, default `false`) `limit` (Number, restrict number of results) `startkey` (String, start key to return documents in a range) `endkey` (String, end key to return documents in a range) `startkey_docid` (String, start document ID of range) `endkey_docid` (String, end document ID of range) `key` (String, only display document that matches key) `stale` (String=ok, don't refresh views for quicker results) `skip` (Number, skip the defined number of documents) `group` (Boolean, Results should be grouped, default `false`) `group_level` (Number, level at which documents should be grouped) `reduce` (Boolean; if exists, display result of reduce function; default `true`)
Description:	Performs a query on the database using a temporary view
Sample Request URI:	`http://127.0.0.1:5984/employees/_temp_view`

The following is a sample response:

```
{"total_rows":2,"offset":0,"rows":[
{"id":"2d32010cc35bdeb92dac4872746628","key":"2d32010cc35bdeb92dac487274662809","value":null
},
{"id":"e24d6da28466cf136242b150f8e2dcb","key":"e24d6da28466cf136242b150f8e2dcb","value":null
}
]}
```

Query Permanent View

Request Method:	GET
Request URI:	/[db_name]/_design/[design_doc_name]/_view/[view_name]
Request Headers:	None
Request Body:	None
Request Parameters:	descending (Boolean, reverses order of results, default false) include_docs (Boolean, include full document, default false) limit (Number, restrict number of results) startkey (String, start key to return documents in a range) endkey (String, end key to return documents in a range) startkey_docid (string, Start document ID of range) endkey_docid (String, end document ID of range) key (String, only display document that matches key) stale (String=ok, don't refresh views for quicker results) skip (Number, skip the defined number of documents) group (Boolean, results should be grouped, default false) group_level (Number, level at which documents should be grouped) reduce (Boolean; if exists, display result of reduce function; default true)
Description:	Executes a permanent view stored in a CouchDB design document
Sample Request URI:	http://127.0.0.1:5984/employees/_design/myviews/_view/getall

The following is a sample response:

```
{"total_rows":2,"offset":0,"rows":[
{"id":"2d32010cc35bdeb92dac4872746628","key":"2d32010cc35bdeb92dac487274662809","value":null
},
{"id":"e24d6da28466cf136242b150f8e2dcb","key":"e24d6da28466cf136242b150f8e2dcb","value":null
}
]}
```

Query a Permanent View Specifying A Key Set

Request Method:	GET
Request URI:	/[db_name]/_design/[design_doc_name]/_view/[view_name]
Request Headers:	None
Request Body:	{"keys":["docid1","docid2",...,"docidN"]}
Request Parameters:	descending (Boolean, reverses order of results, default false) include_docs (Boolean, include full document, default false) limit (Number, restrict number of results) startkey (String, start key to return documents in a range) endkey (String, end key to return documents in a range) startkey_docid (String, start document ID of range) endkey_docid (String, end document ID of range) key (String, only display document that matches key) stale (String=ok, don't refresh views for quicker results) skip (Number, skip the defined number of documents) group (Boolean, results should be grouped, default false) group_level (Number, level at which documents should be grouped) reduce (Boolean; if exists, display result of reduce function; default true)
Description:	Executes a permanent view stored in a CouchDB design document
Sample Request URI:	http://127.0.0.1:5984/employees/_design/myviews/_view/getall

The following is a sample response:

```
{"total_rows":2,"offset":0,"rows":[
{"id":"doc1","key":"2d32010cc35bdeb92dac487274662809","value":null},
{"id":"doc2","key":"e24d6da28466cf136242b150f8e2dcb","value":null}
…
]}
```

Execute a Show Function

Request Method:	GET
Request URI:	`/[db_name]/_design/[design_doc_name]/_show/[function_name]/[doc_id]`
Request Headers:	None
Request Body:	None
Request Parameters:	`format` (String, file format to show document in) `details` (Boolean, show the document's details, default `false`)
Description:	Presents a CouchDB document in a defined format, as set out in a show function
Sample Request URI:	`http://127.0.0.1:5984/employees/_design/myshows/_show/payslips/200`

The response is the document represented in the format set in the show function.

Execute a List Function

Request Method:	GET
Request URI:	/[db_name]/_design/[design_doc_name]/_list/[function_name]/ [view_name]
Request Headers:	None
Request Body:	None
Request Parameters:	descending (Boolean, Reverses order of results, default false) include_docs (Boolean, include full document, default false) limit (Number, restrict number of results) startkey (String, start key to return documents in a range) endkey (String, end key to return documents in a range) startkey_docid (String, start document ID of range) endkey_docid (String, end document ID of range) key (String, only display document that matches key) stale (String=ok, don't refresh views for quicker results) skip (Number, skip the defined number of documents) group (Boolean, results should be grouped, default false) group_level (Number, level at which documents should be grouped) reduce (Boolean; if exists, display result of reduce function; default true)
Description:	Presents a list of the results of a CouchDB view, as defined in a list function
Sample Request URI:	http://127.0.0.1:5984/employees/_design/myviews/_list/browse/getall

The response is the results of the view, in a format as set out in the list function.

Execute a List Function Specifying a Key Set

Request Method:	GET
Request URI:	`/[db_name]/_design/[design_doc_name]/_list/[function_name]/[view_name]`
Request Headers:	None
Request Body:	`{"keys":["docid1","docid2",...,"docidN"]}`
Request Parameters:	`descending` (Boolean, Reverses order of results, default `false`) `include_docs` (Boolean, include full document, default `false`) `limit` (Number, restrict number of results) `startkey` (String, start key to return documents in a range) `endkey` (String, end key to return documents in a range) `startkey_docid` (String, start document ID of range) `endkey_docid` (String, end document ID of range) `key` (String, only display document that matches key) `stale` (String=ok, don't refresh views for quicker results) `skip` (Number, skip the defined number of documents) `group` (Boolean, results should be grouped, default `false`) `group_level` (Number, level at which documents should be grouped) `reduce` (Boolean; if exists, display result of reduce function; default `true`)
Description:	Presents a list of the results of a CouchDB view, as defined in a list function
Sample Request URI:	`http://127.0.0.1:5984/employees/_design/myviews/_list/browse/getall`

The response is the results of the view, in a format as set out in the list function.

Further Information

The CouchDB API is constantly evolving. With each version, new features are added, and older features are deprecated. You can find out more information on the CouchDB API in the handlers section of the `default.ini` configuration file or on the official CouchDB wiki at `http://wiki.apache.org`.

APPENDIX B

HTTP and curl Reference

CouchDB's API is made available using a RESTful HTTP interface. This appendix outlines how an HTTP request is processed.

HTTP Request Message

An HTTP request comprises the following elements:

- The request line, indicating the method, resource, and HTTP version of the request

- Headers, such as Content-type and Content-length

- An empty line

- The message body

Listing B-1 shows an example of an HTTP request with all four of these properties.

Listing B-1. A Sample HTTP Request

```
POST /db HTTP/1.1
Content-type: application/json

{"type":"category","name":"Web Tutorials","slug":"web-tutorials"}
```

HTTP Request Methods

Table B-1 describes the HTTP request methods that are used in CouchDB. Please note that the COPY method is not part of the HTTP standard but is rather an extension to HTTP used by CouchDB.

Table B-1. HTTP Request Methods

Method Name	Description
GET	GET requests are usually used for side-effect-free transactions, such as retrieving data. In CouchDB, GET requests are used to request data from the database.
POST	POST requests are used to submit data to a resource, with the data included in the message body. In CouchDB, POST requests are used to create new resources, typically where the URI of the request is different to the resource that is to be created.
PUT	PUT requests are also used to submit data to a resource, with the data included in the message body. Unlike POST requests, PUT requests are generally used to update existing data, at the same resource the URI is requested from. PUT requests are also used in CouchDB where you want to specify the resource name where the data will be accessible, that is, when you want to specify the document ID when creating a document, rather than have one automatically assigned by the server.
DELETE	DELETE requests are used to delete the specified resource. CouchDB uses DELETE requests to delete databases and documents.
COPY	This nonstandard extension to HTTP is used by CouchDB to copy one resource to another resource.

HTTP Response

An HTTP response consists of a status line, headers, and a body. The headers usually provide information such as the time of the response, information about the server, the type of content contained in the response body, and more meta-information. The response message is returned in the body.

Listing B-2 is an example of an HTTP response.

Listing B-2. A Sample HTTP Response

```
HTTP/1.1 200 OK
Server: CouchDB/0.9.0 (Erlang OTP/R13B)
Date: Sun, 04 Oct 2009 20:50:00 GMT
Content-Type: text/plain;charset=utf-8
Content-Length: 40
Cache-Control: must-revalidate

{"couchdb":"Welcome","version":"0.9.0"}
```

HTTP Response Status Codes

Table B-2 describes the HTTP status codes that CouchDB uses to indicate the success or failure of a database transaction.

Table B-2. HTTP Response Status Codes

Status Code	Description
200 (OK)	The request was successfully processed.
201 (Created)	The document was successfully created.
202 (Accepted)	The database was successfully compacted.
304 (Not Modified)	The document has not been modified since the last update.
400 (Bad Request)	The syntax of the request was invalid or could not be processed.
404 (Not Found)	The requested resource was not found.
405 (Method Not Allowed)	The request was made using an incorrect request method; for example, a GET was used where a POST was required.
409 (Conflict)	The request failed because of a database conflict.
412 (Precondition Failed)	Could not create database—a database with that name already exists.
500 (Internal Server Error)	The request was invalid and failed, or an error occurred within the CouchDB server that prevented it from processing the request.

Performing HTTP Requests with curl

The curl command-line utility provides a convenient way to make HTTP requests. The following is an example of the most basic curl HTTP request to CouchDB:

```
curl http://127.0.0.1:5984
```

This command makes a GET request to the URL http://127.0.0.1:5984. By default, curl outputs the message body of the HTTP response, as shown here:

```
{"couchdb":"Welcome","version":"0.9.0"}
```

curl has a series of command-line arguments that can be used to modify part of the HTTP transaction. For example, if you want the response header to be displayed, you can use the -v (verbose) argument, for example:

```
curl -v http://127.0.0.1:5984
```

Although you are requesting the same resource as before, the response is much different:

```
* About to connect() to 127.0.0.1 port 5984 (#0)
*    Trying 127.0.0.1... connected
* Connected to 127.0.0.1 (127.0.0.1) port 5984 (#0)
> GET / HTTP/1.1
> User-Agent: curl/7.16.3 (powerpc-apple-darwin9.0) libcurl/7.16.3 OpenSSL/0.9.7l zlib/1.2.3
> Host: 127.0.0.1:5984
> Accept: */*
>
< HTTP/1.1 200 OK
< Server: CouchDB/0.9.0 (Erlang OTP/R13B)
< Date: Sun, 04 Oct 2009 21:08:36 GMT
< Content-Type: text/plain;charset=utf-8
< Content-Length: 40
< Cache-Control: must-revalidate
<
{"couchdb":"Welcome","version":"0.9.0"}
* Connection #0 to host 127.0.0.1 left intact
* Closing connection #0
```

By default, if a request method is not supplied, curl will perform a GET request. To make an HTTP request with a different method, such as PUT, you can use the -X argument. The following command makes a PUT request to the URI /mydb, which will create a new database named mydb:

```
curl -X PUT http://127.0.0.1:5984/mydb
```

If you need to specify headers in your HTTP request, you use the -H argument. The following example uses the Destination header to define where a document should be copied to:

```
curl -X COPY http://127.0.0.1:5984/mydb/doc1 -H 'Destination: doc2'
```

Many of CouchDB's API methods require you to include data in the message body. You can supply this data using the -d argument, as shown in the following replication example:

```
curl -X POST http://127.0.0.1:5984/_replicate -d '{"source":"db_one","target":"db_two"}'
```

The previous example works quite nicely, because the data being supplied in the request body is short. But what if you need to supply a large set of data, such as a number of documents being added using the bulk document API? In this case, you can save the data in a file, for example documents.json, and then tell curl to load the data from this file. The following is an example of this type of request:

```
curl -X POST http://127.0.0.1:5984/mydb/_bulk_docs -d @documents.json
```

curl has a host of other command-line arguments, far too many to list here. A final argument that you may find useful, however, is the -o flag. You can use this to output the response to a file, as follows:

```
curl http://127.0.0.1:5984/mydb/mydoc -o mydoc.json
```

This will store the document with document ID mydoc in the file mydoc.json.

Index

You Need the Companion eBook

Your purchase of this book entitles you to buy the companion PDF-version eBook for only $10. Take the weightless companion with you anywhere.

We believe this Apress title will prove so indispensable that you'll want to carry it with you everywhere, which is why we are offering the companion eBook (in PDF format) for $10 to customers who purchase this book now. Convenient and fully searchable, the PDF version of any content-rich, page-heavy Apress book makes a valuable addition to your programming library. You can easily find and copy code—or perform examples by quickly toggling between instructions and the application. Even simultaneously tackling a donut, diet soda, and complex code becomes simplified with hands-free eBooks!

Once you purchase your book, getting the $10 companion eBook is simple:

❶ Visit **www.apress.com/promo/tendollars/**.

❷ Complete a basic registration form to receive a randomly generated question about this title.

❸ Answer the question correctly in 60 seconds, and you will receive a promotional code to redeem for the $10.00 eBook.

233 Spring Street, New York, NY 10013

Offer valid through 4/10.